The
JOHN COLTRANE
Companion

The **JOHN COLTRANE** *Companion*

Five Decades of Commentary

Edited by
CARL WOIDECK

SCHIRMER BOOKS

New York

Schirmer Books

1633 Broadway
New York, New York 10019

Library of Congress Catalog Number: 98-15919

Printed in the United States of America

Printing number
10 9 8 7 6 5 4 3 2

Library of Congress Cataloging-in-Publication Data

The John Coltrane companion : five decades of commentary / [edited by] Carl
  Woideck.
      p.   cm.
    Discography: p.
    Includes bibliographical references (p.   ) and index.
    ISBN 0-02-864790-4
    1. Coltrane, John, 1926–1967—Criticism and interpretation. 2. Jazz musi-
cians—United States—Biography. 3. Jazz—History and criticism. I. Woideck,
Carl.
ML419.C645J65   1998
788.7'165'092—dc21   98-15919
[B]   CIP
                                                                        MN

This paper meets the minimum requirements of ANSI/NISO Z39.48-1992
{Permanence of Paper}.

For John Coltrane

Contents

PART THREE: COLTRANE'S RECORDING CAREER

PART FOUR: NIGHTCLUB AND CONCERT REVIEWS

PART FIVE: RECORD REVIEWS

Acknowledgments

Sincere thanks go to Richard Carlin, my editor at Schirmer Books. Although I encountered some significant and unplanned obstacles in preparing this anthology, he was both understanding and firm as I moved toward completion.

An anthology like this one comes together with the cooperation of many individuals. Warm thanks go to Lewis Porter of Rutgers University for helping me find this opportunity to edit and publish. Lewis was already aware of most of the Coltrane articles, interviews, and resources before I even undertook this project, and his generosity in sharing information with me made this book take shape much more quickly. Dan Morgenstern, director of the Institute of Jazz Studies, helped me to move this project forward with the right gestures and help. The staff at the Institute, Don Luck, Ed Berger, and Vince Pelote, gave valuable in-person and long-distance aid. Thanks to Michel Delorme for steering me in the right direction about a key interview. Thanks also go to the contributors to this collection who gave permission to print their material for this anthology: Zita Carno, David Wild, August Blume, Valerie Wilmer, Frank Kofsky, and Lewis Porter. Thanks also to Pam Bendich, Louise Boundas, Philippe Carles, Scott Asen, Patrick Milligan, and Frank Alkyer for their help in obtaining the rights to print such excellent Coltrane articles.

Finally, heartfelt thanks go to my wife, Marian Smith. Marian's understanding of what it takes to create a book like this and her appreciation of great music helped me immeasurably in bringing this book to fruition.

Introduction

John Coltrane's significance in jazz history—as a saxophonist, composer, and bandleader—is comparable with only a handful of other figures. His improvisational and compositional contributions were so broad that his music influenced players on all instruments, not just the saxophone. More than thirty years after his death, young jazz musicians several generations removed from Coltrane are still inspired by his dedication to music, pursuit of musical knowledge, and pursuit of instrumental technique.

John Coltrane (1926–1967) was the principal link between the song-based techniques of saxophonist Charlie Parker and the more abstract expressions of saxophonist Ornette Coleman. Born just six years after Parker, Coltrane chose Parker's instrument and modeled his early alto saxophone style after Parker's. As had Parker, Coltrane mastered the repertoire of the American popular song and of the African-American blues, and he cultivated the ability to play this repertoire with both exhilarating velocity and poetic depth. Parker spent his last years in a period of premature artistic consolidation, hastened by drug and alcohol addictions. Coltrane, who gained his first national exposure in the year that Parker died, chose a different aesthetic and personal path. He was one of relatively few musicians in jazz history who embraced the ideal of continuous artistic evolution. The search was an integral part of his musical journey.

By 1955, when he joined Miles Davis's group, Coltrane had long since switched to the tenor saxophone, which made him more independent of the pervasive Parker influence. Then in 1957 Coltrane rid himself of his drug addiction; in a spiritual awakening, he consciously devoted his life to the study of music: "At that time, in gratitude, I humbly asked to be given the means and privilege to make others happy through music." This moment was a turning point in Coltrane's artistic odyssey. His strong desire to research, practice, master, and apply musical concepts led him to acquire a stunning command of the saxophone and of the materials of jazz.

Coltrane's insatiable curiosity about music and its structures found expression in his work-in-progress approach to his music. Perhaps influenced by Miles Davis in this regard, Coltrane seemed to celebrate musical style as a process, not as an arrival point. If the ideal of steady change was one of the positive hallmarks of his style, it was also a potential liability. Coltrane could be obsessive in his need for change and in his perpetual dissatisfaction with what he had found in his search. His audience needed familiar musical guideposts, which was sometimes at odds with Coltrane's appetite for change; Coltrane felt pulled in two directions.

After Coltrane formed his own group in 1960, his music became more intense. Reactions by musicians, critics, and listeners varied radically. Some found Coltrane's improvisations compelling to the point of being hypnotic; others (such as critic John Tynan) dismissed this difficult music as "anti-jazz." Many found the force of his musical searching to have overtones of spiritual seeking—confirming this in a 1961 interview, Coltrane said, "I am interested in all the sciences: metaphysics, astrology, astronomy. . . ." After citing his astrological chart and its negative aspects in some detail, Coltrane predicted, "I won't live to be old." (After his death, listeners who looked to John Coltrane as a spiritual guide formed a church partially dedicated to Coltrane in San Francisco.)

In the mid-1960s Coltrane grappled with the music of a younger generation—high-energy music made by players who had been inspired by him, albeit more by his intensity than by his discipline and love of study. Coltrane's artistic struggles of the period seemed to be mirrored by a feeling of unresolved tension in his performances. (Indian musician Ravi Shankar used the words "turmoil" and "turbulence" to describe this quality). Although Coltrane expressed some characteristic doubts about his musical direction, he was also committed to seeing the process through.

John Coltrane died of liver cancer in 1967 without resolving many of the musical issues he was dealing with. Because his music was indeed a work-in-progress, his last musical statements were by no means final. Coltrane's death had a profound effect on the community of jazz musicians. He had been an inspiration to musicians as an ideal of musical exploration. Since Coltrane's death, no single jazz figure has emerged to serve as such a unifying force and catalyst for change.

Carl Woideck
July 1997

PART ONE

Profiles and Surveys

Most jazz listeners and jazz writers became aware of saxophonist John Coltrane after he joined Miles Davis's group in 1955. From then until his death in 1967, Coltrane's music was enthusiastically and critically discussed in print many times. This section contains some of the best profiles of Coltrane and surveys of his music to appear from the 1950s to the 1990s. The first four (Gitler, Carno, Gardner, and Goldberg) were written during Coltrane's lifetime. The others (Williams, Hentoff, Watrous, Crouch, and Davis) were written later, ranging from several months to twenty-five years after Coltrane's death.

Note: Some of the dates in these articles may be somewhat contradictory or simply inaccurate. In many cases, these dates represented the best recollections of Coltrane or others. The latest scholarship (especially by Lewis Porter), however, has in many cases supplied the correct dates or at least more accurate estimates. The reader, therefore, is directed to this anthology's chronology for such information. See also Porter's excellent *John Coltrane: His Life and Music,* listed in the Bibliography.—CW

IRA GITLER
'TRANE ON THE TRACK
Down Beat, *October 16, 1958*

Ira Gitler has long been part of the New York jazz scene, first as a keen listener, then as a writer and occasional record producer. His writing on jazz always shows love for the music and sympathy for the musicians. Gitler writes with musical insight into jazz, perhaps because of his experience playing the alto sax. In fact, earlier in the year that this article was published, Gitler loaned his alto sax to Coltrane for a Gene Ammons 1958 record date, for Prestige.

Ira Gitler elicited some very thoughtful responses from Coltrane while interviewing him for this article. Immediately, Gitler tackles an issue that followed Coltrane for years—because the saxophonist played with great intensity, he must be "angry." Given that much of Coltrane's later music was considered to be heavy, serious, and intense, it's interesting that the saxophonist says jazz "used to be happy and joyous" and that he'd like to return to and project those qualities.—CW

Asked about being termed an "angry young tenor" in this publication's coverage of the 1958 Newport Jazz festival, John Coltrane said, "If it is interpreted as angry, it is taken wrong. The only one I'm angry at is myself when I don't make what I'm trying to play."

The 32-year-old native of Hamlet, N.C., has had his melancholy moments, but he feels that they belong to a disjointed, frustrating past. The crucial point in his development came after he joined Dizzy Gillespie's band in 1951.

Prior to that, he had studied music and worked in Philadelphia, assuming many of the fashionable nuances of the Charlie Parker–directed groups. When the offer to join the Gillespie band came, Coltrane felt ready.

The feeling turned out to be illusory.

"What I didn't know with Diz was that what I had to do was really express myself," Coltrane remembered. "I was playing clichés and trying to learn tunes that were hip, so I could play with the guys who played them.

"Earlier, when I had first heard Bird, I wanted to be identified with him . . . to be consumed by him. But underneath I really wanted to be myself.

"You can only play so much of another man."

Dejected and dissatisfied with his own efforts, Coltrane left Gillespie and returned to Philadelphia in search of a musical ideal and the accompanying integrity. Temporarily, he attempted to find escape in work.

"I just took gigs," he said. "You didn't have to play anything. The less you played, the better it was."

Plagued by economic difficulties, he searched for a steady job. In 1952, he found one, with a group led by Earl Bostic, whom he admires as a saxophonist even though he disliked the rhythm-and-blues realm the band dwelt in. But this job did not demolish the disillusion and lethargy that had captured him.

"Any time you play your horn, it helps you," he said. "If you get down, you can help yourself even in a rock 'n' roll band. But I didn't help myself."

A more productive step was made in 1953, when Coltrane joined a group headed by Johnny Hodges.

"We played honest music in this band," he recalled. "It was my education to the older generation."

Gradually, Coltrane rationalized the desire to work regularly with the aim of creating forcefully. In 1955, he returned to Philadelphia and, working with a group led by conga drummer Bill Carney, took a stride toward achieving his goal. As he recalled, "We were too musical for certain rooms."

In late 1955, Miles Davis beckoned. Davis had noted Coltrane's playing and wanted him in a new quintet he was forming. He encouraged Coltrane; this encouragement gradually opened adventurous paths for Coltrane. Other musicians and listeners began to pay close attention to him. When Davis disbanded in 1957, Coltrane joined Thelonious Monk's quartet.

Coltrane will not forget the role Davis and Monk played in assisting his development.

"Miles and Monk are my two musicians," he said. "Miles is the No. 1 influence over most of the modern musicians now. There isn't much harmonic ground he hasn't broken. Just listening to the beauty of his playing opens up doors. By the time I run up on something, I find Miles or Monk has done it already.

"Some things I learn directly from them. Miles has shown me possibilities in choosing substitutions within a chord and also new progressions."

Enveloped in the productive atmosphere of both the Davis and Monk groups, Coltrane emerged more an individualist than ever before. In early '58, he rejoined Davis. In the months since he did so, he has become more of an influence on other jazz instrumentalists. His recordings, on Prestige, Blue Note, and with Davis on Columbia, often are matters for passionate debate.

Yet, there is no denying his influence. There are traces of his playing in that of Junior Cook, with Horace Silver's group, and in Benny Golson, previously a Don Byas–Lucky Thompson–out-of-Hawkins tenor man.

Coltrane's teammate in the Davis sextet, Cannonball Adderley, recently said, "Coltrane and Sonny Rollins are introducing us to some new music, each in his own way. I think Monk's acceptance, after all this time, is giving musicians courage to keep playing their original ideas, come what may."

When the jazz audience first heard Coltrane, with Davis in 1955 and '56, he was less an individualist. His style derived from those of Dexter Gordon (vintage mid-'40s), Sonny Stitt, Sonny Rollins (the Rollins of that time and slightly before), Stan Getz (certain facets of sound), and an essence of generalized Charlie Parker.

As he learned harmonically from Davis and Monk, and developed his mechanical skills, a new more confident Coltrane emerged. He has used long lines and multinoted figures within these lines, but in 1958 he started playing sections that might be termed "sheets of sound."

When these efforts are successful, they have a cumulative emotional impact, a residual harmonic effect. When they fail, they sound like nothing more than elliptically phrased scales.

This approach, basic to Coltrane's playing today, is not the result of a conscious effort to produce something "new." He has noted that it has developed spontaneously.

"Now it is not a thing of beauty, and the only way it would be justified is if it becomes that," he said. "If I can't work it through, I will drop it."

Although he is satisfied with the progress he's made during the last three years, Coltrane continues to be critical of his own work. Dejection is no longer a major part of this self-criticism. Now, he seeks to improve, knowing he can do so.

"I have more work to do on my tone and articulation," he said. "I must study more general technique and smooth out some harmonic kinks. Sometimes, while playing, I discover two ideas, and instead of working on one, I work on two simultaneously and lose the continuity."

Assured that the vast frustration he felt in the early '50s is gone, Coltrane attempts to behave in terms of a broad code, which he outlined:

"Keep listening. Never become so self-important that you can't listen to other players. Live cleanly. . . . Do right. . . . You can improve as a player by improving as a person. It's a duty we owe to ourselves."

A married man, with an eight-year-old daughter, Coltrane hopes to meet the responsibilities of his music and his life without bitterness, for "music is the means of expression with strong emotional content. Jazz used to be happy and joyous. I'd like to play happy and joyous."

ZITA CARNO
THE STYLE OF JOHN COLTRANE
The Jazz Review, *October/November 1959*

This landmark article was the first to examine John Coltrane's art from a technically accurate musical perspective. Coltrane's saxophone style had been criticized from the time of his first recordings with Miles Davis, and as Coltrane's approach became more intense it became controversial with jazz critics. Jazz listeners of the 1950s, however, didn't seem to have as much trouble appreciating Coltrane as the critics did. Carno tackles these responses head-on, and concludes in part that Coltrane's style is sometimes difficult to appreciate because it is not conventional and familiar—and therefore it requires concerted listening.

Pianist Zita Carno was introduced to jazz by trumpeter Donald Byrd, a fellow student at the Manhattan School of Music. (Carno in turn introduced Byrd to the music of Paul Hindemith.) Carno's keen musical ear led her to transcribe the solos of jazz musicians, and later she transcribed Coltrane's improvised solo on his composition "Blue Train." Although she and Coltrane had never met, "just for a joke" she mailed him a copy of the solo with an anonymous note reading, "Does this look familiar?" After a few weeks, she called Coltrane one evening and identified herself as the sender. He said that he had been waiting to hear from the anonymous transcriber: "He wanted to know who had ears like that." Coltrane invited Carno to his home, where she asked him if he could read the solo down. He replied with some humor, "No, it's too difficult."

Carno and Coltrane became musical friends, and in the 1960s she visited him at his home in Queens. As he practiced she would slip onto the piano bench and begin to spontaneously harmonize with his playing. So quick and accurate was her ear that Coltrane said wryly, "You're hearing things that I don't want you to hear." Carno recalls, "That was his way of saying 'what big ears you have.'"

Zita Carno lives near Los Angeles and has been the keyboardist with the Los Angeles Philharmonic since 1975.

Note: The notated musical examples in the original printing of this article have been replaced with bracketed CD timings for easy location of the passages discussed. The version of "Blue Train" referred to is the master take (see the Discography at the end of this anthology). "Straight, No Chaser" can be found on Miles Davis's Milestones *(Columbia CK 40837).—CW*

The only thing you can, and should, expect from John Coltrane is the unexpected; that is what makes listening to his tenor style hard for people who look for the familiar and the conventional, for clichés. They are puzzled when they fail to find such things. They are thrown off by his frequently arrhythmic phrasing. His unusual harmonic concept baffles them. They are forced to listen with both ears and an alert mind. Many are not accustomed to having to do this, and they give up.

I have been asked, goodness knows how many times, how I would compare Coltrane to Sonny Rollins, the other leader on the hard blowing school. My answer has always been that you cannot compare Coltrane with anyone else. He has a completely personal style.

Even the least informed in the ways of the "hard cookers" could fail to notice the influence he has exerted upon many other musicians. Benny Golson, and to a lesser extent, Hank Mobley and Junior Cook, have been most strongly affected. Especially interesting is Golson because until recently he sounded like a cross between Lucky Thompson and Coleman Hawkins, with other elements thrown in. Such a complete switch as this is as clear an indication as any of Coltrane's influence. Cannonball Adderley is by now classic proof that you can't play with Coltrane without being influenced by him. Even Miles Davis and Horace Silver have picked up a few things from him and have been working around with them.

Just what is it he's doing that has such an effect? A lot of people may be moved to think of Charlie Parker as the widespread influence. Everyone tried to imitate him as much as possible, to sound as nearly a carbon copy of him as they could—which was only natural when you consider that he revolutionized jazz.

But what Coltrane has been doing is to get the ones he has influenced into the "hard" groove and then stimulate them to think for themselves, to work out ideas of their own within the framework of this style. For one there's Wayne Shorter, a tenor man from New Jersey whose style is as close to Coltrane's as any, yet doesn't sound like his.

Coltrane's style is many-faceted. There are many things to watch for in his playing, and the fact that he is constantly experimenting, always working out something new—on and off the stand—leads to the conclusion that no matter how well you may think you know what he's doing, he will always surprise you.

To begin my discussion of the various aspects of Coltrane's playing, I would like to elaborate a bit on the remarks I made above concerning the failure of listeners to find anything "familiar"—any clichés—in his solos.

He does have a few pet phrases that he will use in his solos. But you could hardly refer to them as clichés. They are his own, and he never even plays them exactly the same way twice. True, I have heard other instrumentalists—tenor men, trumpeters—pick them up and try to play them, but there is a certain inflection in the way he plays these phrases that no one could ever hope to duplicate.

Perhaps the most familiar of these phrases is the one in Example 1a ["Moment's Notice," 2:08–2:12].

But very often he will employ it sequentially in the course of building up a solo (or reaching the climax of one), and he is an expert in the subtle use of sequences for this purpose. Notice what he does with that same phrase towards the end of his solo on "Bass Blues," Example 1b [3:06–3:12]. Notice how he alters the phrasing. You will find the same sort of thing in tracks like "Straight, No Chaser" and "Soft Lights and Sweet Music."

Another phrase that recurs frequently in his playing is this one, which undergoes even more alterations: Example 2a [1:50–1:53] gives it in a portion of his solo on "Blue Train." Example 2b [5:02–5:09] shows what happens to that same phrase at the beginning of his second chorus on "Bakai."

Before I go any further, I would like to discuss a most controversial aspect of Coltrane's playing: his technique. It is an excellent one—one of the finest. His command of the instrument is almost unbelievable. Tempos don't faze him in the least; his control enables him to handle a very slow ballad without having to resort to the double-timing so common among hard blowers, and for him there is no such thing as too fast a tempo. His playing is very clean and accurate, and he almost never misses a note.

His range is something to marvel at: a full three octaves upward from the lowest note obtainable on the horn (concert A-flat). Now, there are a good many tenor players who have an extensive range, but what sets Coltrane apart from the rest of them is the equality of strength in all registers which he has been able to obtain through long, hard practice. His sound is just as clear, full and unforced in the topmost notes as it is down at the bottom.

That tone of his, by the way, has been, and doubtless will continue to be, a subject of debate. A result of the particular combination of mouthpiece and reed he uses plus an extremely tight embouchure, it is an incredibly powerful, resonant and sharply penetrating sound with a spine-chilling quality. There are many who argue that it is not a "good" saxophone sound. Exactly what is a good saxophone sound? Are we to go along with those who hold that the only really good sound is of the Lester Young or of the Coleman Hawkins variety and therefore assume that none of the younger "hard" tenor players has a "good" sound? Lester Young's sound suited Lester Young, and Coleman Hawkins' sound is great for Coleman Hawkins. A sound is good if it suits the player's style and conception. So it is with Coltrane.

A word about his intonation. Those listeners who say that he doesn't play in tune have been deceived by that sharp edge in his sound. Of course, I don't mean to imply that his horn is immune to weather changes—no instrument is. And there are days when he has some intonation difficulties. But he plays in tune.

I mention all these things because they have a direct connection with a good many things that Coltrane does. A technique like his seems essential to his approach, as we shall see.

There is far more to Coltrane's style than "hard drive." Hard drive is only one aspect of it, and even then it is an entirely different kind from that of, say, Sonny Rollins. Coltrane seems to have the power to pull listeners right out of their chairs. I have noticed this terrific impact on the various rhythm sections he has played with; he pulls them right along with him and makes them cook too. An interesting phenomenon is what happens to rhythm sections when Coltrane takes over from another soloist. Say Miles Davis is the first soloist. Notice that the rhythm section doesn't push. They are relaxed behind him. Now Coltrane takes over, and immediately something happens to the group: the rhythm section tightens up and plays harder. The bass becomes stronger and more forceful, as does the ride-cymbal beat; even the pianist comps differently. They can't help it—Coltrane is driving them ahead. This is most noticeable on medium and up tempos where he is most likely to cut loose. (It would be most interesting to see what would happen to a typical West Coast rhythm section should they find themselves having to play behind him.)

Coltrane's kind of "funk" drives, rather than swings. And it is less obvious. Listen carefully to his solos on such tracks as "Blue Train" and "Bass Blues" and you will hear some excellent examples. But listen carefully, because it won't be as easy to spot as Horace Silver's kind. That solo on "Blue Train" is such a revealing example of so many facets of his style and conception that I will transcribe it in its entirety [omitted here], with accompanying explanatory notes.

Coltrane's harmonic conception is perhaps the most puzzling aspect of his style, inasmuch as it is so advanced. For one thing, he really knows what to do with the changes of the tunes he plays. This is apparent not only in his playing, but also—as we shall see—in his writing. He knows when to stick with the basic changes and when to employ those unusual extensions and alterations that a lot of people refer to as "blowing out of the changes" because they don't quite hear just what he is doing. He is very subtle, often deceptive—but he's always right there.

An excellent insight into these harmonic devices of his can be found in that weird phenomenon which has been variously referred to as "sheets of sound," "ribbons of sound," "a gosh-awful lot of notes" and other things. These are very long phrases played at such an extremely rapid tempo that the notes he plays cease to be mere notes and fuse into a continuous flow of pure sound. Sometimes they do not come off the way he wants them to, and that is when the cry of "just scales" arises. That may be, but I dare anyone to play scales like this, with that irregular, often arrhythmic phrasing, those variations of dynamics, and that fantastic sense of timing.

But more often they work out the way he wants them to, and then one hears things. There is an unbelievable emotional impact to them; plus a fantastic residual harmonic effect which often is so pronounced that in many instances the piano wouldn't be missed if it weren't playing. A perfect example of this occurs halfway through Coltrane's solo on "Gold Coast" (Example 3 [4:14–4:29]). The piano plays the changes behind this, but it seems that just drums and bass would be sufficient, because in this section the changes are right there, as you can see.

An example of implied changes occurs in the unaccompanied run he plays in the tag of "Russian Lullaby" (Example 4 [4:58–5:05]). Look at the transcription [omitted here] carefully, and you will be able to pick out a definite chord progression. It is probably the one Coltrane had in mind.

Some fantastic things happen when he plays on blues changes, the most basic ones. Example 5 [3:59–4:31] is his first two choruses on "Straight, No Chaser." The changes are regular blues in F. Keeping that in mind, notice the way Coltrane subtly plays all those extensions and alterations of the chords. It does seem at first as if he were "blowing out of the changes." Actually he is not. That is a very important part of Coltrane's harmonic concept: his awareness of the changes and what to do with them. The same sort of thing occurs with telling effect in the middle of his solo on "Blue Train" as we will see. You will also notice it in certain portions of his solo on "Bass Blues" if you listen carefully.

Coltrane's sense of form is another source of wonderment. He has very few equals at building up a solo, especially on a blues—and building up a good solo on a blues is not easy.

There are a number of devices which Coltrane employs in building a solo which are by no means obvious, and which would take repeated hearings to spot. But once you know what they are, you will be able to understand more fully just how he goes about it.

One of them—and it shows up at once on "Blue Train"—is his little trick of building up on a single note (as in this case) or a short phrase, then taking off from there. It is personal with him, like so many of the things he does.

Another is his wonderful use of sequences—which I mentioned earlier in the end of his solo on "Bass Blues" wherein he employs one of his pet phrases this way. Another excellent illustration is his tag on "Locomotion" (Example 6 [6:52–7:10]).

Coltrane has a way of starting his solos in the least expected places. What is more, he never does anything exactly the same way twice. He also has a peculiarly individual way of altering the phrasing, unlike anything ever heard before. It is almost impossible to describe it, but if you look back at Example 1b, in part one of this article, you will see something of it. It involves an extremely subtle shifting of accentuation (you'll see this also in Examples 2b, 4 and 5, as well as in the solo on "Blue Train"), which results in previous often arrhythmic phrasing that will throw the unwary listener off the track.

At this point I am going to do what I said I'd do earlier—quote Coltrane's complete recorded solo on "Blue Train," inasmuch as it is a perfect example of so many of the previously mentioned aspects of his style and a good blues solo.

The tune itself is a revealing sample of Coltrane's writing, being as direct and straightforward as his playing, and offering a tremendous insight into his overall conception. It is a most powerful blues line, brooding, mysterious, almost like an eerie chant; someone has remarked that it is more than just a blues, that it has other meanings in it. This is true of everything he does.

There are some unusual things about this solo.

For one thing, this recording was done during his tenure with Thelonious Monk, and here and there are isolated flashes of certain aspects of his current work—sort of a preview of things to come, as it were. I refer particularly to the "sheets of sound," which, it is interesting to note, is a spontaneous development.

This solo continues to build up all the way to the last chorus. It reaches its peak at the sixth chorus, where the other two horns come in with a riff (Example 72 [2:18–2:22]), which repeats six times, and adds even more impetus. This constant building-up is a most striking feature of Coltrane's work, and has been apparent even from his earliest days with Miles Davis. Then, too, notice how he tends to stay in the high register of his horn. Well, he can be justly proud of that register. It is strong, clear and—in his hands—full of a terrific emotional impact.

He does one thing that is unusual in that it is difficult to do well: he slurs those long phrases all the way and plays them so clearly. There is ample evidence of how solid his technique is—that fluid, unerring finger action.

Lest you think that Coltrane's playing consists of cooking and more cooking, I'd like to say a few words about the way he handles slower tempos. I mentioned earlier in discussing various aspects of his technique, his fantastic control which enables him to play a ballad without having to double-time on it. But that control isn't all. Except for the fact that he is more intense, his ballad concept could be likened to that of Miles Davis. He has the same straightforward, thoughtful approach. And I'm not just talking about the classic "'Round Midnight" he did with Miles; there are plenty of other tracks which provide a fine demonstration of this kind of lyricism: his unusual interpretation of the seldom-done standard "While My Lady Sleeps," for instance, or "Slow Dance," to give two examples. They are object lessons in how to play a ballad without unnecessary "cooking."

That is Coltrane the instrumentalist—powerful, sensitive, ahead, and always experimenting. Now I'd like to talk a bit about Coltrane the jazz composer and arranger, inasmuch as it may throw still further light on certain other aspects of his conception.

Coltrane's writing may not be quite as familiar as his playing, except to his most avid followers. He is, like Horace Silver and Benny Golson, always experimenting with different structures and unusual chord progressions—but his writing is easily distinguishable from that of the other two.

For one thing, his melodic lines—blues or not—are all very powerful, direct and straightforward, with strong emotional impact. When he gets "funky" (the theme of "Blue Train" is a perfect example) it is, as I said earlier, hard, driving, intense—not like any other kind. Even "John Paul Jones," which he composed a few years ago, could never be taken for a line by someone like Horace Silver, despite the fact that it is slower and more relaxed (Example 8 [0:00–0:08]). Among other tunes of this kind is one called "Straight Street," which, although based on twelve-bar phrases, could never be mistaken for a blues (Example 9 [0:00–1:05]). The chord progression, by the way, is a characteristic one. If you look closely, you will notice that it is the old familiar II-V changes—with a twist not instantly noticeable. Of course, you know that it's this II-V business, because I told you so, and there it is in front of you. But if you were listening to it for the first time, you might notice only that the changes *seem* out of the ordinary. Coltrane handles this so cleverly that you don't realize just what it is. Another example of this occurs in "Moment's Notice." Example 10 [0:00–0:15] gives part of the introduction.

The deceptiveness that is part and parcel of Coltrane's writing also shows up in his blues "Locomotion." The structure of this tune is not too unusual: 12-12-8-12 blues is now almost standard on the East Coast. But even here he has a little twist: he has each succeeding soloist take an unaccompanied eight-bar break before going into his solo.

But it is the rhythm of that eight-bar riff in the line itself that is really confusing (Example 11 [0:07–0:15]). You hear it on the recording, and it sounds as if the accented E-flat were on the first beat of the measure. As you can see, it isn't. (I was thrown off by it on the first couple of hearings, and I'm supposed to have a good ear!)

His approach to arranging is just as different as everything else he does. Very often what he does amounts to an almost complete reharmonization or reconstruction of a tune or part of it, and right there you get another view of his harmonic conception.

For instance, the first few bars of his arrangement of "While My Lady Sleeps" (Example 12 [0:00–0:33]). Another illustration of the reconstructive process he uses can be seen in what he does to the familiar Latin-beat introduction so often played on "Star Eyes" (Example 13 [from an unrecorded live performance]).

As I said in the first part of this series, the only thing to expect from John Coltrane is the unexpected.

BARBARA GARDNER
JOHN COLTRANE
Down Beat Music 1962

In this article, written a few years into John Coltane's career as a leader, Barbara Gardner looks back at Coltrane's youth and early career before discussing the saxophonist's current directions. She interviewed not only Coltrane but also several individuals who had known him at various stages of his life and musical development. As expected, Coltrane answers questions about his life and music with sincerity and candor.

The "trail of self-destruction" mentioned in the first paragraph was Coltrane's drug addiction and alcoholism. In his liner notes to his recording A Love Supreme, *Coltrane writes of a spiritual awakening in 1957; part of that experience involved giving up alcohol and drugs. Also in 1957, Coltrane recorded his first LP solely under his name; his philosophy about that event is touched on here.—CW*

He walked a fast trail of self-destruction for much of his early adulthood. By the time he was 31, he had about physically and spiritually burned himself out, and he just lay there, smoldering in deterioration. One day in 1957, he made up his mind to "Get some fun out of life for a change." He rose out of the ashes of his life to become one of the most controversial contributors to modern jazz . . . John Coltrane.

John William Coltrane was born on September 23, 1926, in Hamlet, North Carolina. He was an only child. When he was still an infant, his parents moved to High Point, N.C. There was nothing spectacular about their life there. His father, a tailor, saw his son enjoying music as he himself did. The Coltrane home was filled with musical instruments. In time, young John learned to play clarinet, alto saxophone, and ukulele.

When Coltrane was 12, his father died, leaving him little but a love of music. The high school he attended did not have a school band, but he played alto saxophone and clarinet in a community center band after school.

In 1943, Coltrane and his mother moved to Philadelphia. He continued his studies at Granoff Studios and Ornstein School of Music. In 1945, he entered the Navy, serving in Hawaii, where he played in a Navy Band. He was discharged in the middle of the following year.

A quiet, introspective musician of 21, who had never played the tenor saxophone in his life, John Coltrane was hired on tenor by Eddie (Cleanhead) Vinson. Pianist Red Garland, who was working with Vinson at the time, was instrumental in getting him the job. Coltrane objected mildly that he was an altoist but made the switch without trauma.

The multinote soloist of today is in direct contrast to the shy, reluctant instrumentalist of the late '40s.

"Yeah, little ol' Coltrane used to be in my band," Vinson remembers with a paternal smile. "He never wanted to play. I used to have to play all night long. I'd ask him, 'Man, why don't you play?' He'd say, 'I just want to hear you play.'"

It was partly sincere admiration that made the newcomer hesitate to play in the presence of the pros, but much of the reluctance could be attributed to the stage of his development, which he alone knew. There was little individuality or personal creation in his early playing.

"At that time, I was trying to play like Dexter Gordon and Wardell Gray," Coltrane said. "I liked what they were doing. I heard in them lots of the ideas of Lester Young, who was my first influence. So when I made the switch to tenor, I was trying to play like them."

In 1949, Coltrane began accumulating jazz experience with the giants. He joined the Dizzy Gillespie big band as an altoist. Later he was to work in a Gillespie combo playing tenor. About the time of his first Gillespie stay, the fleeting, biting tenor of Sonny Stitt caught his ear. Again, the exploring musician attempted to find his direction in another man's course.

"Sonny's playing sounded like something I would like to do," Coltrane recalled. "He sounded like something between Dexter and Wardell, an outgrowth of both of them. All the time, I thought I had been looking for something and then I heard Sonny and said, 'Damn! There it is! That's it!'"

And he thought it was and set about developing that brand of tenor playing that drew on Lester Young and Charlie Parker for its chief points of departure. He was more than competent in this style. Several jazzmen of stature kept an eye on him. In turn, he was snapped up by Earl Bostic,

Johnny Hodges, Jimmy Smith, and in 1957, Miles Davis. He left Davis briefly to work with Thelonious Monk in 1958 but returned later the same year.

With Davis, the bubble of false security burst, and Coltrane again was forced to view those repressed aspirations for musical freedom and individuality.

"I began trying to add to what I was playing because of Miles's group," he said. "Being there, I just couldn't be satisfied any longer with what I was doing. The standards were so high, and I felt that I wasn't really contributing like I should."

Then he added a thought that reflects his concern for musical truth:

"About this time, I got the recording contract with Prestige, and I decided that if I was going to put anything on record, then it ought to be me."

This was the beginning of the emergence of John Coltrane as one of the most individual of musicians.

Once the decision was made, Coltrane wasted no time in beginning at the core of his frustrations. He put his mental and physical health on the mend by stopping two destructive habits—alcoholism and narcotics addiction—simultaneously and immediately. Not only was this the turning point in John Coltrane's life, it reflected the great inner strength of the man.

"He never clarified his direction, verbally," remembers Cannonball Adderley, who worked with him in the Davis group. "He did suggest that he was going to change all around, both personally and musically.

"All of a sudden, he decided that he was going to change the John Coltrane image. Along with changing the physical and spiritual things, he encountered Monk along the way musically, and played with him for near a year. I'm sure that he heard a lot of things he's playing now, even back then."

Then Adderley expressed a prevalent admiration for the strength of conviction that led to Coltrane's musical direction:

"You've got to hand it to him, you know. In the middle of a successful career, Coltrane decided that he wasn't playing anything and made up his mind to go ahead and develop something that had been in the back of his mind all along."

There was no outside influence demanding that Coltrane move on from his comfortable, accepted position as a rising young tenor man in the pattern of Gordon, Gray, and Stitt. He was being accepted, even welcomed, on this basis. Adderley describes the Coltrane of the Miles Davis era as "not so much commercially successful, as commercially acceptable.

He played quite a few solos back then that the hippie-in-the-street began to hum. I challenge them to hum some of his solos now."

Exactly what the spark was that ignited Coltrane into new flamboyant motion is yet unknown, even to the reed man himself. Adderley attributes part of the answer to the acceptance being given Sonny Rollins.

"Coltrane had appeared on most of the commercially successful records with Miles Davis, and his material was becoming more and more popular," Adderley said. "People were beginning to say 'John Coltrane' with some degree of serious feeling about it. At that time also, Sonny Rollins had broken through with a little thing of his own in vogue, and I guess John thought that the time was right for him to start fooling around with his own stuff."

If Sonny Rollins can be referred to as a fresh breath of wind in the static tenor scene, then the post-1958 Coltrane must be regarded as a tornado.

He bombarded the listener with a rapid-fire succession of 16th notes; long, apparently unrelated lines; interchanging, reversible five-note chords; and constantly altering tone. Some charged he was repetitious. He played an idea over and over, turning the notes around in every possible combination, summoning every imaginable tone from his instrument, trying to coax out of the horn the thing he felt, trying to attain that certain feeling that would tell him that he was on the right track.

"I work a lot by feeling," Coltrane still admits. "I just have to feel it. If I don't, then I keep trying."

This musical and physical renaissance was not without its outside problems and disappointments. Coltrane found that to be different and distinctive, to dare to step outside the pale of the accepted, overworked pattern of tenor playing was to inspire, most often, the wrath of those writers and listeners who complained loudest about the clichés and imitation existing in tenor playing at that time.

Coltrane's repetition and constant trial and error reaped criticism from within the charmed music circle as well. Musicians occasionally cloaked in criticism their admiration for his daring.

Adderley remembers that occasionally Miles Davis would question Coltrane about his long solos:

"Once in a while, Miles might say, 'Why you play so long, man?' and John would say, 'It took that long to get it all in.' And Miles would accept that, really. Miles never bothered anybody much about what to play or how to play it."

Initially, much of the jazz world laughed. This man could not be serious, was the attitude even though there perhaps never has been a jazzman with a greater reputation for sobriety about his work. Coltrane never deviated from his newly charted course.

"He was serious about everything—everything he played," Adderley says. "Where sometimes Miles would take on some humor in his playing—or lots of times I might feel lighter than usual—John was heavily involved with being just serious and musical, all the time."

Donald Garrett, a Chicago musician who works with Coltrane as the second bassist occasionally, has said:

"He is a meticulous musician. He will often play a tune seven or eight different ways before he decides on just how he wants to play it."

Coltrane's wife, Juanita, remembers that during the early period of experimentation, Coltrane sometimes would woodshed for 24 hours straight without food or sleep. He stopped only when he was physically unable to practice anymore. And when he was too exhausted to play, he talked music.

Gradually, the first wave of critical laughter passed and was replaced by a general outrage or a sophisticated mockery. Writers articulate in their craft referred to him as an "angry young tenor," to his sound as "the bark of a dog," to his ideas as "epileptic fits of passion."

One compassionate writer, Ira Gitler, in 1958 described Coltrane's playing as "sheets of sound," and in *Jazz Review* Mimi Clar elaborated on this years later to describe the saxophonist's music as "yards of accordion-pleated fabric hastily flung from the bolt."

When Coltrane's name was breathed in the same context as Charlie Parker's, one writer retorted, "Charlie Parker's playing is like an electric fan being switched on and off; Coltrane's playing is like an electric fan being turned on and left."

There were a few Coltrane champions in those days, but they were almost consumed in the raging heat of controversy. By 1960, the general attitude of most jazz writers and listeners was succinctly expressed in a Martin Williams record review:

". . . patience for all may be the best thing to suggest. When the plant is growing, it doesn't do to keep pulling it up to look at the roots."

Following this metaphoric admonition, most jazz listeners, professional and otherwise, settled back to await the maturation of the "angry young tenor." The wait has not been a quiet or uneventful one. In April 1960, Coltrane formed his own combo. Since that time, he has changed personnel and instrumentation often in his search for new sounds and new musical concepts.

"John is one of the most brilliant jazz musicians of all times because he has the rare combination of originality and the ability to make profound decisions, musically," Adderley said. "By profound decisions, I mean that he can think of so many things to play, a whole variety of things, before he plays anything; and he can instantly make a good selection from this wide choice. He is a brilliant soloist, but he is also a good, original, all-around musician. His concept is altogether different.

"He has a tremendous influence and will have on the young tenor players coming up now. He is a definite departure. I don't mean that he was a radical departure from the tenor played by, say, Coleman Hawkins because there were some radical departures before him. But there was a generally accepted, established style of play that was a mixture of Charlie Parker, Dexter Gordon, Lester Young, and some of Coleman Hawkins' style. And John decided, all of a sudden, that although he was one of the most successful of these modern jazz players, that wasn't good enough for him."

A well-discussed departure that Coltrane has made from the accepted jazz pattern has been the addition of a second bassist.

Young Garrett maintains that this is an idea Coltrane had toyed with for several years. Garrett himself takes credit for having interested Coltrane in the idea.

"Well, we have been friends since 1955, and whenever he is in town, he comes over to my house, and we go over ideas," Garrett said.

"I had this tape where I was playing with another bass player. We were doing some things rhythmically, and Coltrane became excited about the sound. We got the same kind of sound you get from the East Indian water drum. One bass remains in the lower register and is the stabilizing, pulsating thing, while the other bass is free to improvise, like the right hand would be on the drum. So Coltrane likes the idea."

To Garrett, Coltrane represents more than a successful tenor man.

"Coltrane has individual freedom without sacrifice of musical message," he said. "He just proves that if you've really got something to say, you don't have to cheat."

The bassist is too good a musician not to recognize and acknowledge many of the early limitations of the renovated saxophonist. But Garrett has a simple and sympathetic explanation:

"He just had a sound in his head that he couldn't get out of his horn. His direction has always been the same. He is just getting able to express it better. Just like Sonny Rollins. When Sonny started, he used to squeak a lot. He was just trying to play what he heard in his head. Any time one is an innovator, there are lots of defects in the early playing because nobody's ever tried it before."

Coltrane says that he plans to continue extending his harmonic growth, but, at the same time, he does not turn his back on rhythmic developments. He wrote in 1960, "I want to be more flexible where rhythm is concerned. I feel I have to study rhythm some more. I haven't experimented too much with time; most of my experimenting has been in a harmonic form. I put time and rhythm to one side, in the past."

Others recognize rhythmic development as one of Coltrane's most fertile areas.

"His growth has to be basically rhythmic," said bassist Garrett. "His harmonic conception will be limited until his rhythmic concept is fully developed. This is one of the reasons for his success now. He is extending in all rhythmic directions which give him more area for climactic development."

For all practical purposes, Coltrane has arrived. No one is asking for further extension from him. Perfect that which you have introduced, he is asked today. Coltrane himself surveys his lot and answers in confusion:

"I haven't found it yet. I'm listening all the time, but I haven't found it."

Where is it? What is it? How will he know it when he has it?

"I don't know what I'm looking for," he answers frankly. "Something that hasn't been played before. I don't know what it is. I know I'll have that feeling when I get it. I'll just keep searching."

Two years ago, Coltrane said he had something "that I'm afraid to play. People won't let me get away with it."

"I don't remember what I was talking about specifically," he says now. "I guess I must have tried them already. I've gone through all the things I used to want to do. Some I liked and am still working on. Others I had to set aside."

Restless and discontented, he says he does not feel dissatisfied with his present contribution, but, at the same time, he does not feel completely satisfied. He still feels the tenacious tug of incompleteness that spurred him to walk away from his "commercial acceptance" in 1957 and begin moving in a more self-satisfying direction. But he knows no guaranteed answers to fulfillment.

"I just can't seem to find the right songs," he said. "I'm listening everywhere. I listen to other groups, records, the men I work with, trying to find what I'm looking for. I learn a lot from the fellows in the group. Eric Dolphy is a hell of a musician, and he plays a lot of horn. When he is up there searching and experimenting, I learn a lot from him, but I just haven't found exactly what I want yet."

There is the obvious solution a musician can employ when available material ceases to provide the musical stimulus or outlet for expression.

"I just have to write the tunes myself," he said flatly, without any show of arrogance. "And I don't really want to take the time away from my horn. Writing has always been a secondary thing for me, but I find that lately I am spending more and more time at it, because I can't find the proper tunes."

Friends and associates closest to the quiet, withdrawn reed man are holding their breath, hoping that he begins to catch a glimpse of his elusive rainbow. There is perhaps not a bolder, more aggressive, more volitant tenor player anywhere among the leading musicians of today. The Coltrane experimental and effectual use of the soprano saxophone is held by many to be a further step in modern-jazz coloration. Yet his personal acquaintances are waiting for some sign of that abrupt, venturesome departure that hurtled Coltrane into the spotlight almost two years ago.

Some remarks are clothed in blind faith, and some rare speculation, like Adderley's: "You never know what he's going to do next. He may come out in a few months with a whole new thing."

Garrett observes with admiration, "He's always going to be new and fresh and ahead of everything. He isn't going to sacrifice anything. He's always learning, trying new things."

Eddie Vinson remembers from years back and repeats today, "That ol' boy was something. He changed his playing every six months almost. Even now, you never can tell what he's going to be playing six months from now."

Constant change, this is the basic characteristic with which John Coltrane has impressed every person who knows him well. And dedication to music—he lives and breathes music. An interview with Coltrane must be something like intruding into a human being's soul. His honest love and respect for his work and his unembarrassed humility in his current dilemma gush forth, almost unasked for. He seems to want to share his stalemate with the world in the faint hope that someone someplace might have a key to unlock for him the entire world of music.

Beyond the ambition to find "something," he has no further plan. At the moment he has no new ideas for further direction. He wants to improve and refine those he has. His next album may contain only material written by him. He is not sure, but he may or may not return the alto saxophone to his horn kit. This may help him to extend his harmonic development. One thing of which he is certain, he will definitely have to write more, whether he wants to or not.

In the meantime, he continues to pour into his craft a dedication born of intimate knowledge of neglect and its devastation. He does so even knowing that he is marking time, at least according to his own criteria. That much of the world hasn't caught up to his work is its problem. He does not want to bask in belated glory. Coltrane says he very well may be looking into the sinking sun and cannot feed on the plaudits of the late risers.

"I just want to play all I can," he said, almost desperately. "Sometimes an entertainer just has a certain span of productivity. I hope that never happens to me, but you never know, so I want to keep playing as long as I possibly can."

JOE GOLDBERG
JOHN COLTRANE
Jazz Masters of the Fifties, *1965*

Goldberg's book was published two years before Coltrane's death. At the time, Coltrane's "classic" quartet with McCoy Tyner (piano), Jimmy Garrison (bass), and Elvin Jones (drums) was at its peak and had already released several LPs that are now considered jazz classics. The year 1965 would be an important one for Coltrane and his group. Coltrane's four-part suite A Love Supreme *(recorded in December 1964) was released, and in some ways the record summed up the explorations of the Coltrane quartet. As this chapter makes clear, Coltrane had for several years been adding guests including Eric Dolphy (reeds and flute), Wes Montgomery (electric guitar), and Art Davis (bass), to his basic group. In June 1965, Coltrane expanded on this practice by adding seven guests for the recording of his Ornette Coleman–influenced composition* Ascension. *In the following transitional period, Coltrane often added guest musicians to the quartet nucleus. However, by early 1966 Tyner and Jones had left the band, and Coltrane became thoroughly committed to the new instrumentations, personnel, and musical practice that would characterize his group to the end of his career.*

Note: The August Blume interview quoted here has been retranscribed and appears on pages 86 to 95 of this volume.—CW

"He played quite a few solos back then that the hippie-in-the-street began to hum," Julian Adderley said, recalling John Coltrane's tenure in the Miles Davis group. "I challenge them to hum some of his solos now."

No statement more accurately reflects the problem that critics and fans have with John Coltrane's music; it comes close to isolating the problem that Coltrane himself has with it. A writer in the December, 1960 issue of the men's magazine *Nugget* remarked that "One of the best things that ever happened to John Coltrane was the discovery of Ornette Coleman by the jazz avant garde . . . Coltrane . . . has been able to continue his search for his own musical personality without the onus of having everything he does, missteps and all, hailed as evidence of genius." It would have been nice had it been true. By comparison, the Ornette Coleman controversy was an argument carried on by physicists on the blackboard of the Princeton Institute for Advanced Study; discussions about Coltrane can take on some of the truculent, hysterical aspects of political arguments in neighborhood bars.

Often, the participants in arguments about Coltrane have about the same amount of accurate information as barroom philosophers. Coltrane is as undecided about his music as those who discuss it. Since 1959, he has run through several musical ideas so rapidly that a given Coltrane record may be obsolete before its release; it will almost surely be outdated before reviews of it are published. He therefore identifies with very little of what he reads about himself.

The tenor saxophonist first came to prominence in the middle fifties, reflecting compulsion, anxiety, anger, and fear, what pianist Cecil Taylor calls "the realities of the day." For all its seeming chaos, the music had deep and direct emotional meaning for many listeners, and some insiders began to mark Coltrane as "the man." But it did not become Coltrane's year until 1961, when he won three divisions in *Down Beat*'s International Critics' Poll, best tenor saxophonist of the year, and, in the "New Star" division, "Miscellaneous Instrument" (for soprano saxophone) and "New Combo." It behooves a musician to take such "honors" with a grain or two of realism. For as often as not, some of the same writers who make a current victory possible are those who once maintained that their favorite did not know how to play his instrument. The experience of Sonny Rollins, for one, indicates that it can be detrimental to read one's own press notices. It would have been disastrous for Coltrane too, had he taken his to heart, for his early notices were frequently negative, and he has been under fire several times since. That he continues to progress in the inexorable glare of a scrutiny that invests his most casual acts with significance is evidence of unusual conviction. Coltrane is probably the first major soloist of the contemporary era whose development largely took place under such scrutiny, and it should be of some value to examine that development.

Very little is known about Coltrane's personal life; on the face of it, there is not much to tell. As his wife Juanita, who is an avid partisan of her husband and his playing, puts it, "He doesn't think about anything else but his music." He was born John William Coltrane on September 23, 1926, in Hamlet, North Carolina. His father was a tailor who loved music, and played several instruments around the house. John himself played a variety of reed instruments: the E♭ alto horn, the clarinet, and then the tenor saxophone in high school. A few years after his father died, Coltrane's family moved to Philadelphia, and he continued his studies there at the Granoff Studios and the Ornstein School of Music. By 1945, he was playing professionally in that city with a cocktail combo. Then in 1945–46 he was in the Navy, and despite what writers were later to say of his playing, he had evidently mastered the rudiments of his instruments enough to satisfy the more conservative elements of our society, for he toured with a Navy band in Hawaii during those years.

He once outlined his early professional experience for August Blume in *The Jazz Review*: "My first job was with a band from Indianapolis, led by Joe Webb. This was in 1947. Big Maybelle, the blues singer, was with this band. Then King Kolax, then Eddie Vinson, and Dizzy's big band. Earl Bostic, Gay Cross from Cleveland. He used to be with Louis Jordan. He sang and played in Jordan's style. Then I was with Daisey May and The Hep Cats, and then with Johnny Hodges in 1953 for six or seven months. Richie Powell was on piano, Lawrence Brown on trombone, Emmett Berry on trumpet, Jimmy Johnson on drums and I can't seem to remember the bass player's name. . . . I enjoyed that job, we had some true music. I didn't appreciate guys like Bostic at the time because Bird had swayed me so much. After I'd gotten from under his spell I began to appreciate them more. After Hodges I spent a couple of weeks with Jimmy Smith. Wow, I'd wake up in the middle of the night and hear that organ. Those chords screaming at me. Back in 1949 I worked one job with Bud Powell. It was a dance gig at the Audubon in New York. Sonny Rollins and Art Blakey were with him. Those guys you can call really great."

In tone and style, that extract is reminiscent of nothing quite so much as the recitations of past battles which club fighters give reporters. Understandably so, for any talented young Negro hoping to achieve some stature is likely to be telling a reporter either of drummers he has played with or welterweights he has fought.

Coltrane's early experience, which for the most part could be dismissed superficially as local rhythm-and-blues work, all points in one direction. If one looks in the windows of record stores in Harlem, Chicago's South Side, or any other of the large Negro areas of the country, he will see such music on display—tenors, organs, vocalists, and a few comedy or "party" records. This music has been given different names, but as soon as one admits that the Negro and the white have largely different cultures, then it becomes apparent that it is simply Negro popular music; the equivalent, in a sense, of Lawrence Welk, Les Brown or Doris Day.

Local Negro bands around the country play for social situations. In the small clubs and roadhouses, the patrons are drinking, dancing, talking, and laughing, often paying little or no attention to the musicians. The music becomes, in the most exact sense, background, and the performing musician must first of all cater to the taste of his public and try within that framework, if possible, to satisfy whatever private esthetic standards he holds.

It is perhaps this sort of training, still evident even in Coltrane's most advanced work, which accounts for two extremely revealing remarks he has made. I once questioned him about an album he had recorded, one side of which was a trio with only bass and drum accompaniment. When I first heard these performances, I wondered why he had chosen to record that way. Did he feel more freedom, or was there constriction? Sonny Rollins had made considerable impact by recording and playing personal appearances without piano; was Coltrane challenging Rollins? His answer was brief and to the point: "The piano player didn't show up." Another time, he was speaking of the writers who were nearly unanimous in their dislike of his first widely-heard efforts, seeming to feel that he did not know how to play. "I was hurt by it," he says, "but I was surprised. I don't know why they talked about me the way they did. I wasn't original then; I wasn't playing anything new or different."

In the light of what Coltrane has done since, the statement is true. But it is puzzling when one thinks of the turbulent saxophonist heard on the Miles Davis Quintet record which first brought him to public notice. The conductor Ernest Ansermet once remarked on "what a moving thing it is to meet" Sidney Bechet, the first great jazz virtuoso of the soprano saxophone, ". . . who is very glad one likes what he does, but can say nothing of his art except that he follows his 'own way' . . . ." At one time, the same could have been said of Coltrane, and it might account for the self-deprecation. But one is also reminded of some remarks apropos guitarist

Charlie Christian which novelist Ralph Ellison printed in *Saturday Review:* "More often than not (and this is especially true of its Negro exponents) jazz's heroes remain local figures known only to small-town dance halls, and whose reputations are limited to the radius of a few hundred miles. . . . Some of the most brilliant of jazzmen made no records; their names appeared in print only in announcements of some local dance or remote 'battles of music' against equally uncelebrated bands. Being devoted to an art which traditionally thrives on improvisation, these unrecorded artists very often have their most original ideas enter the public domain almost as rapidly as they are conceived, to be quickly absorbed into the thought and technique of their fellows. . . . Thus, because jazz finds its very life in an endless improvisation upon traditional materials, the jazzman must lose his identity even as he finds it—how often do we see even the most famous of jazz artists being devoured alive by their imitators, and, shamelessly, in the public spotlight?"

Those remarks belong on Coltrane's wall, next to the *Down Beat* plaques which hang there, for he has been living them for years. It seems quite likely, for one thing, that Coltrane was simply playing out of a background which was known to him but not to the writers who found him so unusual. Ira Gitler, the first critic to recognize that Coltrane was not an imitator of Sonny Rollins, feels that the saxophonist is indebted to Dexter Gordon and Sonny Stitt for much of his style, but Coltrane himself has acknowledged Lester Young, Johnny Hodges, and Charlie Parker, and has said—significantly, in the light of Ellison's remarks—"I have listened to about all the good tenor men, beginning with Lester, and believe me, I've picked up something from them all, including several who have never recorded."

But Ellison was talking about Charlie Christian, and the situations in which Christian and Coltrane came to prominence are different. Roughly twenty years separate the influence of the two men, a fact whose importance can best be judged by noting that even though Christian's music is universally acknowledged to be a source of modern jazz, there is no complete LP by him currently in print.

Even though Christian died young, it is unlikely that there would have been so few recorded examples of his playing had he worked in the fifties. As one recording executive puts it, "A man can get on an album if he's had two lessons; if he's had three, he can be a leader." It is highly unlikely that any musician of real talent will remain unknown today, as companies beat the bushes in a desperate search for new people to record. One could say that several young musicians have not received the exposure warranted by their talent, but most of them have had their music committed to disc at least once. Today's young jazzman believes that if he is to be successful, he ought to come to New York. During the fifties, there were mass exoduses to New York from both Detroit and Philadelphia. The danger now is more likely to be that the young musician will be over-recorded, perhaps before he is ready to be recorded at all. It seemed, for a time, that this was happening to Coltrane.

When he came to New York with the Miles Davis Quintet in 1955, Coltrane encountered difficulty, at first, in trying to get a recording contract. At that time, Davis has recalled, "people used to tell me to fire him. They said he wasn't playing anything." Coltrane presented himself to the officials at Blue Note, who were unwilling to sign him to a contract, but agreed to make one album, which, ironically enough, contain some of his best and most famous early work. In April 1957, he recorded one piece with Thelonious Monk which impressed Riverside's A & R man, Orrin Keepnews, so much that he offered Coltrane a contract on the spot. But Coltrane had signed with Prestige two weeks previously. And he has never lacked for work since. The problem with which he then became confronted was one I attempted to discuss in a piece written in 1958:

When John Coltrane is left to shift for himself, those facets of his style that make him a candidate for greatness and those that may well keep him from achieving it are both thrown into sudden relief. On the back liner of his new Blue Note album, Robert Levin speaks of Coltrane's "spearing, sharp and resonant" sound that creates an "ominous atmosphere," and of his "veering, inconsistent lines." Those phrases, I think, characterize Coltrane about as well as it could be done, and highlight the qualities of original thinking that have made him the first major new saxophone innovator since Sonny Rollins, who in turn was the first since Bird. But change is not always progress, and to a large degree Coltrane contains within himself the elements that make his kind of jazz the most exciting being played, and the elements that often seem to be leading it (and him) down a blind alley.

Excitement is there, certainly, of an incomparable nature, and surprise. Most often, at the beginning of a solo, Coltrane enters from the unexpected place, creating a shock effect in the first phrase that leaves the listener limp for two or three choruses. Listen to him on "Blues By Five" on the Miles Davis *Cookin'* album (Prestige 7094). He is also possessed of an unmatched energy by which, in two choruses, he can lift an average, flaccid bop record out of its rut and into the realm of major jazz. Hear his solo on "Light Blue," in the album *Interplay for Two Trumpets and Two Tenors*.

Two new Coltrane records have just been released which illustrate the right and wrong ways to present his music. The title piece on *Blue Train* is an exceptional blues, loaded with menace, perhaps the best Coltrane has ever recorded. Few current bop releases have the musical value of that one solo, which sounds in many ways like back-country guitar. Unfortunately, on the rest of the record, his material seems casually put together, and the other musicians are of no great assistance. The soloists, in particular, have little on-the-job familiarity with each other's work. *John Coltrane with the Red Garland Trio* (now called *Traneing In*) is another matter. Here he is surrounded exclusively with sympathetic musicians—men who have played and recorded as a unit and with Coltrane over long periods of time. All four men—Coltrane, Chambers, Garland, and Taylor—have Miles Davis as a common mentor. The result is a cohesive, thoughtful album which represents Coltrane's most consistent recorded work to date. Only one track, "Soft Lights," is at all disappointing. His second appearance on the blues "Traneing In" might well be the most advanced statement of his ideas. On the two ballads, he displays a delightful sound and approach, reminiscent of the small local bands which gave him his start. It is, literally, a dancing approach, a wonderful ballad style which record-date musicians never have the chance to learn.

His attributes are to be admired and respected, and if Coltrane played always what he only plays at times, he would be great. But he has all the lack of discipline of jazz itself. He has his standard runs and phrases, as does everyone, and often must play them for quite a while before they take him to the point in his solo that is art. Although he has worked extensively with Miles Davis and Thelonious Monk, he has not yet mastered the sense of compression that is at the center of their music. When Monk, for instance, takes a solo, it is often a very short one, getting as much exceptional music out of one chorus that Coltrane gets in three. If that is the way Coltrane plays, that is how he plays, and we should be glad we have him, whatever his limitations. . . . But why has Coltrane been a part of one unorganized blowing session after another?

Of his role as everybody's recording sideman, Coltrane says, "I wouldn't do it now." At the time, he needed the money. The result is that he appeared on a few records on which his is the only music likely to last.

(Johnny Griffin's *A Blowing Session,* for example, which has a fascinating solo on "All the Things You Are"; and *Tenor Conclave,* which has a "How Deep Is the Ocean?" that is the best early recorded instance of Coltrane's unique ballad style.) He also played on many others on which he merely juggles his own stock of pet phrases from one tune to the next, justifying his own assessment of himself as not "playing anything new or different." There are two Gene Ammons records on which he even reverts to his original instrument, the alto.

Aside from his regular work with Davis, his best musical opportunity at that time was the chance he got to record an album of Tadd Dameron compositions with the composer on piano.

He profited from contact with musicians who, like Dameron, were more adroit than himself, and his main source of knowledge in those days was his work with Miles Davis. An uncertain musician when he joined the quintet, Coltrane has been reluctant to talk about exactly what he learned from Davis, but it was obviously a great deal. The record of the original Davis group called *'Round About Midnight* first brought Coltrane to the attention of that segment of the jazz public which had been ignoring him. Davis has always been the star of his own group, but as Cecil Taylor said on first hearing the Davis set, "Coltrane's what you hear on *that* record." He had gotten his style under control, and for the first time, it seemed sure that he would fulfill his promise as a soloist.

The major turning point in Coltrane's career seems to have come in the summer of 1957, when he left Davis, who was temporarily dissatisfied with his group, to join Thelonious Monk. "Working with Monk," he wrote in *Down Beat,* "brought me close to a musical architect of the highest order. I felt I learned from him in every way—through the senses, theoretically, technically. I would talk to Monk about musical problems, and he would sit at the piano and show me the answers just by playing them. I could watch him play and find out the things I wanted to know. Also, I could see a lot of things that I didn't know about at all.

"Monk was one of the first to show me how to make two or three notes at a time on tenor. . . . It's done by false fingering and adjusting your lip. If everything goes right, you can get triads. Monk just looked at my horn and 'felt' the mechanics of what had to be done to get this effect."

The Monk group apparently had its origins in that single track, "Monk's Mood," which Monk recorded with Coltrane and bassist Wilbur Ware in April 1957. That summer, Monk added another Davis sideman, drummer Philly Joe Jones, and formed a quartet which he took into New York's Five Spot Café. Coltrane recalls that rehearsals consisted largely of his going to Monk's house and waking the pianist up. Monk would play a piece, and wait while Coltrane tried to learn it on the saxophone, preferring not to produce sheet music unless aural methods failed. "I always had to be alert with Monk," Coltrane has said, "because if you didn't keep aware all the time of what was going on, you'd suddenly feel as if you'd stepped into an empty elevator shaft." The unit which resulted, one of the greatest in modern jazz, was unfortunately never recorded, although Riverside released three tracks with Jones' replacement, the late Shadow Wilson. Coltrane, however, has some tapes made at the club, and "I really treasure them."

In the fall of 1957, Coltrane, a greatly improved musician, returned to Miles Davis, who was now beginning the modal experiments which were, in their use of fewer and fewer chords, to affect Coltrane greatly. The saxophonist had also changed. He had previously fallen prey to self-destructive practices that lurk in the jazz world but had, by now, suddenly and definitively stopped. An interview with Ira Gitler reflected his new attitude: "Live cleanly . . . do right. . . . You can improve as a player by improving as a person. It's a duty we owe to ourselves."

Not surprisingly, it was at this time that Coltrane began to be an influence on other players. He had also become a careful student of his own work, analyzing it to a point that once caused him to remark, "I'm worried that sometimes what I'm doing sounds just like academic exercises, and I'm trying more and more to make it sound prettier."

In *Down Beat*, he was able to dissect his style in a way that he had never done before: "About this time," he wrote, referring to his second stint with Davis, "I was trying for a sweeping sound. I started experimenting because I was striving for more individual development. I even tried long, rapid lines that Ira Gitler termed 'sheets of sounds' at the time. But actually, I was beginning to apply the three-on-one chord approach, and at that time the tendency was to play the entire scale of each chord. Therefore, they were usually played fast and sometimes sounded like glisses.

"I found there were a certain number of chord progressions to play in a given time, and sometimes what I played didn't work out in eighth notes, sixteenth notes, or triplets. I had to put the notes in uneven groups like fives and sevens in order to get them all in.

"I thought in groups of notes, not of one note at a time. I tried to place these groups on the accents and emphasize the strong beats—maybe on 2 here and on 4 over at the end. I would set up the line and drop groups of notes—a long line with accents dropped as I moved along. Sometimes what I was doing clashed harmonically with the piano—especially if the pianist wasn't familiar with what I was doing—so a lot of time I just strolled with bass and drums.

"I haven't completely abandoned this approach, but it wasn't broad enough. I'm trying to play these progressions in a more flexible manner now."

In those days, Coltrane was in marked contrast to the other two horns in the Davis sextet, sometimes taking interminable solos that seemed little more than scales. One speculated on how much of some men's personalities are released only in music: the quiet, pleasant Coltrane played fierce slashing lines in direct opposition to the gentle, delicate phrases of the often blunt, arrogant Miles. "Cannonball" Adderley, the group's other saxophonist, recalls of those solos, "Once in a while, Miles might say, 'Why you play so long, man?' and John would say, 'It took that long to get it all in.'" Coltrane himself told Gitler of the "sheets of sound" that "Now it is not a thing of beauty, and the only way it would be justified is if it becomes that. If I can't work it through, I will drop it."

It is unfortunate that a phrase like "restless search" has become a cliché used to describe anyone who plays a solo differently from one time to the next, for it accurately describes the thing in which Coltrane has long been involved. At this time, when his whole life had become music, he turned his back on his own considerable achievement and attempted new advances in his style.

By now, he was recording regularly as a leader for Prestige. As he became better known, Coltrane placed himself on the recording auction block (which had then begun to hear wild excesses in the bidding for major jazz performers) and left Prestige to record for Atlantic. His first Atlantic record, *Giant Steps,* showed a more assured Coltrane than ever before, on an album made up entirely of his own compositions.

In the summer of 1959, the growing critical and public dispute over whether Coltrane or Sonny Rollins was the most influential modern tenor-man was settled, at least temporarily, by Rollins' retirement. Coltrane, once maligned, was now indisputably on top. Early in 1960, he made the obvious move: he left Miles Davis to form his own group.

In the group's early stages, it was, according to reports, a chaotic venture. Coltrane, driven by his own needs, was experimenting publicly with his method of playing two or more notes at once on his instrument. It was apparently an extremely exciting experience when it came off, but when it didn't, he would play for a few minutes and walk off the bandstand, disgusted. Recorded examples of the technique are to be found on the Atlantic record, *Coltrane Jazz.*

But he had another idea, one which was eventually to place him so firmly in the public eye that he received a feature story in *Newsweek,* something which rarely happens to a jazzman. "Three of us were driving back from a date in Washington in 1959," he told that magazine's interviewer. "Two of us were in the front seat and the other guy, a saxplayer, in the back. He was being very quiet. At Baltimore, we made a rest stop, then got back in the car and 30 miles later realized that the guy in the back wasn't there. We hoped that he had money with him, and drove on. I took his suitcase and horn to my apartment in New York. I opened the case and found a soprano sax. I started fooling around with it and was fascinated. That's how I discovered the instrument."

Eventually, he got a soprano of his own ("It helps me get away—lets me take another look at improvisation. It's like having another hand"). Until Coltrane, the instrument had been irrevocably associated with the New Orleans style of Sidney Bechet (Coltrane's lovely "Blues to Bechet" is a demonstration of the linkage); only Steve Lacy had attempted to adapt the difficult, hard-to-tune instrument to the modern idiom.

His use of the soprano not only brought him greater popularity, it helped make him an influence so powerful that one thinks of another of Ansermet's remarks about Bechet: ". . . perhaps his 'own way' is the highway along which the whole world will swing tomorrow." And Ellison's comment—"how often do we see even the most famous of jazz artists being devoured alive by their imitators, and, shamelessly, in the public spotlight?"—is brought forcibly home every time one hears the younger players—even some of the older ones who have revamped their styles to accommodate the pervasive Coltrane impact. It might be expected that the soprano saxophone should become a more popular instrument; not so expected is the presence of one young man in Greenwich Village who plays Coltrane lines on a kazoo.

The first Coltrane recording to employ soprano was *My Favorite Things.* Some idea of the effect it creates is indicated by the experience of Cecil Taylor, who heard Coltrane play the piece in a club and was unable to convince several young musicians present that it was a Rodgers and Hammerstein song made famous by Mary Martin, rather than the East Indian folk music they took it to be.

Coltrane had, indeed, become deeply involved with the music of India, going so far as to study briefly with the Indian musician Ravi Shankar. Although he is not what he calls "an astute observer of the music," he has found much of what he has learned of it applicable to the sort of jazz he wants to play. Indian music is based on ragas, Indian scales which ascend differently than they descend. There are countless ragas, and each has a particular significance, concerned with religion, time of day, etc. Coltrane had found that "My Favorite Things" could be played almost as a raga. His next soprano recording, "Greensleeves," also played on principles of the raga, was an even more eerily hypnotic performance. Coltrane had been fascinated by the Indian water drum, essentially a drone instrument which keeps a steady tone going while others improvise around it. To simulate this, he used two bassists ("I like music to be heavy on the bottom"), one of whom was virtually imprisoned while the other remained almost completely free. Coltrane was quite pleased when he later discovered that Ali Akbar Khan, considered the greatest Indian musician, likes to play "Greensleeves." "I wish I could hear him do it," was his disarming remark. "Then I'd know if I was playing it right.

"Most of what we play in jazz," he continues, "has the feeling of just that one raga. The Indian musicians don't play the melody, they just play their scales. But maybe that's the melody to them. But what they do with it, the little differences, that's the improvisation." For a time, Coltrane pursued this so far that he would call off a chord sequence for his sidemen to play on, rather than an actual tune. They would then improvise on the mood suggested by the chord sequence and the tempo. "Yeah, I did that," he admits somewhat ruefully.

To be able to keep the feeling of the raga, but yet not play just chord changes ("I want to play tunes," he says, "I want to play the feeling of the song"), he began looking through old song books for folk tunes, perhaps turning to folios rather than recordings so that he would not be influenced by another's interpretation. He came up with "Olé," based on the Spanish folk song "Venga Vallejo." It is a remarkable synthesis of Indian elements, ideas propounded by Miles Davis in *Sketches of Spain,* and a growing concern with multiples of 3/4 time. Coltrane contributes one of his most furious solos, and Art Davis plays some of the most intricate, superbly musical bass that has ever been heard on a jazz record. In another song book, he found a piece he calls "Spiritual," which he plays with the irreducible minimum of one chord.

Coltrane's approach may owe as much to Miles Davis as to India. Davis had become preoccupied with "modal" jazz, based on scales rather than chords. As he remarked to Nat Hentoff in 1958, "When you go this way, you can go on forever. You don't have to worry about changes and you can do more with the line. It becomes a challenge to see how melodically inventive you are. When you're based on chords, you know at the end of 32 bars that the chords have run out and there's nothing to do but repeat what you've just done—with variations. I think a movement in jazz is beginning away from the conventional string of chords, and a return to emphasis on melodic rather than harmonic variation. There will be fewer chords but infinite possibilities as to what to do with them." Davis thus predicts the development of both Coltrane and, to a lesser degree, the more extreme, more melodic Ornette Coleman.

Coleman, who is also interested in the music of India, has, conversely, been an influence on Coltrane. It is not surprising that Coltrane's insatiable curiosity and insistence on fewer and fewer chords should have led him to Coleman's music. For Coleman, who has all but done away with traditional harmony, had taken the step which Coltrane's deeply harmonic sensibilities might not allow him to take. As the composer George Russell put it, "Coltrane, it seems to me, is just bursting at the seams to demolish the chord barrier, and because of this, he is enlightening everyone to what can happen on a single chord."

Coltrane and Coleman are good friends, and when they were working a few blocks from one another in New York, each would leave his own club between sets to hear the other man play. Coltrane said of Coleman to French jazz writer François Postif, "I have only played with him once in my life; I went to listen to him at a club and he asked me to join him. We played two pieces—twelve minutes to be exact—but I think that was the most intense moment of my life."

It was quite likely Coltrane's interest in Coleman which led him, in 1961, to invite the late Eric Dolphy to "come on in and work" in his band. Dolphy, who played alto, clarinet, bass clarinet and flute, was as addicted as Coltrane to long solos. Although Coltrane was delighted with the association, there was such a storm of critical protest that Coltrane's advisors eventually convinced him to ask Dolphy to leave. Coltrane had tremendous respect for Dolphy's formal education ("I'm into scales right now," he said one evening, and when asked if Dolphy was doing the same, replied proudly, "Eric's into everything"), and, when his explorations led him into a new area, traces of Dolphy's work began to show up in his own playing. Dolphy, for his part, felt that "I can't say in words what I've learned from John, the way he handles things. He's such a pro."

One remarkable example of Coleman's influence on Coltrane is a fifteen-minute blues accompanied only by bass and drums, called "Chasin' the Trane." Recorded when Coltrane had only recently become interested in Coleman, it is, as is usual when a new idea strikes him, pure music, exhibiting a concern with notes and sound for their own sake, going painfully through ideas which a more sophisticated musician such as

Dolphy might long ago have worked out. Later, significantly enough, Coltrane hired an ex-Coleman bassist, Jimmy Garrison.

A synthesized recorded statement of Coltrane's musical ideas was made after Garrison joined the group. This is not surprising, since each of his musical discoveries has immediately been reflected in changing personnel. Adding, subtracting, changing players, he gathered around him an impressive cadre of young musicians. "I keep looking," he explains, "for different ways to present my music. I don't think it's as presentable as it could be." He once mentioned that "I'd like to add an instrument that can play melody and percussion, maybe a guitar." Thus, Wes Montgomery joined the band, but the guitarist soon noted that the spaces between his solos were longer than the intervals between sets, and left. For a time, the second bassist was Art Davis, a brilliant young musician from Harrisburg, Pennsylvania. When Coltrane became involved with his new ideas about the use of the bass, he got into the habit of driving over to Davis' home and picking him up for a practice session. But Davis will not travel, preferring to remain in New York, where he often works in a non-jazz context. Coltrane uses Davis when he can. "I don't think Trane thinks of anything but music," Davis says. "He'll come back off the road and call me up to say, 'We're opening at the Vanguard tonight.' I say, 'We are?' and then I have to tell him that I'm working somewhere else. He never seems to think to let me know in advance, so I can stay free." Asked one night during a one-bass engagement in New York, why Davis was not with the group, Coltrane replied with some puzzlement, "Art's a very busy guy." For such reasons, he generally bills himself as "John Coltrane and his Group." "I'm playing it safe," he says.

Long permanent fixtures were the heavily chordal pianist McCoy Tyner ("McCoy has a beautiful lyric concept that is essential to complement the rest of us") and Elvin Jones, the most fiery, compulsively brilliant of modern drummers, in many ways the finest now playing. "Even I can't play with him," Coltrane says bemusedly. "He uses so many accents."

With these two and Garrison, Coltrane produced a nearly shattering recording of "Out of This World." Critic-saxophonist Don Heckman said of it in *Jazz* magazine, "Some of the principles that seem to be basic to (Coltrane's) music are: (1) he rarely cares to explore the development of extended harmonic variations drawn from the chords of a stated melody; (2) color, rhythms, and emotional tensions (often expressed by nontraditional instrumental sounds) replace harmony as cadential signposts; (3) like the improvising musicians of the East, Coltrane prefers that his tonal accompaniment remain static, and that motion be derived from a sympathetic and nearly equal rhythmic percussion—in this case, Elvin Jones. When this happens all at once, the results are very startling indeed. 'Out of This World' is surely one of the best things Coltrane has ever done, and its success is as much due to the brilliant drumming of Jones as it is to Coltrane. In combination they have very nearly solved the problem of the essential differences between Eastern and Western improvisatory music. One of the strengths of Indian music is a long, regular metric pulse that stimulates a constant interplay of tension and release between the soloist and the percussionist. By opening up the rhythms of their material (in this case to a rather complex 6/4) Coltrane and Jones are finding a successful solution to the problems of overextension and listening tedium that had nagged much of their earlier work in this vein. The problems for the listener are increased, however, in that he must now meet the music on its own terms."

Not all criticism has been this sympathetic. Coltrane is puzzled by the fact that one critic may praise him for exactly the same qualities another writer uses to damn him. Too often, the opposition to his work has assumed a hysterical cast, his detractors employing words like anarchistic, nihilistic, gobbledegook, confusion, amorphism, nonsense, and the dread epithet, antijazz. More reasoned questioning of his approach dealt with the extreme length of his solos, his use of suspensions ("vamps," he calls them) and the essential emotional sameness of his performances, no matter what the material. As Martin Williams summed up reviewing *Africa/Brass* in *Down Beat,* "Coltrane has done on record what he has done so often in person lately, make everything into a handful of chords, frequently only two or three, and run them in every conceivable way, offering what is, in effect, an extended cadenza to a piece that never gets played, a prolonged *montuna* interlude surrounded by no rhumba or *son,* or a very long vamp 'til ready."

With this in mind, it is extremely enlightening to listen to a Miles Davis album, *Someday My Prince Will Come,* recorded during the time that Coltrane was making such controversial music. Coltrane appears on two of the selections ("I sneaked down one afternoon and made it," he says of the record), the title track and a Spanish-influenced piece called "Teo." In the stricter, long-familiar setting of the Davis group, Coltrane contributes not only the most exciting, impassioned music on the set, but two of the best solos he had played in a long time. What Nat Hentoff called the "cry" in his playing, each note sounding incomplete, only a link between the surrounding ones, was once again present, and he displayed his talent in magnificent relief against another man's contrasting discipline, just as he had been able to do in former years. There were rumors that Davis wanted Coltrane to rejoin him, but even though Davis consistently outdrew Coltrane in the same clubs ("He has a wonderful name," Coltrane says, "he'd hire Sonny, he'd hire me, he'd hire all of us, just to hear us play. He's got a lot of money, and he loves to listen to music"), it seemed unlikely that the merger would ever come to pass.

For "everybody's sideman" is now indisputably a leader himself. He has created a music which is identifiably his, even during the long stretches of any selection when he is not soloing. How he has arrived at this new status is a fascinating question.

To see Coltrane in action is only to increase one's puzzlement about him. A quiet, pleasant, shyly friendly man who dresses simply and speaks softly, he is likely to be found between sets seated on his horncase, reading and eating an apple. At the conclusion of a solo, he wanders off-stage, Miles Davis fashion. He may talk to friends who have come to hear him— Ornette Coleman, for instance, or Davis—or he may sit quietly at the far end of the club, listening to his band. But on the stand, he becomes impassioned and engrossed; it is as if setting the instrument to his lips completed an electrical circuit. As the music takes hold, he leans far back, eyes tight shut as if possessed with instant frenzy. Then, after the solo, he may move to the side of the stage, light one of the long, thin cigars he has begun to affect, and adjust a reed.

He once said of his work with Dizzy Gillespie, "I was playing clichés and trying to learn tunes that were hip, so I could play with the guys who played them." It is hard to equate the Coltrane of today with the hip saxophonist he says he was. In a little over a year, he passed rapidly through several different styles of music, a man with a sudden thirst for knowledge, and each new thing he tries only opens up wider areas to explore. Basically a romantic player—the rage in his playing is only the reverse side of the lyricism—he has accumulated in his search, as most romantics do, an ever-growing list of what he knows he does not want. It may be pertinent that he has retained his original slow ballad style. When playing other music, though, he is in a dangerous position. The first attempt at any new thing inevitably involves awkwardness, and the listener on any given night may find Coltrane struggling through his own musical vocabulary. This has caused many to turn away in exasperation, but the saxophonist is apparently willing to take that chance. All he can offer his audience on such occasions is the excitement of participating in the creative process. It is a thrilling thing to be able to share, but obviously not everyone is willing to share it.

This concern with pure music is easily understood. Jazz began as music-at-home, in which almost anyone could participate. Today, when many jazz musicians can in some respects outplay their symphonic counterparts, it has become a virtuoso's music, a music in which one *begins* as a virtuoso and goes on from there. But technical facility is not Coltrane's only concern. He would like, he says, for his music to have "strong emotional content."

Some of that emotion comes out in his compositions. Now determined to play songs instead of chords, he has found none that completely satisfy him, and has turned to writing his own, more from necessity than a desire to compose. One night at the Jazz Gallery, he premiered a new untitled piece (now called "Big Nick"), so simple and charming that several members of the audience immediately began whistling it. Coltrane was unable to believe he had been successful. "I'd like to know what the hell they were whistling," he said, puzzled. "I thought it was mine." Some of his pieces do sound familiar. His "Blue Train" is the prototype of much of his work, and some of his blues sound like classic lines from the thirties. "What John has done," says Cecil Taylor, "is take the concept of time he learned from Miles Davis and extend it. You can hear it on 'Blues Minor.' It's 'Bags' Groove,' sure, but what he's done is tighten it up, take the unnecessary parts out." Coltrane has expressed a desire to write in the twelve-tone system. Asked about the seeming impossibility of improvising serially, he replies, "Damn the rules, it's the feeling that counts. You play all twelve notes in your solo anyway."

Despite the increased emphasis on composition, improvising remains the primary vehicle of Coltrane's emotions. If we are, in Heckman's words, to "meet the music on its own terms," to understand the menace of its almost crushing energy, then some attempt must be made to understand Coltrane himself.

One clue is in his Jamaica, Long Island, home. There are few records in his library, but what he has is almost all folk music from India. For a long time, occupying a considerable part of the livingroom was a large rented harp, which he was learning to play "because it helps me with harmony." His only apparent hobby is a telescope in the back yard, which he looks through on the rare occasions when he has the chance. His group works constantly. "I don't know what you mean by a dedicated musician," his wife says, "but all he does is practice. Many nights he'd fall asleep with the horn still in his mouth." "When you talk to him," adds young trumpeter Freddie Hubbard, "he's always looking off somewhere, like he's thinking of the next note he's going to play."

Scant attention has been paid to furnishing; ceramic wall plaques provide almost the only decor. Coltrane, the most pleasant of men, seems almost naïve; his musical sophistication is not hinted at by his manner. ("A lot of 'literary' people say that," comments Cecil Taylor. "I always feel good about being with John *after* I've talked to him.") "White Americans," James Baldwin has written, "find it as difficult as white people elsewhere to divest themselves of the notion that they are in possession of some intrinsic value that black people need, or want." In that remark may lie the ultimate significance of the power and danger of the jazz of quiet, naïve John Coltrane, who has taken his musical imagination from India, from Africa, and from the blues.

While displaying an ever more voracious appetite for all things new (Coltrane does not tend to think of himself as a leader, but as a student of music who is in the remarkable position of being paid to do what obsesses him), he has still managed to combine commerce and art. Although his playing is basically the same on both his instruments ("I think you have to have musical conviction, rather than let the instrument dictate to you"), his soprano sax is primarily responsible for a popularity that, in 1961, enabled him to appear at all four of New York's major jazz clubs. He has judiciously combined the elements of his success. Early in an evening, he will feature the soprano on pieces like "My Favorite Things" and "Greensleeves." Afterwards, he might say to a friend, "The next set will be different. The next set I'll play all my nonhits." The soprano disappears, to be replaced by the tenor and long, furiously impassioned and basic blues.

Off the stand again, he once more becomes the shy, friendly man whose cigar is the only indication that he knows he is a success. His main concern with his constant work on the road is the protracted absence from his wife ("She really knows me, and understands the problems I have as a leader"). Perhaps he takes his preeminence with such equanimity because, having made it the hard way, he has an extremely realistic view of the business he is in. "Every time I talk about jazz," he says, "I think of prizefighters. One year it's your year, like it's mine now, and the next year everybody's forgotten you. You only have a few years, and you have to stay up there as long as you can, and do the best you can, and be graceful about it when it's someone else's turn."

I was interested to know what John Coltrane would do when the young musicians who are learning so much from him overtook him.

"I'd just keep playing," he said. "It's all I know."

MARTIN WILLIAMS
JOHN COLTRANE: MAN IN THE MIDDLE
Down Beat, *December 12, 1967*

*Appearing soon after John Coltrane's death in July 1967, this arti-
cle was among the first to summarize and evaluate Coltrane's
entire career. Williams later revised it for his book* The Jazz
Tradition *(Oxford University Press, 1970 and 1983). Martin
Williams was one of the most respected jazz critics. He wrote for*
Down Beat, Evergreen Review, Saturday Review, *and the* New
York Times. *In 1958 he and Nat Hentoff were founders and edi-
tors of* The Jazz Review, *often considered to be the finest of all jazz
magazines. In 1970 Williams began working for the Smithsonian
Institution, where his legacy includes the* Smithsonian Collection
of Classic Jazz.

*Note: Williams's reference to pedal tones on "Giant Steps" is in
error. The composition "Naima" uses those pedal tones.—CW*

John Coltrane has had his followers and imitators and popularizers from
the time that he was first a member of Miles Davis's quintet in 1955, and
there are musicians who show the influence of his playing at almost every
period of his career.

That fact reminds us that he was an important jazzman. It may also
remind us of how much his playing changed, or perhaps one should say,
how often it changed during his life, because, on the surface at least, some
of the changes seemed to come abruptly, almost as though some phases of
Coltrane's career were not evolutionary exactly, but deliberate.

When he first attracted attention with Davis, Coltrane was sometimes
spoken of as another "hard" tenor player—hard as opposed to cool—but
he was then already an original musician, and his basic originality was of
the most important sort for a jazzman, which is to say that it was rhythmic.

What Coltrane did rhythmically had to be done, and was even predictable, but to say so is not to belittle his importance in having done it.

Coltrane subdivided jazz rhythm; he did so according to the lines
already laid down by the past. Rhythmically, Louis Armstrong thought in
quarter-notes; Charlie Parker thought in eighth-notes. Coltrane's phrases
and accents imply that he was thinking rhythmically in 16ths; thus,
Coltrane subdivided bebop rhythm.

Equally important is the way he did it and, much as it is the result of gross simplification to speak of so flexible a rhythmic idiom as Armstrong's as "quarter-notes" or so imaginative a rhythmic idiom as Parker's as "eights," so it is also crude to reduce Coltrane's rhythmic language to "16ths." Still, such a description seems the best way—or at least the handiest way—to describe the basis of the rhythmic styles of these men and to indicate the relationships among them.

Otherwise, Coltrane was a vertical player, a kind of latter-day Coleman Hawkins. And that means that he moved somewhat counter to the direction that jazz saxophone had been taking since the mid-40s. Dexter Gordon was the leading player of a generation of tenor men who, receiving guidance from Parker, had made a synthesis of the styles of Coleman Hawkins and Lester Young. They liked Hawkins' big sound but Young's limited vibrato; they liked Hawkins' harmonic sophistication and exactness but preferred Young's linear melodies to Hawkins' arpeggios; they favored Young's variety of rhythm and phrase-length over Hawkins' four-bar, heavy/light/heavy/light regularity.

However, Coltrane owed more to the Hawkins heritage, and to a brilliant Hawkins follower like Don Byas, than to Lester Young or to any of Young's followers, or to Dexter Gordon or any of *his* followers, first- or secondhand. If one doubts this, I think it can be found confirmed in the playing of Coltrane's onetime associate, Benny Golson. For Golson will sometimes slip from a very much Byas-inspired style into a Coltrane idiom, and the transition seems a logical one.

Coltrane's 1955–56 solos with Davis are largely exploratory. He seemed more interested in discovery than in making finished statements, as though for the time being he were occupied with turning up a vocabulary with which future sentences, paragraphs, and essays might be built.

Coltrane's original rhythmic sense, his already evident subdivided beat, would obviously give problems in both melody and swing—it is difficult to improvise melodically and to swing (at least in the traditional sense) when one is thinking in 16th accents rhythmically. But it is to Coltrane's credit that he avoided a direct confrontation of these problems in order to concentrate on his saxophone sound and technique, on his own rhythmic idiom, and on harmonics.

However, there is one aspect of his recorded style, particularly at this period, that might confirm the view that his approach was tentative. It is the tendency for Coltrane's terminal phrases to end with an apparent fumble of notes or to diminish into a kind of mutter or hesitantly delivered cliché. Perhaps the exploratory Coltrane swallowed his endings because he found himself suddenly up against a banality he saw no way of avoiding but did not really want to pronounce.

Even Coltrane's most provocative solo from this period, on the Thelonious Monk *'Round Midnight* (Columbia version), has a hesitant note or two here and there, but it was prophetic of the next step in his career.

In mid-1957, Coltrane became a member of Monk's quartet. The importance of that event to Coltrane's development is not to be underestimated, though the importance of the group itself may more properly belong to a discussion of Monk's career than to Coltrane's. Coltrane's work remained exploratory, and he expanded his techniques along the lines his past work had indicated.

But with Monk's music (as the truism has it) one has to know the melodies and their harmonies, and understand how they fit together, in order to improvise well, and Coltrane understood this. Thus a solo like Coltrane's on "Trinkle Tinkle," for all its bursting virtuosity, which runs into elusive corners of Monk's piece and proceeds to build its own structures, is constantly orderly and keeps us constantly oriented because of the nature of Monk's composition and Coltrane's understanding of it.

Leaving Monk, Coltrane rejoined Davis, and his solo with the trumpeter on the Monk blues in F, "Straight, No Chaser," is a powerful and arresting statement of where Coltrane *was* at the time. But several of the harmonically architectonic solos on the Coltrane LP *Blue Train* give indication of where he might be headed and reveal some of the problems he would encounter.

The title blues, "Blue Train," has a prophetically eerie, almost mysterious statement from the leader. The faster "Locomotion" (a 12-12-8-12 blues) gives an exposition of Coltrane's unique melodic rhythm at perhaps its fullest development. And "Moment's Notice" has a rather undistinguished theme that it uses to set up a series of challengingly difficult chord changes for the soloist.

The post-Monk Coltrane, then, was a prodigious saxophonist and a prodigious harmonicist. He was also a prodigious jazzman in that he had extended the range of his instrument, the textures of sound he was able to evoke from it, and the human quality of his saxophone voice.

Coltrane could superimpose a world of passing chords, substitute chords, and harmonic extensions upon a harmonic structure that was already complex. And at times he seemed prepared to gush out every possible note, find his way step by step through every complex chord, careen through every scale, and go beyond even that profession by groping for impossible notes and sounds on a tenor saxophone that seemed ready to shatter under the strain.

From one point of view, Coltrane had pushed jazz harmonies as far as they could go. From another, such complex, sophisticated knowledge builds its own trap, and Coltrane, still a vertical thinker, was like a hamster trapped in a three-dimensional harmonic maze of his own making. ("You don't have to play *everything!*" Davis is reported to have said to him.)

To this Coltrane, a Davis piece like "Milestones," or pieces like "So What?," "All Blues," and some of the others on the Davis recital *Kind of Blue,* must have come as a revelation.

Here were "modal" pieces, with harmonic challenges cut to an absolute minimum, and with the soloist allowed to invent for 16 measures, or even for as long as he liked, on a single chord or scale. Coltrane sounded a bit hesitant on "Milestones," but he met the challenges of "So What?" and "All Blues" like a man who saw—or thought he saw—an exit from the maze.

Kind of Blue is key evidence of one of the most remarkable events to take place in Western music in this century. Why should a comparable modality suddenly appear—coincidentally and almost simultaneously—in the music of Ornette Coleman, of Miles Davis, and of John Coltrane, of the Detroit rock-and-roll groups, of the British rock groups, of the Chicago blues bands, and of the U.S. quasi-folk ensembles?

Coltrane's first LP as a leader followed *Kind of Blue,* but did not immediately build on it. "Giant Steps," the title piece, echoed "Moment's Notice" in setting up a difficult and ingenious series of sophisticated changes over an E-flat pedal tone, with a B-flat in the bridge, and allowing the soloist to take either course. Coltrane's solo on *Countdown,* in which he several times employs a complex double-motif, has been praised for its form. But I think the solo raises fundamental questions about when the reiteration of a motif is a means to order and when it is a matter of repetition.

At this point in his career, Coltrane encountered "My Favorite Things," and "My Favorite Things" could serve his purposes in almost the same way that "How High the Moon" had served Parker and Gillespie's 20 years earlier.

Here was a popular song that had, built in, so to speak, the sort of things he had been working on: little chordal motion, folklike simplicity, a quasi-Eastern mystery, and incantativeness—simple but still sophisticated, the piece could contain Coltrane's prodigiousness as an improviser.

In no sense was "My Favorite Things" an artistic compromise for

Coltrane—and in no sense should it be a surprise that his first recording of it was a best-seller.

As he pursued modality, however, evenings with Coltrane, a vertical player working with minimal harmonic understructures, began to sound to some listeners like long vamps-till-ready, or furious cadenzas, or lengthy montunas introducing rhumbas, or songs that never got played.

As one wag put it at the time, "I went to hear Coltrane last night. He played 45 minutes of C-minor ninths." And 45 minutes on a C-minor pedal tone, it became increasingly clear, do not lead to musical freedom.

It is true that Coltrane's audiences frequently were enthralled. I know the sincerity, the powerful and authentic emotion, and frequent skill involved. I am aware of the truly astonishing contribution of Coltrane's drummer, Elvin Jones, to his music and of the innovative importance of his style. And yet, to be entirely subjective about his work at this period, I was and am repeatedly disengaged. After three or four minutes, my attention wanders, and giving the records try after try does not seem to help.

Two extended performances from 1961 represent a turning point for Coltrane, "Impressions" and "Chasin' the Trane." On each, his improvising had become more horizontal, more linear than previously. "Impressions" borrows an opening melody from Claude Debussy, to revisit, two years later, the same modes and song-form structure that Davis used on "So What?" Before the performance is over, Coltrane is reiterating a little half-scale figure. Virtually the same figure dominates a portion of "Chasin' the Trane." "Chasin' the Trane" is the key performance from this period for Coltrane, and has become a highly influential one among younger musicians.

It seems that Coltrane's use of such reiterated phrases is not sequential or significantly organizational or truly developmental. His use of them is deliberately repetitive and incantatory. And one man's incantation is perhaps another man's monotony. With Elvin Jones laying down a rich and complex pattern beneath him, Coltrane's sing-song lines sometimes sound thin, and his occasional saxophone cries and shrieks seem protestations, perhaps against that very thinness.

I may hear this Coltrane wrongly, but if I do, perhaps I can at least put questions to those who hear him better, questions that they may find worth answering. And perhaps the key question is whether so able and knowledgeable a vertical player could still walk upright when setting himself so decidedly horizontal a task.

The Coltrane that I better admire from this period is the deliberately conservative Coltrane. The Coltrane who stated Duke Ellington's "In a

Sentimental Mood" so perceptively yet personally and without overembellishment. And the Coltrane of the LP called *Crescent*. There, for the moment at least, he seemed to have profited by the years of complex harmony and by the years of modality, to return like a hero from a perilous but necessary journey, ready to share the fruits of his experience.

Harsh dangers and exotic beauties are related on the title piece, "Crescent," and the once "impossible" saxophone sounds seem natural and firmly established techniques. Reflections and evaluations of the journey take place on "The Wise One." And "Bessie's Blues" might be called a joyful celebration of the new insight the hero had provided. Perhaps it was also an element of comparative calm and of reflection that made Coltrane's *A Love Supreme* a best-seller.

On the other hand, *Ascension* is probably Coltrane's most daring recording. It is a 38-minute performance on which the leader's regular quartet was augmented by two trumpeters, two tenorists, two altoists, and an extra bassist. There is a single, slight thematic idea; there are several turbulent, loose, improvised ensembles; and there are solos by most of the participants. The performance soars, and it sings. And it rages, blares, shouts, screams, and shrieks. It is at the same time a contemporary jazz performance and a communal rite.

Ascension is directly indebted to Ornette Coleman's *Free Jazz,* and that fact inevitably invites comparison between the two. For me, Coleman's work invokes the contemporary demons as unflinchingly as Coltrane's but is a thing of beauty and affirmation and hope. *Free Jazz*—to use James Joyce's superb phrase—better sees the darkness shining in the light.

Thus, some of Coltrane's work from the '60s seems to me brilliant and some of it repetitious and banal. There are times when Coltrane's authentically wild passion seems not so much a part of the music as a part of the musician—it seems to be the reaction of a player who is improvising with a minimum of built-in protections but who sometimes cries out in frustration against the limitations that he has set for himself, limitations that once seemed so necessary.

Sometimes my own impression is of having heard musical statements that have brilliant moments but that may become static and remain unresolved, statements that are contained only by a fantastic and original saxophone technique on one hand or by a state of emotional exhaustion on the other. And it is perhaps indicative that several of his later records were faded out by the engineers rather than ended by the musicians.

I began by saying something about the ways that Coltrane's music changed. There have been several musics—Oriental and African, as well as American—that interested and directly influenced him during his last 12 years.

The changes in his work, of course, may have been signs of growth, and if they were, perhaps no important jazz improviser ever grew and developed as much as Coltrane did in so short a time.

But on the other hand, the changes may have been naive on the face of it, or they may have been signs of indecision or of a deeper frustration.

Does one with Coltrane, then, take his choice between the alternatives of a true artistic growth or of mere change?

Perhaps not, or not necessarily. Perhaps a deeper frustration and tormented indecision are part of the unacknowledged truth of the temper of the times that it was Coltrane's destiny to articulate. And if so, he was an artist of primary rank.

In any case, Coltrane has been bold enough to state his message so that the present knows of him and so that the future must acknowledge that he has been with us.

NAT HENTOFF
JOHN COLTRANE
Jazz Is, *1976*

As he readily points out, Hentoff had criticisms of Coltrane's playing early on. But as this article makes clear, Hentoff's appreciation of Coltrane's art only grew: "I was converted, or educated, from listening first to Coltrane with Miles Davis for many nights."

As of this writing, Nat Hentoff is in his fifth decade of writing about music. In the 1950s he was associate editor of Down Beat, *and in 1958 he and Martin Williams were among the founders of* The Jazz Review. *Since the 1960s Hentoff has written about many social and political issues.—CW*

Coltrane, a man of almost unbelievable gentleness made human to us lesser mortals by his very occasional rages. Coltrane, an authentically spiritual man, but not innocent of carnal imperatives. Or perhaps more accurately, a man, in his last years, especially but not exclusively consumed by affairs of the spirit. That is, having constructed a personal worldview (or view of the cosmos) on a residue of Christianity and infusion of Eastern meditative practices and concerns, Coltrane became a theosophist of jazz. The music was a way of self-purgation so that he could learn more about himself to the end of making himself and his music part of the unity of all being. He truly believed this, and in this respect, as well as musically, he has been a powerful influence on many musicians since. He considered music to be a healing art, an "uplifting" art.

Yet through most of his relatively short career (he died at forty), Coltrane divided jazz listeners, creating furiously negative reactions to his work among some. ("Antijazz" was one of the epithets frequently cast at him in print.) He was hurt and somewhat bewildered by this reaction, but with monumental stubbornness went on exploring and creating what to many seemed at first to be chaos—self-indulgent, long-winded noise. Some still think that's what it was.

Others believed Coltrane to be a prophet, a musical prophet, heralding an enormous expansion of what it might now be possible to say on an instrument. Consider Art Davis. He is a startlingly brilliant bassist, as accomplished in classical music as in jazz. (Because Davis is black, he has been denied employment by those symphony orchestras to which he has applied, and so he has challenged them to pit him against any classical bassist of their choice. The challenge has gone unanswered.) Anyway, Davis, whom I've known for years, is a rationalist, a keen analyzer of music and of life. He is not given, so far as I have ever known, to giant or even small leaps into faith. Davis requires a sound scaffolding of fact and proof for his enthusiasms.

But here is Art Davis, who played for a time with Coltrane, as quoted in the Fall 1972 issue of the periodical *Black Creation* [Institute of Afro-American Affairs at New York University]: "John Coltrane would play for hours a set. One tune would be like an hour or two hours, and he would not repeat himself, and it would not be boring. . . . People would just be shouting, like you go to church, a holy roller church or something like that. This would get into their brains, would penetrate. John had that spirit—he was after the spiritual thing. . . . You could hear people screaming . . . despite the critics who tried to put him down. Black people made him because they stuck together and they saw—look what's going down—let's get some of this. You know all the hard times that John had at the beginning, even when he was with Miles. And when he left Miles, starting out, everybody tried to discourage him. But I'd be there and the brothers and sisters would be there and they supported him. . . . John had this power of communication, that power so rare it was like genius—I'll call him a prophet because he did this."

Coltrane had another power, a power of self-regeneration that also has to do with that power of communication. One evening in the early 1950s, I saw Coltrane in Sheridan Square, in Greenwich Village. He looked awful. Raggedy, vacant. "Junk," said a musician with me. "He's been hooked a while." But, I noted, he had a bottle of wine in his hand. "That, too," said the musician.

And Coltrane stopped using both. By himself. During his huge musical ascent, which was soon to start. Coltrane was clean and stayed clean. That's power. Like Miles.

Coltrane changed jazz in as fundamental a way as Charlie Parker had before him and Louis Armstrong before Parker. One thing he did was to radically reshape—by the overwhelming persuasiveness of his playing—all previous jazz definitions of "acceptable" sounds and forms.

Obviously, through the decades, jazz had encompassed an extraordinary range of sounds—growls, slurs, cries, guffaws, keening wails. And certainly it had been accepted from the beginning that each player had his own "sound." There was never any one criterion for how every trombone or tenor saxophone or singer should sound. Still, at each stage of jazz history certain kinds of sounds were beyond the pale. Or at least they were considerably downgraded. For years, to cite a pre-modern-jazz example, Pee Wee Russell's rasping tone (which, to its denigrators, veered between a squeak and an access of laryngitis) was mocked by a good many musicians as well as listeners. Yet Pee Wee proved to be among the most inventive and seizingly original of all clarinetists.

Lester Young was in disfavor among some of his peers for quite a while because his sound was too "light" compared to Coleman Hawkins' robust fullness. Nor was Lee Wiley the only appraiser to think of Billie Holiday that she sounded "as if her shoes were too tight." At the advent of Charlie Parker one of the many criticisms of his playing by older musicians and by traditionalist listeners was that his tone was "bad," too acrid by contrast, say, with that of Johnny Hodges.

In the case of John Coltrane, a majority of the initial reviews of his recordings in the early and mid-1950s also cited his "strident," "unpleasant" sound. Mine were among them. Later, however, when Coltrane was really under way and pushing his instrument beyond any previous limits of sound possibilities, the intermittent rawness of his tone, the high-pitched squeals, the braying yawps, the screams, generated even more intense hostility along with the denunciation that his extensive solos were structureless, directionless. "Musical nonsense," wrote one critic.

In retrospect, however, it is clear that Coltrane was one of the most persistent, relentless expanders of possibility—all kinds of possibility: textural, emotional, harmonic, and spiritual—in jazz history. And also one of the most totally exposed improvisers in the history of the music.

I was converted, or educated, from listening first to Coltrane with Miles Davis for many nights. This was the Coltrane "sheets of sound" period (a phrase originated by critic Ira Gitler). The term came about, Gitler later explained, "because of the density of textures he was using. His multinote improvisations were so thick and complex they were almost flowing out of the horn by themselves. That really hit me, the continuous flow of ideas without stopping. It was almost superhuman, and the amount of energy he was using could have powered a spaceship."

Miles would sometimes grumble about the constant hailstorms of notes in a Coltrane solo, since Miles himself preferred to work with space, to let his notes breathe. And the length of the solos also occasionally annoyed him. "Why did you go on so long?" he once asked Coltrane after a particularly lengthy flight by the latter.

"It took that long to get it all in," said Coltrane, and Miles accepted the logic of the answer.

Actually, Miles Davis was much intrigued by the sheer will to creativity of Coltrane on his better nights. "Coltrane's really something," Miles told me one afternoon in 1958. "He's been working on those arpeggios and playing them fifty different ways and playing them all at once. However," there was a glint of triumph in Miles, "he *is* beginning to leave more space—except when he gets nervous."

It was important for Coltrane to work with Miles. For one thing, of course, he received attention, with the Davis imprimatur legitimatizing Coltrane for some of those who up to that point had considered Trane either incompetent or a charlatan or both. Miles, it was agreed by nearly all, could not and would not be conned musically. If he hired the man, the man must have something to say. That imprimatur also gave Coltrane confidence. Feeling set upon by the critics, he had passed a far more severe test by being considered worthy of a place in the Miles Davis band.

Even more valuable to Coltrane, however, was his stay with Thelonious Monk—in between stints with Miles Davis in the late 1950s. That collaboration at the Five Spot Café in New York's East Village was a key historic event—of the musical order of Louis Armstrong playing second cornet to King Oliver at the Royal Garden Café in Chicago in the 1920s. I was there nearly every night all the weeks Monk and Trane played the Five Spot, and it was there I finally understood how nonpareil a musician, how dauntless an explorer Coltrane was. The excitement was so heady that soon musicians were standing two and three deep at the bar of the Five Spot nearly every night.

Monk creates a total musical microcosm, and for musicians who play with him the challenge is to keep your balance, to stay with Monk, no matter where his unpredictably intricate imagination leads—and at the same time, play yourself, be yourself.

"I learned new levels of alertness with Monk," Coltrane said, "because if you didn't keep aware all the time of what was going on, you'd suddenly feel as if you'd stepped into a hole without a bottom to it." He learned other things as well. "Monk was one of the first to show me how to make two or three notes at one time on tenor. It's done by false fingering and adjusting your lips, and if it's done right you get triads. He also got me into the habit of playing long solos [longer than with Miles] on his pieces, playing the same piece for a long time to find new conceptions for solos. It got so I would go as far as possible on one phrase until I ran out of ideas. The harmonies got to be an obsession for me. Sometimes I was making music through the wrong end of a magnifying glass."

As a teacher, one of the most liberating teachers in jazz, Monk had another kind of impact on Coltrane, as on practically all the musicians who have played with him. Monk kept insisting that musicians must keep working at stretching themselves, at going beyond their limitations, which really were artificial limitations that came from their having absorbed conventional—and thereby gratuitously constricting—standards of what can and what cannot be done on an instrument.

Before Coltrane came with the band, Gigi Gryce had learned this lesson: "I had a part Monk wrote for me that was impossible. I had to play melody while simultaneously playing harmony with him. In addition, the intervals were very wide besides; and I just told him I couldn't do it. 'You have an instrument, don't you?' he said. 'Either play it or throw it away.' And he walked away. Finally, I *was* able to play it. Another time I was orchestrating a number for him, and I didn't write everything down for the horns exactly as he'd outlined it because I felt the musicians would look at the score and figure it was impossible to play. He was very angry, and he finally got exactly what he wanted. I remember the trumpet player on the date had some runs going up on his horn and Monk said they were only impractical if they didn't give him a chance to breathe. The range was not a factor 'because a man should be flexible on all ranges of his horn.'"

Then came Coltrane. The story, told by Art Blakey, is in J. C. Thomas's *Chasin' the Trane:* "I played drums on the *Monk's Music* album for Riverside, where Monk expanded his group to a septet with both Coleman Hawkins and John Coltrane on tenor. Naturally, Monk wrote all the music, but Hawk was having trouble reading it, so he asked Monk to explain it to both Trane and himself. Monk said to Hawk, 'You're the great Coleman Hawkins, right? You're the guy who invented the tenor saxophone, right?' Hawk agreed. Then Monk turned to Trane, 'You're the great John Coltrane, right?' Trane blushed, and mumbled, 'Aw . . . I'm not so great.' Then Monk said to both of them, 'You play saxophone, right?' They nodded. 'Well, the music is on the horn. Between the two of you, you should be able to find it.'"

Coltrane kept looking and finding, and, never satisfied, looked some more. His audience was growing, especially among musicians, but more nonmusicians were finding that if they *actively* listened to his music, their whole way of hearing jazz might well be changed. This did not mean, however, that they had to listen analytically. In the liner notes for Coltrane's album, *Om,* for example, I suggested that those who were finding Coltrane "difficult" start again, but this time without "worrying about how it is all structured, where it's leading. Let the music come in without any pre-set definitions of what jazz *has* to be, of what *music* has to be.

"If you find yourself responding—and I don't mean necessarily with conventional 'pleasure,' but rather with any strong feeling—listen on. In this music, just as textures are themselves shapes and motion is by colors as well as by time"; so, in the listening, I should have gone on, ingress is by routes that will unexpectedly come upon you in guises other than the usual ways to get into a piece of music. A link of pitches perhaps, an arrhythmic phrase that will lead to a strong subterranean pulsation.

For the last seven years of his life Coltrane continued to make more demands of himself musically than any jazz musician, except perhaps Cecil Taylor, ever has. None of this, so far as I could tell, was done as an act of competition. It was himself, and only himself, Coltrane kept pressuring to hear more, feel more, understand more, communicate more. At home he would practice for hours, sometimes silently—just running his fingers over the keys—and pick up new instruments and meditate and listen to recordings of Indian music and the music of South African Pygmies. Possibilities. Always more possibilities. He decided he wanted two drummers working with him. Then, on an album, he fixed on two bass players. I asked him why. "Because I want more of the sense of the expansion of time. I want the time to be more plastic."

Time. Vast, fierce stretches of time. The music sometimes sounding like the exorcism of a multitude of demons, each one of whom was mightily resisting his expulsion. Yet at other times Coltrane could sound his probes with such gentle luminescence as to fool the voracious spirits, but soon the shaking, smashing, endless battle would begin again.

At night clubs there were scores, hundreds of exhilarating, exhausting nights during which the listeners, along with the musicians, had no resting space but had to keep emotional pace as best they could with the ferociously wheeling, diving, climbing Coltrane.

For better or worse, and that depended on the inventiveness of the musicians who followed him, Coltrane more than any other player legitimated the extended jazz solo. As Archie Shepp, a tenor saxophonist befriended and influenced by Coltrane, said, "That was his breakthrough—the concept that the imperatives of conception might make it necessary to improvise at great length. I don't mean he proved that a thirty- or forty-minute solo is necessarily better than a three-minute one. He did prove, however, that it was possible to create thirty or forty minutes of uninterrupted, continually building, continually original and imaginative music. And in the process, Coltrane also showed the rest of us we had to have the stamina—in terms of imagination and physical preparedness—to sustain those long flights."

I once tried out on Coltrane my theory that one reason he developed such long solos was in an attempt to create and sustain a kind of hypnotic, dervishlike mood so that the listener would in time become oblivious to distractions and end up wholly immersed in the music with all his customary intellectual and emotional defenses removed.

"That may be a secondary effect," Coltrane said, "but I'm not consciously trying to do that. I'm still primarily looking into certain sounds, certain scales. Not that I'm sure of what I'm looking for, except that it'll be something that hasn't been played before. I don't know what it is. I know I'll have that feeling when I get it. And in the process of looking, continual looking, the result in any given performance can be long or short. I never know. It's always one thing leading into another. It keeps evolving, and sometimes it's longer than I actually thought it was while I was playing. When things are constantly happening the piece just doesn't feel that long."

Always looking, Coltrane always tried to be ready for the unexpected revelation, "that feeling." Alice Coltrane told me that "when John left for work he'd often take five instruments with him. He wanted to be ready for whatever came. That was characteristic of John. His music was never resigned, never complacent. How could it be? He never stopped surprising himself."

He was a man who spoke of universal, transcendent peace—becoming one with Om, "the first vibration—that sound, that spirit which set everything else into being." And yet his music, to the end, although sometimes almost eerily serene, remained most often volcanic. Ravi Shankar, who had come to know Coltrane, said: "I was much disturbed by his music. Here was a creative person who had become a vegetarian, who was studying yoga and reading the *Bhagavad-Gita,* yet in whose music I still heard much turmoil. I could not understand it."

Marion Brown, the alto saxophonist and composer, was one of the musicians assembled by Coltrane for his almost unbearably intense set of "free jazz," *Ascension,* and Brown recalls: "We did two takes, and they both had that kind of thing in them that makes people scream. The people in the studios were screaming."

Perhaps Om, the first vibration, is a scream. Perhaps Coltrane wished so hard to transcend all of what he regarded as his baser, antispiritual elements, that he was doomed, from the time his ambition became so otherworldly, to always feel desperately imprisoned. Hence the scream. But part of the scream may also have been the pain, the difficulty, of self-purgation, a process that had become the normative conundrum of thorns in his life.

Whatever the explanation—if there is a discernible matrix of explanations for the phenomenon of Coltrane—by the time he died of cancer of the liver in 1967, he had helped shape a new generation of jazz musicians. He didn't like the term "jazz," by the way, since he felt all music to be one, without labels.

In musical terms Trane's contributions have perhaps been most succinctly described by David Baker, who has long taught black music, and other music, at the University of Indiana. Now that *Grove's Dictionary of Music and Musicians* has at last decided to admit articles on jazz musicians, Baker is writing an entry on, among others, John Coltrane. And the achievements of Coltrane he will cite are: "using multiphonics, playing several notes or tones simultaneously; creating asymmetrical groupings not dependent on the basic pulse; developing an incredibly sophisticated system of chord substitutions; and initiating a pan-modal style of playing, using several modes simultaneously. I've transcribed some of his solos for teaching my students at the University of Indiana. I think all musicians should study Coltrane solos the way we now study the études of Bach and Brahms."

Coltrane, who read theory as well as biographies of the creative (Van Gogh, for instance), might have been pleased to hear that. But at night, on the stand, there would be no abiding satisfaction for him in what he had done in the past. "You just keep going," he told me once. "You keep trying to get right down to the crux."

He even frustrated himself—in addition to knowing the crux would always be beyond him or anyone else—by yearning for yet another impossibility. "Sometimes," Coltrane said to me one afternoon, "I wish I could walk up to my music as if for the first time, as if I had never heard it before. Being so inescapably a part of it, I'll never know what the listener gets, what the listener feels, and that's too bad."

Looking at Coltrane's early background—born in Hamlet, North Carolina; schooling in Philadelphia; rhythm-and-blues work with Eddie "Mr. Cleanhead" Vinson; gathering experience with Dizzy Gillespie, Earl Bostic, Johnny Hodges, Miles Davis, and Thelonious Monk—there would have been no way to predict (before Miles and Monk, anyway) the singular, unyieldingly questioning force that was to revolutionize much of jazz. There never is any way to predict the coming of the next jazz prophet. And that's why nearly all speculation, learned or otherwise, about the future directions of jazz is always futile. The future of jazz has always depended on unexpected individuals with radical (though at first seemingly opaque) questions to ask—questions they eventually proceed to answer: Louis Armstrong on the nature of the jazz solo; Duke Ellington on the nature of the jazz orchestra; Charlie Parker on the obsolescence of the rhythmic and harmonic language that preceded him; and John Coltrane on all manner of jazz constrictions that antedated *him.*

In spending himself on trying to answer the questions that consumed him, Coltrane eventually developed what in jazz terms could be called a large audience. As Martin Williams has pointed out, "It was almost impossible for a man to be as much of a technician, artist, and explorer as Coltrane and still have the kind of popular following he had. What did he tell that audience? In what new and meaningful things did his music instruct them?

"I don't know, of course," Williams continued. "And perhaps as a white man I can't know. But I would venture a suggestion. I don't think Coltrane spoke of society or political theory. I think that like all real artists he spoke of matters of the spirit, of those things by which the soul of man survives. I think he spoke of the ways of the demons and the gods that were always there, yet are always contemporary. And I think that he knew that he did."

Some months after Coltrane died, I was visiting a black college in Delaware. It had been a year during which I had lectured at many colleges—mostly on education and civil liberties. When music had come into the discussion, the emphasis invariably was on rock sounds and players. Only at this black college did the students talk of Bird and Ornette Coleman, and especially of Coltrane.

"You know," one of the black students said, "when Trane died, it was like a great big hole had been left. And it's still there."

In one sense that hole is indeed still there and will continue to be. Obviously, certain artists do leave great big holes when they die, for they are irreplaceable in the size and scope of their originality. Louis Armstrong. Duke. Lester Young. Coleman Hawkins. Billie Holiday. And on and on. There has yet been no successor to Coltrane in terms of having dominant, pervasive influence on the jazz of the 1970s.

On the other hand, as pianist Keith Jarrett said of Trane's death, "Everyone felt a big gap all of a sudden. But he didn't intend to leave a gap. He intended that there be more space for everybody to do what they should do."

And there *is* more space for further generations of seekers. In one way or another they are all children of Coltrane. And, of course, of all those who shaped him. The legacy is long and rich and demanding.

PETER WATROUS
JOHN COLTRANE: A LIFE SUPREME
Musician, *July 1987*

Peter Watrous wrote this survey of Coltrane's musical career just before the twentieth anniversary of the saxophonist's death. His article is insightful and thoughtful, and it makes an important contribution in its original interview material. Watrous conducted interviews with musicians who knew Coltrane well. Jimmy Heath illuminates Coltrane's days as a young professional, and Sonny Rollins makes it clear that he and Coltrane were more cooperative than competitive toward each other. Tommy Flanagan and Art Taylor shed light on how the famous recording of Coltrane's composition "Giant Steps" came about. Included at the end of the article are three statements from saxophonists Wayne Shorter, Ornette Coleman, and Sonny Rollins that were presented in stand-alone boxed form in the original article.—CW

John Coltrane died in 1967. America had seen the rise and assassination of Malcolm X and was about to experience Martin Luther King's death. It was more than just dancing in the streets; there was a riot going on, perhaps the greatest urban turmoil in the country's history. The arts were in upheaval, too: The Beatles were finishing *Sgt. Pepper's* and reshaping notions of pop; the Grand Union, a New York school of dance including

Twyla Tharp and Merce Cunningham, were using improvisation and random motion; junk and pop art were replacing the established abstract expressionists. There was a rupture with the past going on, in other words, and John Coltrane, who'd started out as a saxophonist deep in the jazz traditions, was one of its leaders.

In a sense he is the archetypal 60s artist, the man who reshaped the iconography of jazz genius from the brilliant burnout of Charlie Parker—a 50s beat idea—to that of the abstaining saint, paradoxically meditative and angry, Eastern and yet American. He became the paradigm of the searching artist. Though it can be argued that Coltrane helped end jazz's mass popularity with his expressionistic, visceral approach to music, his own appeal and influence was immense, reaching way beyond the confines of jazz or even music. And after two subsequent decades of often jarring cultural and political cynicism, his trademarks of honesty, forthrightness, and an overwhelming desire to change, to do things that haven't been done before, seem more than just appealing. They seem necessary.

For me, Coltrane's astounding emotional power comes from his sound, that chillingly personal cry that's his identity, the one note that can be heard from his fumbling, early recordings with Dizzy Gillespie to the last dates five months before he died. It's not a warm sound, or a friendly sound, it's simply a fact that carries with it an indifference to acceptability. To me Coltrane has always sounded lonely, a three a.m. blue wail that gives succor and sympathy to those in trouble. There's passion in everything he played—even the hundreds of blowing sessions he tossed off—to remind us what it means to be alive. You feel his rawness, his lack of equivocation, his honesty.

Coltrane was a natural. He also worked extremely hard at cultivating his talent. He didn't "do" anything in a Hollywood sense: His life reflects an almost monastic dedication to learning and to advancing, both as a musician and as a person. The son of a tailor and grandchild of two ministers (his mother's father, also a state senator, was known for fire and brimstone sermons), he grew up in High Point, North Carolina, in what passed for the black aristocracy. In school he played in Reverend Steele's Community Band. By the time he graduated from high school in 1943, he already exhibited the sort of aloofness that made him seem mysterious—actually, he was shy—and he was known as *the* musician in High Point. As choices available for black people to make a living were severely limited, being a musician would be considered risqué in some circles, a source of pride and admiration in others. For Coltrane, it meant giving up college.

In 1944, Coltrane and two of his best friends moved to Philadelphia where he began his fanatical practice routine, from ten to twelve hours a day. Following a Navy stint, he joined an R&B band led by Joe Webb and featuring the great blues shouter Big Maybelle, then twenty-two, who loved Coltrane's tone. He went to California, as part of Eddie "Cleanhead" Vinson's group, where he met and played with his idol Charlie Parker. But Vinson wanted him as a tenor player, not an altoist; the change of instruments allowed him to move away from Parker's influence. "On tenor," said Coltrane, "I found there was no one man whose ideas were so dominant. I listened to almost all the good tenor men, beginning with Lester, and believe me, I've picked up something from all of them, including several who haven't recorded."

Post-war Philadelphia was musically fertile; clubs were everywhere, and since the city was on the black tour circuit, local people were often picked up by big-name groups. "Philadelphia was a mecca [for] bebop," says saxophonist Jimmy Heath, a soft-spoken, intelligent man who was one of Coltrane's best friends. "There was a lot of jamming going on; everybody was trying to learn. It was a family type of affair." That year Miles Davis blew into town; having recorded with Charlie Parker's group, he wasn't quite a star but his style was already well-known. Coltrane sat in with him at the Audubon Ballroom in New York and knew, according to biographer O. C. Simkins, that he'd "one day like to play permanently with him."

"I heard Trane in Philadelphia," says Miles Davis. "When he picked up the tenor, his eyes were on Dexter and Sonny Stitt. I used to have him and Sonny Rollins in the same band, and Art Blakey. That was a *baad* band I had, *Goddamn!* So he started working with me. I got him and Philly Joe. And Paul Chambers. He was playing, you know, like Dexter, kicking out different long phrases. I *loved* when he would do that, when he would imitate, like Eddie Davis. It was so funny."

Heroin was endemic to the jazz community of the time; it was cheap, and the long-term effects of addiction hadn't yet become obvious. Coltrane, twenty-two, was fitting in. "There were a lot of guys that were messed up on drugs," says Sonny Rollins, "[but] I never looked at John in that way. He was never that type of guy. It's incongruous. But I guess it happened, and at times he was messed up. It was out of character." To support himself, Coltrane would play R&B dates around the city, walking the bar and honking. "We all had to walk the bar," says Heath. "That was the fad of the time. People would throw money in the bell of your horn. John could adapt to it, but that wasn't his forté, there was too much repetition, the 'Flying Home' type solos." One night Benny Golson entered a club just as Coltrane was stalking the bar. Embarrassed, Coltrane jumped off the bar, walked out the door and never came back.

Nineteen-fifty-five, when Charlie Parker died, was also the year Miles Davis put together his first famous quintet, with Philly Joe, Paul Chambers, Red Garland and Coltrane. John had been working a two-week stint with organist Jimmy Smith, who asked him to join when Philly Joe called him to make a date with Miles. The same week, Coltrane married Niama Grubbs, after whom he would name two songs. She was both traditionally religious (a Moslem) and into astrology, interests Coltrane himself would pursue for the rest of his life.

The Miles Davis group of 1955 set the course for jazz over the next five years. Though deeply rooted in bop, the two horn players took idiosyncratic approaches to its language, Miles by distilling the essence of a phrase into a few notes, Coltrane by cramming bushels of them into a small harmonic space. His early playing with Miles seems slightly out of control; snatches of undigested Dexter Gordon and Sonny Stitt float by, and Coltrane's lines come at you in all directions, sputtering one moment, graceful the next. But he has the "it" Jack Kerouac wrote about: the sound, the excitement and unpredictability of blowing; the way he puts together notes, the way he's thinking about what phrase makes sense next to what phrase. Mark him, Miles would say to Coltrane's critics, as someone who was finding his own way.

He was starting to record frequently: a Davis date in late 1955 (*New Miles Davis Quintet*), with Elmo Hope for Prestige in 1956, and the *Tenor Madness* date with Sonny Rollins, a legendary match-up of the up-and-coming tenorists.

The session, their only recorded meeting, came about by accident. "John went out to the date with us," says Sonny Rollins, with characteristic off-handedness, "because in those days a lot of musicians hung out together. There were more friendships. People would be immersed in music twenty-four hours a day. You'd be over at somebody's house listening to records for days at a time. John was either with Red Garland or Philly Joe Jones, I believe. Money wouldn't have entered it. John had asked me right after that period to make [another] record together. Much to my regret, we never did."

Much was made about tensions between the two top young tenor saxophonists of the time. Rollins, who considered Coltrane one of his closest friends, never saw it that way. "It was hard to be competitive with John, because he was bigger than that, his playing and his person. [We were] competitive in musical terms, sure, to a degree. I think all guys are judged by who's around you. But I don't think he spent a lot of time trying to consciously compete with other people."

By 1956, Coltrane's drug and drinking problems had worsened; he was looking bad onstage, and using up all his money. In St. Louis, Paul Chambers and Coltrane checked out of their hotel via the window. Miles disbanded the group. "He was no trouble," says Miles. "But when he was there he used to say [*in a hurt tone*], 'You never talk to us.' Well, 'You never sober up enough for me to talk to you.'"

Back in New York, Coltrane was still drinking heavily and playing badly, and Reggie Workman confronted him about it. He went off the bottle, but after three days his thought patterns had screwed up, and he couldn't speak properly. He stayed in his house for about two weeks, prayed a lot, then woke up one day without the urge for a drink. "The person who gets all the credit for helping him to clear up is Niama," says Workman. "She's the one who stayed with him through everything and helped him clear his life."

Nineteen-fifty-seven was the turning point in the Coltrane odyssey, a watershed that only an extremely disciplined person could effect. He set up schedules for studying, practicing, listening to other players. He had a second dream in which Charlie Parker came to him (in the first Parker had told him to give up alto) and suggested he "keep on those progressions 'cause that's the right thing to do."

Prestige Records, not known for its largesse to musicians, offered Coltrane a contract in March, and he began to record regularly (at least thirteen dates in '57 alone, including *Dakar*, his first as a leader). Critics, who for the most part hadn't liked what Coltrane was playing, soon realized he'd achieved a profound mastery of his instrument, that he was crossing musical frontiers. He came in second in the New Star category in *Down Beat*, recorded the well-received masterpiece *Blue Train*, and most importantly joined Monk for his legendary gig at the Five Spot in New York, which drew audiences beyond jazz circles, including painters Franz Kline and Willem de Kooning; the latter called Coltrane "an Einstein of music."

The difference between his tentative solos with Miles the year before is astonishing. His solo on "Chronic Blues," for instance, is angular, rhythmically aggressive, with arpeggios flung right and left. A marvel of technique, he'd started experimenting with different ways to approach the same chords. The moan, the quick upward glance, is there too. Four months later, on the classic *Blue Train* session, he's playing hotter and faster, a sort of hyper-bebopper, draping the changes with waves of notes. By now he'd shed his influences and was deep into harmony, superimposing chord after chord, creating a sheen which critic Ira Gitler would name "sheets of sound." He was working on multiphonics, which he'd learned from saxophonist John Glenn and from Monk. Intrigued by harp music, he would check the paper for Marx Brothers movies, and persistently asked Niama to take up the instrument.

Coltrane rejoined Miles at the end of the year; the group now featured Bill Evans on piano, Cannonball Adderly on alto, and a book which used modes as a way to simplify harmonic movement. It was completely antithetical to what Coltrane was working on at the time—the superimposition of chords, dense harmonic webs—yet he fit in perfectly, using the harmonic spaces to experiment with all the chord substitutions he was thinking about. Miles places Coltrane's development: "I said, 'Trane, you can play these chords against the tonic of another chord,' and he was the only one who could do it. Lucky Thompson, maybe. Plus, when I did *Milestones,* with Bill Evans, I wrote out these little things for Trane, these little things within a mode, to see what he could do on them. It was always a challenge for him. The chords I showed him were just like dominant chords against dominant chords, a minor, diminished and half step . . . he could play that in one chord and the trick is, not the trick, but to play them so you can hear the sound of the chord you're playing against. It's always a challenge if you're up in the air, because you're tired of the suspended diminished chord after everything. It's like not having an orgasm, but holding it in."

By late 1958, Coltrane had become a big enough star to leave Prestige and ask for a $1,000 advance per album. Not only was he playing with Miles Davis, which was placing him in front of audiences beyond jazz fans, he was becoming a figure of controversy, acknowledged to be doing something different.

Coltrane's own commitment had gotten to the point where he'd take the saxophone to the dinner table with him, fall asleep in bed with the reed in his mouth. He'd practice until he couldn't play anymore, sometimes for twenty-four hours straight. One result was *Giant Steps,* recorded in May of 1959, and an album which seemed to put an end at the time to the possibilities of chord changes. The title composition sounds like the sort of complicated exercise music students write for themselves to help master chordal playing. Coltrane sounds mechanical; the tune reinforces his occasional rhythmic stiffness. Still, the record has rightly become a masterpiece. Partly it's the writing—listen to the stunning forthrightness of "Cousin Mary"—partly Coltrane's assertive, startling playing.

At the time, the date seemed like nothing out of the ordinary. "I was living on 101st Street and Coltrane was on 103rd Street," pianist Tommy Flanagan recalls. "He came by my apartment with this piece, 'Giant

Steps,' I guess he thought there was something different about it, because he sat down and played the changes. He said, 'It's no problem. I know you can do it, Maestro'—which is what he called me. 'If I can play this, you can.' There *was* no problem just looking at the changes. But I didn't realize he was going to play it at that *tempo!* There was no time to shed on it, there was no melody; it was just a set of chords, like we usually get. So we ran it down and we had maybe one take, because he played marvelous on everything. He was ready. As he said later on, the whole date was tunes he wanted to get out of his system.

"He was using that sequence in the bridge of 'Body And Soul.' I thought it went down very smooth. 'Giant Steps' was just a part of three songs he was going to use called *Suite Sioux*. One was based on 'Cherokee.' It was one of the ones we really didn't get, it posed too much of a problem. It was still at that tempo, and it was supposed to go from 'Giant Steps' to 'Suite Sioux,' to 'Countdown,' which I think was faster yet. Paul [Chambers] had no solo on those pieces, but just keeping up with the sequence of the chords was hard, they were going down so fast.

"I had no idea [how influential the date would become]. A date with Trane, you knew it was going to be important. It seemed like years later people started saying, 'What was it like?' It was like any other date to me. It was a date."

"We had rehearsed at my mother's house in Harlem," says Arthur Taylor, the drummer on the session. "He wanted to rehearse with me before the date. So he brought his horn. We just ran over the pieces for about half an hour or so, and he left.

"I don't put that much importance on the record myself. I've done better records than that with Coltrane. It still remains a heck of a document, people all around the world look to that, and musicians also; that's the thing. I don't like the sound of it. John was very serious, like a magician too. He was serious and we just got down to the business at hand."

Ironically, *Giant Steps* ended Coltrane's dense approach to harmony. *Kind of Blue,* Miles Davis' masterpiece of modality, was recorded at the same time, with Coltrane playing an integral part. Coltrane absorbed a lot of knowledge through mentors—Miles and Monk are just two examples. By late 1959, he was talking with Sun Ra about recording together. Soon after that he began to play the soprano saxophone.

He'd increased his reading to include books on art, music theory, African history, physics, math, anthropology. His record collection had music from Africa, Afghanistan, Russia, France, early England, Greece, American Indians, India, Arabia and all types of black American music.

"He was into Indian music and into African music, and different social groups," says McCoy Tyner, the pianist who charted the idiosyncratic harmonic sound of the classic Coltrane quartet of the 60s. On "Dahomey Dance" (from *Olé*), he had a record of these guys who were from Dahomey, which is why he used two bassists. He showed that rhythm to Art Davis and Reggie Workman. So the influence was there."

By 1960, it was time to leave Miles Davis' group and head out on his own. A live recording from March of that year, done in Europe during Coltrane's last tour with Davis, finds him straightjacketed by Jimmy Cobb's drumming. His intensely detailed, whirling lines seem to be seeking the more mutable, interactive drumming he'd find with Elvin Jones, and a less rigid context for improvisation. On "Green Dolphin Street" he reduces the tune to nothing, unleashing torrents of notes that obliterate the changes.

Giant Steps was well received, and after returning from the European tour, Coltrane gave Miles two weeks' notice. The owners of the Five Spot (the club that had Monk and Coltrane three years earlier) now ran a club called the Jazz Gallery; they offered him a twenty-week engagement, which suggests their appraisal of his drawing power. Coltrane put his first quartet together for the gig, including drummer Pete LaRoca, Steve Kuhn on piano, and Philadelphia bassist Steve Davis. The first set of the first night, during a Coltrane solo, a bald man dressed in a loincloth ran up to the stage, followed by Monk, yelling "Coltrane, Coltrane." The stay lasted nine weeks and proved hugely successful, with Ravi Shankar, Cecil Taylor and others coming by to listen. Coltrane quickly fired Kuhn and LaRoca, replacing them with McCoy Tyner and Elvin Jones (who Coltrane had in mind the whole time anyway). In a few months, Steve Davis was replaced by Reggie Workman (who would later give way to Jimmy Garrison), and the quartet found its sound for the next four years.

Coltrane ran his group like Miles Davis had his, with little or no interference. They rehearsed a total of six or seven times during McCoy Tyner's entire tenure. "He was a great leader," says Tyner. "Never self-imposing. I loved working for him. He was more like a brother. I had a chance to develop. Just playing and listening to him every night and creating something underneath him and creating our own thing when it came time, was quite challenging for a young guy.

"Never did he say how to play piano. He was just not that kind of person. He picked people he didn't have to do that with. Which I thought was very, very smart."

My Favorite Things, his next release for Atlantic, brought Coltrane his widest recognition. Here he embraced the modality he'd learned with Miles Davis, but turned the stark impressionism of Miles' approach into extroverted intensity; his novel treatment of the title track laid the groundwork for the next five years of his life, until the radically different *Ascension*. Completely unlike anything Coltrane, Davis, or, for that matter, anybody had done, the record still swings in a loose, open way. Harmonic vistas open, Coltrane sounds relaxed, his soprano wafting over the pliant background; the fury and impatience of his playing with Miles has been assuaged by a group whose rhythmic liberties match his own.

Just how empathic the group became is spelled out by Tyner, who remembers one night in the early 60s when Miles tried to sit in at Birdland. "There wasn't any room. He didn't quite work. We were very special. It was very difficult for anybody to walk up and come into the band."

Once, with Miles, when Coltrane explained he didn't know how to stop soloing, Davis suggested that he take the saxophone out of his mouth. Now his tunes were getting longer, between an hour or two in live performance. Nonetheless, *My Favorite Things* went gold, and *Newsweek* covered Coltrane's week-long stay in July at the Village Vanguard. Eric Dolphy joined the group that summer, and they recorded *Africa/Brass* for Impulse, a gorgeous, agitated big-band album arranged by Dolphy and McCoy Tyner.

His next record, *Live at the Village Vanguard,* featured "Chasin' the Trane," a side-long blues named by Rudy Van Gelder (who had a tough time following Coltrane's horn for the recording) which caused outrage among critics and listeners, even inciting a double review, pro and con, in *Down Beat.* Critic John Tynan coined the ignorant but telling term "anti-jazz." "Chasin' the Trane" is one of the magnificent recordings of jazz. It begins with a simple opening melody and gradually, maintaining the same level of emotionality, gets more complex. Coltrane starts blowing harmonics, raising the ante; McCoy Tyner keeps out of the way, and what's stunning is the way that Coltrane and Elvin Jones reinvent straight-ahead, 4/4 swing, turning the tune into a tumultuous event.

"He was very much a man of conviction," notes Art Davis, one of Coltrane's favorite bassists, "even though a lot of people said a lot of very bad, hurting things about him. He'd say, 'That's their opinion,' rather than cursing someone out or saying, 'If I see that motherfucker, I'm going to beat the shit out of him.'"

Coltrane had six years to live from the time he made *Africa/Brass.* He recorded an astounding twenty-five albums in that time, not counting the alternate takes and snippets that began to surface after his death, with the overall level of quality virtually unparalleled. After *Live at the Village Vanguard* come a series of albums which take his certain type of oceanic modalism to its limits. *Impressions* (the title track is based on the minimal harmony of Miles Davis' "So What?") and *Coltrane* led into three dates which were suggested by Impulse: *Ballads, Duke Ellington & John Coltrane* and *John Coltrane and Johnny Hartman.*

Bob Thiele, Coltrane's producer, pretty much gave him the keys to the studio, to the point of risking his job. "To the best of my recollection, Coltrane had a contract that called for two albums a year to be recorded and released. Well, hell, we recorded six albums a year. And I was always brought on the carpet because they couldn't understand why I was spending the money. Most of the critics and the various music magazines were putting Coltrane down. And there's one time I did suggest to him, 'Why don't we just go in and show these guys.' I suggested we do an album of popular songs, which became *Ballads,* a beautiful album, and he loved it. And that started to turn the critics around."

By 1962 and 1963, the radical edge was beginning to show on records and American society. Civil rights leader Medgar Evers was murdered in his garage, while in Birmingham, Alabama, four young girls were killed when a black church was bombed. Bob Dylan released *The Times They Are A-Changin'* as the folk movement was aligning itself with the political New Left. Coltrane recorded what may be his most overtly political composition, "Alabama," in memory of the four children killed in the church bombing, and based on the cadences of a Martin Luther King speech about that tragedy.

Politics were integral to being black and a jazz musician: They were integral to the time. Acquaintances could read various meanings into Coltrane's character because he was shy, or political connotations into his music because he rarely clarified himself. These assumptions often have to do with what part of Coltrane's life people knew him from, though they also underscore how Coltrane was accepted by different generations. "He was not involved in politics," says Milt Jackson, who was with Coltrane in Dizzy Gillespie's group and appeared on Coltrane's first album for Atlantic. "I can't draw any parallels between the social times of the 60s and John's playing," says Sonny Rollins. "[But] it may be relevant to somebody that grew up in the 60s and heard Coltrane in the 60s, and was into whatever movements were going on at the time. To me it was just a natural evolution in his own playing."

Rashied Ali, who worked with Coltrane from 1965 to the end, sees it differently. "The younger people embraced the music; the older Coltrane fans, the people who dug the Coltrane from Miles Davis and the Coltrane from the early 60s, they sort of stepped back because they couldn't get with the change. But the connection was there. He wrote songs like 'Reverend King' and 'Alabama'; that whole movement affected everybody. It affected his thinking and his thoughts about what was happening, and the music started getting rougher and tougher. Coltrane wasn't into politics; he wasn't the type of person to speak out about it. But he was playing and writing music about it. And he admired people like King and Malcolm X. He kept up with things."

In an interview with writer Frank Kofsky, Coltrane put it like this: "In my opinion, I would say yes [jazz is opposed to the United States involvement in Vietnam] because jazz to me . . . is an expression of higher ideals. So therefore brotherhood is there; and I believe with brotherhood, there would be no poverty. And also, with brotherhood, there would be no war."

The issues that Malcolm X talked about "are definitely important," he went on. "And as I said, the issues are part of what is at the time. So naturally, as musicians, we express whatever is. Well, I tell you for myself, I make a conscious attempt; I think I can truthfully say that in music I make or I have tried to make a conscious attempt to change what I've found, in music. In other words, I've tried to say, 'Well, this could be better, in my opinion, so I will try to do this to make it better.' We must make an effort. It's the same socially, musically, politically, and in any department of our lives."

Coltrane's main extramusical stimulation came not from politics, but from religion. Deeply influenced by his family background, he maintained an interest in God all his life, exploring different religions, though never settling down and becoming part of one denomination. He was interested in astrology as well and the titles of his compositions—"Psalm," "Song Of Praise," "Ascension," "Dear Lord," "Dearly Beloved," "Amen," "Attaining," "Ascent," "Cosmos," "Om," "The Father and the Son and the Holy Ghost," "Compassion," "Love Consequences," "Serenity," "Meditations," "Leo," "Mars," "Venus," "Jupiter," "Saturn"—tell the story.

By 1963, Coltrane was becoming involved with younger musicians, who saw him as a father figure of the "New Thing"—Archie Shepp (who was to play on a lost version of A Love Supreme a year later), George Braith, Albert and Don Ayler, Bill Dixon and others. He'd separated from Niama and taken up with Alice McLeod, who he'd later marry. But his interest in the spiritual realm had hardly abated; the release of A Love Supreme in December of 1964 included liner notes describing his religious awakening. *A Love Supreme* was awarded *Down Beat*'s record of the year, while Coltrane was "Jazzman of the Year," elected to the Hall of Fame, and voted first place on tenor saxophone. The hagiography was well under way.

For many, Coltrane was the mirror reflecting their dreams or virtues. Withdrawn, quiet, he exuded an air of serenity. His religious song titles and the ascetic quality of his music fit an image many people were eager to impose on him. His personal habits—rigorous practice, vegetarianism, dabbling in odd religions—fit the times, suggesting a sort of monk looking for salvation in art. He was completely honest in his dealings with people. And his music captured the revolutionary spirit of the 60s, epitomizing uncommon ideals.

"I liked him because he was a musician and a serious person," says Sonny Rollins, "almost a religious person. He had a nice unassuming quality to him. This to me was about as good as you can get in this life. As far as his personality goes, he had everything that I think was the best. He was looking for dignity. And respect as a human being. He didn't seem to be interested in self-aggrandizement. He was very young and he was just trying to get out all that music."

For young musicians, his effect was more direct. "To be honest," remembers Rashied Ali, "Coltrane changed my whole concept of playing music. It made me want to play a freer, more searching type of music. I started broadening my scope of listening; it was like a refreshing breeze.

"He was kinda cool because he would be so shy," says Ali, who got to know the less formidable Coltrane. "Because he was such a great artist, people never really found out how the man was. They would say to me, 'Should I speak to him?' and they'd stand there dumbfounded, not knowing what to say. They'd ask me, 'Will you say something to him?' and I'd say, 'Why don't you go over there yourself?' All they had to do was say 'hello,' because the guy was ready to talk, he was just a real down-home, country-type guy. Loved to laugh, loved sweet potato pie, collard greens, stuff like that. He was really what you would call a soul brother, he didn't have any weird stuff about him. He was an alright cat, the type of a person you can really call a friend.

"He would do things for people. So many musicians were damn near living off of Trane. Guys would just call him up and say, 'I'm not working,' or 'I'm broke,' or 'I need this, I need that,' and he'd send them a money order. He paid people's rent for them, anything he could do. He wasn't stupid, but he was definitely there if you needed him. He was just like a regular person who liked to laugh a lot."

Coltrane broke through to another level with *Ascension,* a large group date recorded in 1965 that essentially did away with regular pulsed meter and signaled Coltrane's interest in both density and musical simplicity. Unlike *Giant Steps,* the people on the date knew it was a momentous musical occasion. "When he said that it was very important," remembers Art Davis, "I didn't doubt him. I didn't know what direction he was going. When I saw these people—I knew some of them, and others I didn't know—I knew . . . something's important here. When I heard it, *that* was convincing."

A month later, in September, Coltrane added Pharoah Sanders to his group, and along with Donald Garrett, he recorded *Om* under the influence of LSD. Two weeks later came *Kulu Se Mama,* and on the next date *Meditations.* With the addition of Rashied Ali on drums, Coltrane continued the forward motion he'd begun with *Ascension.* (That record also received the double treatment in *Down Beat.*) This ever-ballooning ensemble caused problems however; conflicts between Rashied Ali and Elvin Jones pushed the volume up and up. Then Elvin Jones and McCoy Tyner left and were replaced by pianist Alice Coltrane (who also played harp).

"At the beginning we were doing the tunes Trane was famous for, 'My Favorite Things,' 'Impressions,'" says Ali. "After a while he started writing new music for the band, and that's when I started playing drums in the band alone. It was a whole different change in the music; very spiritual, and sometimes very harsh on the listeners who had been into Trane previously. Because his whole style changed."

"I really thought it was a bit too much sometimes," remembers McCoy Tyner. "I really did. I couldn't hear what I was doing. I'd look around and about five saxes would be onstage. Where did these guys come from? Norman Simmons, who was working opposite us with Carmen McRae, said to me, 'Man, that F♯'s the sharpest note up there, really out of tune, horrible.' And I said 'Really? I can't hear it.' I could not hear my instrument. So I said, 'Well, it's time for me to exit.'"

In February and March 1967, Coltrane went into the studio for the last times. The result was *Expression,* yet another new direction. Spare, mostly calm and rhythmless, it sounds as if Coltrane had reached a level of contentment. The music has neither the exploratory fervor of his earlier 60s works, nor the technique obvious from his music of the late 50s. With *Expression* and *Interstellar Space* (a duet with Ali), Coltrane had reached, through enormous self-discipline and dedication, his last plateau. In July 1967 he died of liver cancer.

It's extraordinary for anybody to have attempted this kind of odyssey, from junky be-bopper to 60s experimentalist and cultural icon. It's also extraordinary that he even mattered: A less musical person would have been bogged down by the programmatics of his art. But he did matter and the question remains, what does he mean to us now?

One of the unfortunate things that happened to John Coltrane's music in the 70s was the assimilation of his style into the mainstream. All pianists played like McCoy Tyner, all saxophonists worked Coltrane's pentatonic flurries, and they all helped reduce his music's potency. The effects he'd used to elicit certain emotional responses were out of place; the moment had passed, and in the America of Gerald Ford and Jimmy Carter, where complacency was the rule, his sounds were out of context. But his time is coming around again; in the era of Contragate and Bakkergate and Boeskygate, and a renewed awareness toward the outrage of apartheid, John Coltrane's music sounds real, functional again. The beautiful fury has walls to crush.

What we can glean from Coltrane is his steadfast dedication to learning and personal dignity. He absorbed knowledge so he could change, to eradicate the clichéd and stale. His honesty lets us know it's possible to keep going; his music can be heard as inspiration. In his dedication to ideals we can imagine our own capacities. It's an old jazz virtue, but it applies.

"When there's something you don't understand, you have to go humbly to it," John Coltrane once observed. "You don't go to school and sit down and say, 'I know what you're getting ready to teach me.' You sit there and you learn. You open your mind. You absorb. But you have to be quiet, you have to be still to do all of this."

SONNY ROLLINS (tenor sax):

"I first heard him in a band with Kenny Clarke. I remember very well. John and Kenny, it was fantastic. And I recall thinking that John was a puzzle. I could never figure out how he arrived at, how he came up with, what he played. It was one of the things that made him unique. I never got a better fix on it through the years. Like any genius, it's hard to get a handle on how they come up with their ideas.

"His influence was very pervasive. But I don't think it's necessarily bad to have influences. It's inevitable. Any guy who's that much into music is bound to be listening heavily to someone before him, like I did with Coleman Hawkins. The individuality will come out if it's there. It depends whether or not the individual player can transcend the influence. To play what we call modern music, you need some antecedents.

"Although he had a sense of humor, he was quite serious most of the time. Almost like a guy who would be a minister, especially about music. You realized you were in the presence of someone who held the sacred in high regard. His humor wasn't about cracking jokes or anything like that, he was more droll or wry.

"I remember when I heard the news of his death. I was working somewhere and I took some people back to Brooklyn. In those days we wouldn't get out of the clubs until four in the morning. By the time I got back home it was light out. I was listening to WOR and there was a quote from Elvin to the effect that John never hurt anybody. It was a shock; I had just talked to him two weeks earlier. We were always close."

ORNETTE COLEMAN (alto & tenor sax):

"He called me up and asked if I would join his band. I was very interested in trying to get the things I was playing in the public's eye, but I was having too much trouble with the business, so I hadn't been out in clubs for a long time. I thought I'd better go out and see what's going on. When I went to the Vanguard, Max Gordon called me over and said, 'Somebody just cancelled—could you bring in a band?' And that's the only thing that stopped me from joining Coltrane.

"In the early 60s he was studying with me. He was interested in non-chordal playing, and I had cut my teeth on that stuff. He later sent me a letter which included thirty dollars for each lesson, and thanked me. [That influence] showed up very clearly because all of a sudden a guy who had been playing very 'legitimately' started playing strictly from his own spiritual and emotional state without worrying about his past. Had he lived, Trane would probably have legitimized that concept. I thought he had a beautiful tone. I thought it was very humane."

WAYNE SHORTER (tenor & soprano sax):

"He invited me to his house after we met and said he wanted to get together with me because we were playing . . . not the same way, but in the same areas of the horn. He said, 'You're playing some funny stuff.' He wanted to sit down and talk about it. He was playing the piano mostly, I think it was the beginning of 'Giant Steps,' those augmented thirds over and over. He'd get his horn and play two notes for a long time. Then two others, then two others. We also talked about doing impossible things with your instrument. We also talked about starting a sentence in the middle, and then going to the beginning and the end of it at the same time.

"George Tucker, the bassist, would come by, Cedar Walton too, Freddie Hubbard. He'd ask me to spend the night. That happened more than once. We'd cook food. Then he came to Jersey to my parents' house, on Thanksgiving. He'd talk with Ayler, he liked him. He wanted to check out what was going on with the scene. Not just tenor, but flute and other things; I think that's why he grabbed that bagpipe toward the end. It was all-encompassing. Charlie Parker was realizing that before he died, too.

"From 1955 on, he had a sense of urgency. Like he couldn't get everything he wanted out. I think Trane knew something about his health, even if he couldn't pin it down.

"I think one of John's legacies is that any melody has a flexibility beyond what it initially seems. Nothing is frozen. He said that everything can be opened up but it's a lot of work. There are people who say you've got to do 'Nature Boy' just the way it is. And the 'Star Spangled Banner.' Hey, you can really take the 'Star Spangled Banner' out!"

STANLEY CROUCH

JOHN COLTRANE: TITAN OF THE BLUES

Village Voice, *October 6, 1987*

As was the previous piece, this article was also written around the time of the twentieth anniversary of John Coltrane's death. Stanley Crouch uses a review of several Coltrane CD reissues as his point of departure for an assessment of the saxophonist and his groups of the early 1960s. The "classic" quartet was considered quite exploratory in its time but also maintained contact with the traditions of blues, swing, ballads, and the "Spanish Tinge." Crouch writes that while it was Coltrane's "appetite for freedom" that led him to explore artistically, it was his essential feeling for the blues that made him a musical giant.

Crouch, a jazz journalist and artistic consultant to Jazz at Lincoln Center, is author of Notes of a Hanging Judge, The All-American Skin Game, *and* Always in Pursuit.

Note: The MCA-label CDs discussed here are now available on the Impulse label, manufactured by GRP.—CW

Like all serious jazz musicians, John Coltrane invented a remarkable personal style, but his status also stems from the fresh conception he developed for an entire band. Probably his most artistically successful period as a bandleader was between 1961 and 1965, when he fronted the classic quartet, which included drummer Elvin Jones, pianist McCoy Tyner, and bassist Jimmy Garrison. At its best, the art of that ensemble at least equals the finest music written for or performed by any foursome, regardless of idiom. Over the last year, MCA has reissued digital versions of Coltrane albums made between 1961 and 1964. Of the reissues, *Impressions* finds the saxophonist experimenting with different-sized ensembles, while *Coltrane, Crescent,* and *A Love Supreme* best capture the quartet's contribution. That contribution was the fusion of passion and intellectual depth that distinguishes jazz from the music of the concert or popular worlds, neither of which offers the combination of the inflamed soul and the mind in such perfect synthesis.

So much enduring music was produced by Coltrane's group because he grasped how essential *hearing* is to improvising. It is at the center of the *action* that is improvising, the source of vitality. Detailed hearing draws upon the aesthetic feeling that brings music alive and separates it from the academic and merely virtuosic. Hearing is the way knowledge, experience, and technique are given structure and function. It informs taste, sensitivity, and passion; determines the clarity of the melodic, harmonic, rhythmic, and textural choices available. Given the necessary discipline, those who hear best sound best.

But one can hear well enough to become an extraordinary improviser, as did Art Tatum or Don Byas, and still have a style that is compatible with the conventions of group playing. In fact, most jazz musicians organize bands around chemistry, and though the individual styles included might be unique, the ensemble approach is usually generic in the best sense of the word. The listener experiences personal versions of different schools—New Orleans, swing, bebop, etc. Yet with Coltrane's quartet, the saxophonist and his musicians could hear their way through the materials and make collective variations on them that redefined the strategic aspects of the aesthetic. That is the differences between an individual and a group conception—the former, however wonderful, is but one musician's way; with the latter the means must be sufficiently large to include roles for traditional ensemble instruments (especially the rhythm section, if the music is jazz). The upshot was the redefinition of blues, swing, ballads, 4/4 (fast, medium, and slow), and what Jelly Roll Morton called "the Spanish Tinge," which had evolved by the '60s to include African-derived rhythms and elements of Third World music from as far east as India.

No musician of Coltrane's era was better prepared to extend the jazz aesthetic. Born September 23, 1926, he had worked with many masters, learning the particulars of their music from the inside. Everything he drew from Eddie "Cleanhead" Vinson, Dizzy Gillespie, Earl Bostic, Tadd Dameron, Johnny Hodges, Miles Davis, and Thelonious Monk was put to specific use with such expanding facility that saxophone technique was revolutionized. Coltrane wanted to have every register, corner, fingering, overtone, and possible note on call at will. By working through blues, swing, bebop, and the architecture of Monk, as well as the precise ensemble conceptions of Miles Davis, Coltrane synthesized a broad range of music with an inherent scope missing from almost all so-called avant-garde jazz. Unlike most associated with the avant-garde, he knew what the essences of the tradition were—blues, idiomatic lyricism, and swing—and was able to remake them rather than avoid their demands.

Coltrane's appetite for freedom of expression drove him to learn all that he did, yet his understanding of and feeling for the blues made him a giant. From working with blues singers and with supreme blues instrumentalists (Hodges, Davis, and Monk), Coltrane obviously concluded that the blues essentials could provide the foundation upon which to build his saxophone style and the style of his band. In blues, the form is simple, the harmony limited, and the expression often arrives through overt and subtle use of texture and rhythm. With such insight, Coltrane separated himself from other saxophonists who also used sweeping arpeggios by bringing an increasing complexity of timbre to his epic sashes of notes—the keening to grunting to rasping to wailing colors of the blues. In that sense, saxophone and all, Coltrane became the champion blues shouter of his era, a man whose enormous harmonic resources were made idiomatic by their order and the molten timbres that coated them.

Just as Miles Davis once made simple, songful phrases more musically and emotionally intricate by calling on the tonal resources trumpeters had so superbly refined before the bebop era. Coltrane made his own dense passages earthy through blues coloration and blues intensity. And as he matured, Coltrane took advantage of the blue *mood* that had been brought into jazz by Ellington (and where better to hear that source than in the band of Hodges?). The melancholy, sophistication, and bittersweet swing of that mood had been best personalized in the wake of the bebop era by Monk and Davis. In fact, the greatest contribution of Davis's influential *Kind of Blue* was conceptual: if limited harmony and scales were to replace numerous chords and arpeggios, then modal jazz should ground itself in the three elements mentioned above—blues, idiomatic lyricism, and swing.

Aware of all of that, Coltrane had to find musicians whose hearing and invention were passionate enough to both inspire him and also express their own personalities. Though his players have often said that he never told anyone what to do, it is obvious that Coltrane knew how important personnel is to composition. Therefore, if his musicians *hadn't* been doing what he wanted, they would have been fired. For his purposes, the fact that a conception is an imaginative way of using knowledge meant that he had to hire musicians whose sensibilities fitted the vision he was pursuing.

Because Ahmad Jamal's group conception was as important to Coltrane as it was to Miles Davis, enlisting McCoy Tyner was pivotal. On *Coltrane Plays the Blues* (Atlantic), one hears the vamps, block-chords, and uses of rhythms other than those conventionally used to swing a band. Hearing it right after Jamal's *But Not for Me* is illuminating. Then one can easily notice how Tyner made his own style out of Bud Powell, Jamal, Red Garland, and Wynton Kelly. The percussiveness of his distinctly original accompanying style moved the music closer to a point at which the roles of drums and harmony instruments were profoundly reinterpreted. Tyner took on the role of a percussionist with tonal resources in the rhythm section, sharing heavily rhythmic vamps with the bass, which supplied the dominant ground beats upon which Coltrane and the drummer built their own improvisations (hear "Out of This World" and "Tunji" on *Coltrane*). Most of all, he swung harder than any other young pianist of the day, could truly hear the blues, and his playing had an extraordinary elegance of sound, phrasing, and a stretch of feeling (hear "Lonnie's Lament" on *Crescent*) that could encompass the noble and the incendiary.

Then Coltrane got Elvin Jones, who made the music cohere and swing with nearly peerless fury. Jones didn't play time, he voiced it. Expanding upon the innovations of Art Blakey, Kenny Clarke, Max Roach, Roy Haynes, and Philly Joe Jones, he began to hear the drum set as an ensemble in which time was orchestrated across the entire trap set. Jones's rhythmic tension perfectly complemented Coltrane, whose stacking of harmonies or scales often resulted in cones of phrasing that whirled like drum rolls, suggesting an expanded definition of percussive attack that can be heard perfectly as the tenor and drums mirror and echo each other on "Out of This World," from *Coltrane*.

Just as a pianist, or Coltrane himself, could weave together apparently unrelated chords that seemed to move outside the tonality but were inevitably resolved. Jones would stagger time all over the drum kit then resolve the rhythms at the end of four- or eight-bar sequences. Instead of conducting only a linear dialogue with the horn or the other players, Jones created a vertical approach, one that called for rhythms to appear simultaneously as notes do in chords. Each limb executed a moving part in an improvisational style that leaned, beat, and pulled time on different levels at the same moment, surrounding the group in the way big-band brass and reed sections do. If one listens to Jones in that way, it isn't difficult to hear how his rhythmic complexity countered the harmonic simplicity that underlay many of the *modal* forms used by *Coltrane*.

Once Jimmy Garrison joined the quartet, the redefinition of swing took place with collective precision and refinement. His was a big tone and the force with which he plucked his notes expanded upon the percussive function the bass always had in jazz. He knew how to play the *bottom* and the ferocity of his spirit melded with that of Jones. Garrison was not taken in by the Scott LaFaro phenomenon, never slicing the rump roast off the boom of the beat. Though he wasn't opposed to strumming his instrument, Garrison never forgot the *power* jazz bass is supposed to have (listen to him on the title track of *Impressions*, or "Miles' Mode" on *Coltrane*, either of which outswings almost anything else recorded during that period). As his remarkable time and sense of Negroid elegance show on *Crescent*, he could chug, he could lope, he could dance, he could chant, or he could *charge* in tempo. His ability to keep the time and change the texture, the angle, and the motion of the beat fitted so well with the piano and the drums that the collective phrasing of the rhythm and the form was given a fresh dimension of swing.

By bringing together the hardest-swinging rhythm section in jazz, Coltrane met the demands of his muse for a stretch of expression akin to Ben Webster. Like the older man, Coltrane mastered the timbral physics of his instrument, was an extraordinary balladeer and bluesman, and could rise to imposing levels of intensity. All of those inclinations are contained in *Impressions, Coltrane, Crescent,* and *A Love Supreme*. Each record contains at least one indelible classic, and *Crescent* provides a perfect opening for the new Coltrane listener. That album finds the quartet at a peak of expressive clarity, effortlessly remaking the blues, the ballad, 4/4, and the Spanish Tinge. Few ensembles have ever made such lasting music.

Francis Davis uses the occasion of the then-upcoming twenty-fifth anniversary of the saxophonist's death and two Coltrane CD reissues to discuss two poles of Coltrane's career—his early, more traditional music of the 1950s and his late, more exploratory music of the mid-1960s. Davis feels that a majority opinion downplays Coltrane's post-1965 music as less understandable or less successful than the earlier work. However, to really hear this later Coltrane music, Davis writes, "you have to go the distance with him."

Note: An edited version of Carl Woideck's liner notes praised here is included in this anthology as "The Prestige Coltrane Sessions."—CW

I heard John Coltrane in person only once, a concert he gave at Temple University in the fall of 1966. Despite losing the druggies and white activists to Allen Ginsberg, who read elsewhere on campus that night, Coltrane drew a reverent, overflow crowd about equally divided between students (both black and white) and North Philadelphia bloods. As though in unconscious emulation of McCoy Tyner, Jimmy Garrison, and Elvin Jones, all of whom had fled Coltrane's band earlier that year (only Garrison eventually returned), the walkouts began 15 minutes or so into the evening's first tune, which lasted approximately an hour—I think it was "Naima," although it hardly mattered, because Coltrane had abandoned song form, even if still playing songs. What was shocking about the exodus was that these were Coltrane addicts presumably undaunted by the turbulence and complexity of his music to that point, but grief-stricken by what they were hearing now: a spew of untempered and unmetered sound from Coltrane, Pharoah Sanders, two other unidentified saxophonists—neither of them Albert Ayler or Archie Shepp, the holy terrors then sitting in on many of Coltrane's New York gigs—and a rhythm section featuring an inaudible bassist named Sonny Johnson; Rashied Ali on traps; Coltrane's wife, Alice, on piano; and three or four hand drummers.

To many of Coltrane's fans, including some who looked as though they wanted to leave but sat rigid with disbelief, this concert and others like it amounted to a breach of trust for which he still hasn't been completely forgiven. On any visit to Tower or J&R, you're likely to find upwards of a dozen unauthorized Coltrane concert recordings, but none from later than 1965, the cut-off point even for many of those who pay him lip-service as the ultimate musical seeker. For those hardbop heads who reject Coltrane as mystic, his career begins to ebb in 1960, or around the time he added modes to his sheets of sound. It says something about Coltrane's capacity for change that his recorded output—which spanned just 12 years if we overlook inconclusive early sides with Dizzy Gillespie, Johnny Hodges, and Earl Bostic, and start with his first session with Miles Davis, in November 1955—can be divided into as many as three distinct periods.

During Coltrane's lifetime, the contemporary to whom he was most often likened was Malcolm X, also in the process of redefining himself at the time of his assassination. Today, both men's identities are still up for grabs. Malcolm's meaning will be debated in book and film reviews later this year. Meanwhile, with the 25th anniversary of Coltrane's death looming as the most newsworthy event on this year's jazz calendar (only Dizzy's 75th birthday figures to receive as much coverage), reappraisals of Coltrane, early and late, seem inevitable, with the 16-CD reissue *John Coltrane: The Prestige Recordings* (Prestige) and the mostly new-to-America 4-CD *John Coltrane Live in Japan* (GRP/Impulse!) supplying the corroborating data.

Excluding two 1956 dates with Miles already accounted for in a Davis box, the Prestige retrospective includes everything that Coltrane recorded for Bob Weinstock's label as leader or sideman between May 7, 1956 (Elmo Hope's *Informal Jazz,* with Hank Mobley as the other tenor) and December 26, 1958 (the "Bahia" session with Red Garland and Freddie Hubbard). Owing to Weinstock's disdain for alternate takes and his cut-and-paste marketing of Coltrane albums well into the '60s, the box adds nothing new to Coltrane's discography, though several items, including an unexceptional 1957 date led by tubist Ray Draper and never reissued on vinyl, make their first appearance on CD. The set's value lies in tidying up a body of material originally released willy-nilly, thus charting Coltrane's maturation to the point at which he not only overtook Sonny Rollins as the era's saxophone god (their clash on "Tenor Madness" opens the set, in one of its few departures from strict chronology) but challenged Davis as the era's main man.

The format also lends cachet to performances that have always seemed tangential, if not downright inferior, to Coltrane's work with Davis and Thelonious Monk from the same period, and to *Blue Train* (1957), his only session as a leader for Blue Note. In his excellent session notes, Carl Woideck—one of those rare jazz academics who write gracefully and actually have something beyond the obvious to say—speculates that the scarcity of Coltrane originals here has something to do with his having signed away his publishing rights to Prestige Music. The seven compositions he had ready to go for *Giant Steps,* recorded for Atlantic just months after the expiration of his Prestige contract, seem to confirm this suspicion, as does the glimpse of "Naima" (copyrighted in 1959) at the end of Alonzo Levister's "Slow Dance" (recorded in 1957). The evidence to the contrary begins with the originals on *Blue Train,* licensed to Prestige Music but recorded for Blue Note's Alfred Lion, a producer willing to provide adequate rehearsal time, in contrast to Prestige's rush-hour aesthetic. Despite charmed dates such as the one with Tadd Dameron from 1956 that introduced six of Dameron's most winsome pieces, the rule of thumb at Prestige seemed to be to forgo anything complicated for easily sight-read ballads and blues.

Given the eloquence Coltrane brought to both, this worked to his advantage. The most luminous of the ballads, along with Dameron's "Soultrane," are "How Deep Is the Ocean?," from the 1956 *Tenor Conclave* with Mobley, Zoot Sims, and Al Cohn; and "Why Was I Born?," a crystalline duet with Kenny Burrell that makes you sorry Coltrane recorded no other one-on-ones with guitarists or pianists. (The only thing comparable to it is his intro to "I'm Old Fashioned" on *Blue Train,* with Kenny Drew harmonizing on piano.) The blues, even when they're just thinly disguised rip-offs of "Bag's Groove" or "Now's the Time," are redeemed by Coltrane's improvisational ardor, and the most ardent of them, the loomy "Traneing In" for example, hint at the modality he would soon embrace. Although Philly Joe Jones, Coltrane's teammate with Miles Davis and the drummer most in sync with him before Elvin, disappears after the tunes with Dameron (bad blood between Philly Joe and Weinstock, Woideck conjectures), the rhythmic differences between Coltrane and some of his sidemen become the source of fascination. On a two-tenor date with Lester Young man Paul Quinichette, for example, Coltrane's superimposed chords and 16th notes create the illusion that he's speeding along at twice Quinichette's tempo. His haste seems understandable, considering where he was going.

Ranging beyond the music at hand in the booklet's lead essay, Doug Ramsey voices what I'm afraid is becoming the majority position on post-'65 Coltrane: "[He] was often surrounded by sidemen who were not qualified to be in his company. His music had virtually become pure energy. For the most part, it was impenetrable." In other words, Coltrane at his best was Sonny Stitt to the nth power, an unequaled craftsman who, at the end, gave into the musical and sociopolitical insanity of an era whose battle cry (*viz* Albert Ayler) was "It's not about notes anymore." Although I agree with Ramsey (and the Wyntonites) that Coltrane needs to be demystified, I hear his late music quite differently.

Live in Japan, which presents two complete 1966 concerts by Coltrane's quintet with Alice, Garrison, Ali, and Sanders, comes closer to capturing the frenzy of that night in Philadelphia than anything else I've heard, with the possible exception of *Ascension* (just reissued and reviewed by Gary Giddins elsewhere in [this newspaper]). The four discs include just six lengthy performances, two of which—an elegiac "Crescent" and a churning "My Favorite Things" with Coltrane and Sanders testing altos given to them by Yamah only days before—clock in at close to an hour each. Sanders's upper-register screams, which were shock treatment then, sound contrived now. Garrison's extended intros qualify as filler, as do Alice's edgy piano solos, though she shines at her chief ensemble task, that of adding thickness to Ali's cymbal swirls behind the saxophone solos.

Coltrane himself, reportedly in pain from the liver cancer that took his life the following year, emerges as heroic—the duration of his solos (always a point of contention) amounting to less of a feat than the expansiveness of his phrases, which tend to start as simple three- or four-note rhythmic chants (as on the earlier *A Love Supreme*) before expanding into lines at once majestic and severe. You can hear *Live in Japan*'s epic-length improvisations as evidence of a self-indulgence as prodigious as Charlie Parker's, although it took the form of music, not drugs. Or you can hear them, as I do, as Coltrane's attempt to simplify. As though heeding Ornette Coleman's injunction to "play the music, not the background," even if that meant abandoning all remaining harmonic and modal signposts, he was becoming a thematic improviser at the end.

But in order to hear Coltrane's late solos as uninterrupted melody, you have to go the distance with him. Those who walked out on him in Philadelphia did so thinking that he had, in effect, already walked out on them by turning his band into an open forum for a despised and divisive avant-garde to which he seemed both role model and acolyte. In an era in which many dismissed Coleman and Ayler as amateurs and others accused Miles Davis of holding back his younger sidemen, Coltrane had been the magic figure of consensus—the man in whose music recent tradition and the urge to explore further reached a workable truce. I was one of the people up on my feet and cheering at the end of that Temple concert, and I still am. But I think I realized even then that if those of us devoted to jazz could no longer agree on Coltrane, we were never going to agree on anything else again.

PART TWO

In His Own Words

Jazz is often considered to be an intense music, and the music of John Coltrane raised that intensity several degrees. Although some critics second-guessed Coltrane's state of mind or motivation for creating his music—he was called an "angry young tenor" and was later said to have "contempt for an audience"—few of these detractors actually approached Coltrane for insight into his music. Coltrane, in fact, was quite open to discussion, and at one point he publicly invited critics to meet with him. Here is Coltrane in his own words (and in one case his own handwriting) from a variety of perspectives.

Note: Although Coltrane had a generally good memory, a few of the dates given in this section seem to be inaccurate. See the Chronology for the most up-to-date research on Coltrane dates.

JAZZ ENCYCLOPEDIA QUESTIONNAIRE
Institute of Jazz Studies

Beginning in the 1950s, Leonard Feather began distributing questionnaires to jazz musicians, and the information he gleaned was eventually used in his pioneering Encyclopedia of Jazz. *Later, Feather donated the original forms to the Institute of Jazz Studies, and those forms have proven to be a great resource for researchers, containing as they do the musicians' own thoughts in their own writing.—CW*

PLEASE FILL IN VERY CLEARLY IN BLOCK LETTERS:

PROFESSIONAL NAME: JOHN COLTRANE   FULL LEGAL NAME: John William Coltrane

PERMANENT ADDRESS: 1511 N. 33rd St. Phila. Pa. TELEPHONE: ST-4-9921

INSTRUMENTS PLAYED: Tenor Saxophone

EXACT BIRTHDATE: MONTH 9 DAY 23 YEAR 26 WHERE BORN: Hamlet N.C.

ANY PARENTS, BROTHERS, SISTERS OR OTHER RELATIVES MUSICALLY
INCLINED? GIVE DETAILS. My Father, A Tailor, Enjoyed his
Spare Time Playing Violin, ukelele + Clarinet.

WHERE AND WHEN DID YOU STUDY MUSIC? WHAT INSTRUMENTS FIRST?
In high school. Eb Alto horn — Clarinet + Finally
Alto Saxophone. Later at Granoff Studios + ornstein school of Music.
HOW DID YOU GET INTO THE MUSIC BUSINESS? In Philadelphia with
a cocktail Trio. This Job was in 1945, I also
Joined The musician's union at That same Time.
GIVE FULL DETAILS, WITH DATES, OF ALL BANDS OR COMBOS YOU HAVE
WORKED WITH.
   1947 — Eddie Vinson's Band Through mid 1948.
   Dizzy Gillespie — 1949 — 1951
   Earl Bostic — 1952 — 1953
   Johnny Hodges — 1953 — 1954
   Miles Davis — 1955 — Present Date

HAVE YOU EVER WORKED OVERSEAS? IF SO, STATE WHAT TOWNS, COUNTRIES
AND DATES

   only In The Naval Band In Hawaii.
   Dec. 1945 Through June 1946.

WHERE AND WHEN DID YOU MAKE YOUR DEBUT ON RECORDS? In Detroit with Dizzy Gillespie in 1950.

GIVE FULL DETAILS OF ALL IMPORTANT RECORDINGS YOU HAVE MADE, STATING FOR WHAT COMPANIES, AND STATE WHICH YOU THINK IS YOUR OWN BEST SOLO PERFORMANCE ON RECORD. I have only made a few That I Liked. These were A Group Made with Paul Chambers In los Angeles For Alladin + A Recent Album with Miles Davis For Columbia.

ANY MOVIE, RADIO OR TV APPEARANCES?
A Few TV Dates with The Dizzy Gillespie + Miles Davis Bands.

EVER WON ANY MAGAZINE AWARDS? IF SO, WHAT YEAR?
No

WHO ARE YOUR FAVORITE MUSICIANS ON YOUR INSTRUMENT? (IF AN ARRANGER, NAME YOUR FAVORITE ARRANGERS.)
Sonny Stitt, Dexter Gordon, Sonny Rollins, Stan Getz.

GIVE ANY OTHER DETAILS ABOUT YOURSELF, YOUR BACKGROUND, YOUR AMBITIONS THAT YOU THINK WOULD BE OF INTEREST FOR INCLUSION IN "JAZZ ENCYCLOPEDIA".

I'm very happy To Be in This Music world + I have Been Lucky in Being close To Many creative Musicians. IT IS A very Great Pleasure To Play in a Good, well Knit Group + I hope That I will Be Able To Stay at iT For A Long Time.

PLEASE RETURN THIS QUESTIONNAIRE PROMPTLY TO   LEONARD FEATHER
340 RIVERSIDE DRIVE
NEW YORK 25, N. Y.

AN INTERVIEW WITH JOHN COLTRANE

The Jazz Review, *January 1959*

In June of 1958 August Blume heard the Miles Davis quintet fea-
turing John Coltrane at a nightclub in Washington, D.C. Blume
struck up a conversation with Coltrane, and found the saxophon-
ist to be "a warm and open person." Blume invited the saxophon-
ist to a Sunday dinner with Blume and his wife at their home in
Baltimore. On Sunday, June 15, 1958, Blume picked up Coltrane
for dinner, and after their meal, Blume interviewed Coltrane with
a tape recorder taking down their conversation. Coltrane had
picked up some books on philosophy or religion that Blume had
around. Blume had read the Bible, the Torah, and the Upanishads,
and recalled that Coltrane's shared interest in such topics helped
establish a rapport for the interview:

August Blume: Have you ever read anything about philosophy?

John Coltrane: Well, I—

August Blume: What have you read?

John Coltrane: I'll tell you what I've read. You know those books that
they put out, let's see, books—*This Made Simple, That Made Simple?*
[unintelligible]

August Blume: Oh, yeah. Uh huh.

John Coltrane: Well, they got one called *Philosophy Made Simple.*

August Blume: Uh huh.

John Coltrane: Well, I read that. Well, that's the only thing that I actually read all the way through. And I bought a few books, little things.
Something I picked up called *Language, Truth and Logic.* Well, like,
stuff like that I just picked up. Some I get into, man, and I don't get any
further than the first few pages, [laughs] you know, then I start looking
around, trying to find things.

Parts of Blume's interview were edited and arranged for publication in The Jazz Review. This new transcription from the interview tape includes just the topics that Blume published in 1958. Ellipses [. . .] mark where Blume skipped portions of the tape. At the author's request, a few of his sentences have been streamlined for easier reading. Coltrane's words, however, have been transcribed as accurately as possible, with unintelligible portions so identified.—CW

August Blume: What do you think of Johnny Hodges and of Lester Young today?

John Coltrane: I like them just as well as I did.

August Blume: As you used to.

John Coltrane: Yeah, just as well as I did fifteen years ago.

August Blume: Well, Rabbit [Hodges] certainly is—he has to be in the front ranks of any group of musicians you name, because—

John Coltrane: Sure.

August Blume: —he's always played so prettily, man, he's always a beautiful player. I know Bird [Charlie Parker]—I remember reading an interview with Bird in a magazine one time—

John Coltrane: Mm hm.

August Blume: —and Bird was very, very enthusiastic about Hodges's playing, said that Hodges was one of his major influences.

John Coltrane: Yeah, he's great. Very much soul, man, a lot of soul.

August Blume: A lot of people say that Lester doesn't play as well today as he used to. I don't know, to me he's always played great.

John Coltrane: I think so, too.

[. . .]

August Blume: Well, who had you worked with before you worked with Miles and Red and Paul and Philly Joe? Who had you been with before that?

John Coltrane: Well, [pause] you want the whole string of it? [laughs]

August Blume: [laughs] If you feel like it.

John Coltrane: Man, let's see.

August Blume: I know one thing that's for sure and certain: you worked with an awful lot of people.

John Coltrane: Yeah, I did.

August Blume: And it's spread out over a pretty good span of time.

John Coltrane: Yeah, well.

[. . .]

August Blume: Well, like take for example, like, you said fourteen years ago, '44, was when you first started playing. [Coltrane may have meant playing in public; he had actually started playing saxophone by 1939.]

John Coltrane: Yeah.

August Blume: When did you have your first professional gig with anybody?

John Coltrane: Well, I usually call my first professional job was a band from Indianapolis led by Joe Webb. This was in '47. Big Maybelle was in this band, you know, Big Maybelle the blues singer. This was, I don't know, this was—I don't know what the heck we were rhythm and blues, or *everything*. [laughs] I don't know [about] that band. Anyway, that band, and then King Kolax. You've heard of Kolax, right? Trumpet. And Eddie Vinson, Dizzy, Earl Bostic, Gay Cross—

August Blume: Who?

John Coltrane: Gay Cross.

August Blume: I'm not familiar with him.

John Coltrane: He was from Cleveland. He had a little band. He used to be with Louis Jordan one time, his band. He had a little band that was patterned after Louis' band. He sang and played something like Louis. And Daisy Mae and the Hepcats.

August Blume: There's another group I don't know.

John Coltrane: Johnny Hodges.

August Blume: You did work with Hodges?

John Coltrane: Yeah.

August Blume: When was this?

John Coltrane: In 1953. [Coltrane's tenure with the Hodges band extended well into 1954.]

August Blume: For how long?

John Coltrane: Oh, seven months, I think.

August Blume: Who else was in the band?

John Coltrane: Oh, there was Richard Powell on piano, and Lawrence Brown, Emmett Berry, and a guy named Jimmy Johnson on drums and a bass player, I've forgotten his name.

August Blume: That surprises me. I had no idea that you'd ever worked with Hodges.

John Coltrane: Sure, man.

August Blume: I bet that was a real gas for you, wasn't it?

John Coltrane: I enjoyed it, yeah, I enjoyed it. Yeah, they had some true music. [both laugh] Man. Lawrence Brown, I like him immensely, man. A great trombonist. Yeah. Emmett Berry, he impressed me too. And Johnny Hodges, I still like him. And Earl Bostic is kind of tremendous, too. I didn't appreciate guys—men like Earl—after I heard Charlie Parker, because Charlie, he swayed me so much. But, after I'd come out from under it a little bit, after I'd been under it a little bit, under his spell, then I actually tried to listen to other people too. When I played with these men, I found I learned a lot from them. The main thing was trying to just see how things *were,* see how well a guy is who plays altogether different. You say, "well, that's so-and-so," I'd know him anywhere. Then you hear something, and say "well, that's so-and-so," yeah, I'd know him anywhere. Then you sit down and maybe you can see where—try to see where they both came from and you find maybe they came out of the same tree somewhere along the line. So I might start looking at jazz like that, too, at it collectively, looking at the whole thing. And then after Johnny Hodges, there was Miles, that was the next one. I worked with Jimmy Smith for about a couple of weeks before I went with Miles, the organist.

August Blume: Yeah.

John Coltrane: Wow! I'd wake up in the middle of the night, man, hearing that organ. [both laugh]

August Blume: Gives you nightmares.

John Coltrane: Yeah, man, chords screaming at me!

August Blume: You didn't work with Bud Powell.

John Coltrane: I played with Bud. I never worked with him. I played about—I think I played one gig with him. Back in 1949, Miles would get these dance jobs in the Audubon in New York, uptown, way up on Broadway. And I think on one of the jobs he had Sonny Rollins and Bud and Art Blakely [Blakey] and I forgot the bass man and myself. On this dance job. That was the only time I worked with Bud. He was *playing,* too.

August Blume: Whew.

[. . .]

August Blume: Well, when you first started with [Thelonious] Monk, before you actually went to work down at the Five Spot, did Monk used to hold rehearsals so that you could learn all the tunes?

John Coltrane: Yes.

August Blume: How do these things go? I'm kind of curious as to how he more or less made you familiar with the tunes.

John Coltrane: Well, I'd go by his house to—by his apartment, and get him out of bed, maybe, or [laughs]—he'd wake up and roll over to the piano and start playing. He'd play anything, it might be just one of his tunes. He'd start playin' it and he'd look at me, I guess, and so when he'd look at me, I'd get my horn and start trying to find what he was playing. And, he'd tend to play it over and over and over and over, and I'd get this part, and then next time I'd go over it, I'd get another part, and, he would stop and show me some parts that were pretty difficult, and if I had a lot of trouble, well, he'd get his portfolio out, show me the music, he's got music, he's got all of it written and I'd read it and learn it. He would rather a guy learn without reading 'cause that way, you feel it better. You feel it *quicker*, when you memorize it, when you learn it by heart, by ear. And so, he'd, when I almost had the tune down, then he would leave, leave me with it, he'd leave me to practice it alone and he'd go out somewhere, maybe he'd go to the store or go back to bed or something. And I'd just stay there and run over the tune. [When] I had it pretty well, then I'd call him and we'd play it down together. And sometimes, we'd get just one tune a day.

August Blume: How long did it take before you actually thought you were ready to go down to the Five Spot and actually work as a regular unit?

John Coltrane: Well, as soon as we got—as soon as he got the job at the Five Spot, we went right in because this going over things had started earlier—we just—I was just—I met him and I just started hanging around with him, I went down, I started going down to his house because I like that music. And we'd already recorded one song, "Monk's Mood."

[. . .]

August Blume: How did you used to feel when you were working down at the Five Spot? I know I had seen you a couple of times down there, and in the middle of a tune, Monk would get up from the piano and walk around to the side of it and do his little dance—

John Coltrane: [laughs]

August Blume: —and leave you holding the bag.

John Coltrane: [laughs] I feel [laughs] kind of lonesome! [laughs] Yeah, I felt a little lonesome up there! [laughs]

August Blume: Well, when you're standing up there playing like that, how do you hear the [chord] changes? Do you think of the changes as you're going along, or does the bass player suggest them to you with what he's playing?

John Coltrane: Yeah, the bass player, he—I count on him.

August Blume: What does he actually do? When Wilbur would be playing bass, would he play, like, the dominant note in each chord, or—I don't know how you phrase this, but—

John Coltrane: Well, at times. But a bass player like Wilbur Ware, he's so inventive, man. Like, he doesn't always play [laughs] the dominant note. He—

August Blume: But whatever he plays is a suggestive note that gives you an idea of which way the changes are going?

John Coltrane: Yeah, it may be. It might *not* be. 'Cause Wilbur, he plays the *other* way sometimes. He plays things that are kind of—they're for-eign. Well if you didn't know the song, you wouldn't be able to find it [laughs] because he's superimposing things, he's playing around and under and over or something. Building tension, so that when he comes back to it, you feel everything sucks [?] in. But, usually I knew the tune, so I mean it was all right. I knew the changes anyway, so we managed to come out—to end together anyway [laughs].

August Blume: [laughs] Which always helps!

John Coltrane: Yeah, we managed to finish on time. Lot of fun playing that way, though.

August Blume: I can imagine that—

John Coltrane: Lot of fun. But sometimes, he would play—he would be playing altered changes, and I would be playing altered changes. And he would be playing some other kind of altered changes from the type I'd be playing. And neither one of us playing the changes of the tune until we reach a certain spot and then we—if we get there together, we're lucky.

August Blume: [laughs]

John Coltrane: Then Monk comes back in to save everybody, and nobody knows where he is.

August Blume: [laughs]

John Coltrane: That's what—in fact, a lot of people [unintelligible] they say, man, how do you guys remember all that stuff? We weren't really remembering much, just the basic changes and then everybody else just tried anything they wanted to try on it, that's all. And Monk, he's always doing something back there that sounds *so* mysterious. And it's not mysterious at all, when you know what he's doing. Just like those little things, just like simple truths. Like he just—he might take a chord, a major chord, a *minor* chord, and leave the third out. Well, he says, "this is a *minor chord*, man!" [I'd] say, "you don't have the minor third in there, so you don't know what it is." He says, "How do you know it's a minor chord? Well, that's what it is, a minor chord with the third out!" [laughs] [unintelligible] And when he plays the thing, man, it will just be in the right place and voiced the right way to have that minor feel.

August Blume: Uh huh.

John Coltrane: But still, it's not a minor, because the third is not there. Little things like that.

August Blume: Did he pull that on you, actually working on the job, or has he done this before, previously with you, where he'd gotten up and left the piano and left you, so to speak, holding the bag?

John Coltrane: Well, he just started that on the job.

August Blume: How did you feel [laughs] when he first did that?

John Coltrane: Well, I was—I started looking around for him the first time he did it [laughs], but after that, I got used to it and I just tried to hold up 'til he got back.

August Blume: Why do you think he did it?

John Coltrane: I don't know. He said he wanted to hear us, and he said *he* wanted to hear the band. When he did that, he'd be—he was in the audience himself, man, he was listening to the band. And then he'd come back. He got something out of that thing.

August Blume: I used to get the biggest kick out of the way he'd do this little shuffle dance on the side.

John Coltrane: Yeah, I wanted to see that myself. I couldn't see it. [laughs]

August Blume: Did it ever occur to you to pull your horn away from your mouth and walk over and stand by [laughs] him and then Wilbur and Shadow [Wilson] to do it?

John Coltrane: Yeah, I should have done it, man, I wanted to see it myself. Like, it was so interesting, everybody was talking about it, and every once in a while, I'd open up one eye and peep at it. He was really enjoying it. He was getting a big kick, then.

August Blume: Well, I'm sure that he must have really enjoyed your playing. I know, because—

John Coltrane: Well, he said he did, anyway. I don't know.

August Blume: I spoke to him once or twice, I know, and each time he'd say [of Coltrane], "Yeah, he's the man."

John Coltrane: [long pause] Yeah, I learned a lot with him. Learned, like, little things, learned to watch the little things. He's just a good musician, man. It's like, you watch as you work with a guy who watches the finer points of things, it kind of makes you—helps you a little bit. You try to watch the finer points sometimes. And the little things mean so much in music, like everything else. Like the way you build a house, starting with building the little things. You get the little things together and then the whole structure will stand up, you see. Goof the little things and you don't have—

August Blume: [pause] Well, is it the same kind of playing experience playing, say, with Miles now as you say it was with Monk?

John Coltrane: It's an altogether different thing. I don't know what it is, but it's just another great experience.

August Blume: But of a slightly different nature.

John Coltrane: Yeah, slightly different. I can't quite explain the difference, either.

LEONARD FEATHER
BLINDFOLD TEST: HONEST JOHN
Down Beat, *February 19, 1959*

This was the only time that John Coltrane participated in a Leonard Feather Blindfold Test. Coltrane was given no information about the recordings before they were played, and his careful and varied listening habits are apparent—he correctly identifies most of the principal soloists in question. Coltrane also discusses his early saxophone influences in Lester Young and Charlie Parker, and his regard for Coleman Hawkins and Ben Webster.—CW

The *Blindfold Test* below is the first interview of its kind with John Coltrane. The reason is simple: though he has been a respected name among fellow musicians for a number of years, it is only in the last year or two that he has reached a substantial segment of the jazz-following public.

It is the general feeling that Coltrane ranks second only to Sonny Rollins as a new and constructive influence on his instrument. Coltrane's solo work is an example of that not uncommon phenomenon, an instrumental style that reflects a personality strikingly different from that of the man who plays it, for his slow, deliberate speaking voice and far-from-intense manner never would lead one to expect from him the cascades of phrases that constitute a typical Coltrane solo.

The records for his *Blindfold Test* were more or less paired off, the first a stereo item by a big band, the next two combo tracks by hard bop groups, the third pair bearing a reminder of two early tenor giants, and the final two sides products of miscellaneous combos. John was given no information before or during the test about the records played.

The Records

1. **Woody Herman. "Crazy Rhythm" (Everest Stereo). Paul Quinichette, tenor; Ralph Burns, arranger.**

Well, I would give it three stars on the merit of the arrangement, which I thought was good. The solos were good, and the band played good. As to who it was, I don't know . . . The tenor sounded like Paul Quinichette, and I liked that because I like the melodic way he plays. The sound of the recording was very good. I'd like to make a guess about that arrangement—it sounded like the kind of writing Hefti does—maybe it was Basie's band.

2. **Art Farmer Quintet. "Mox Nix" (United Artists). Benny Golson, tenor; Farmer, trumpet, composer, arranger; Bill Evans, piano; Addison Farmer, bass; Dave Bailey, drums.**

That's a pretty lively sound. That tenor man could have been Benny Golson, and the trumpeter, I don't know . . . It sounded like Art Farmer a little bit.

I enjoyed the rhythm section—they got a nice feeling, but I don't know who they were. The composition was a minor blues—which is always good. The figures on it were pretty good, too. I would give it 3½.

3. **Horace Silver Quintet. "Soulville" (Blue Note). Silver, piano, composer; Hank Mobley, tenor; Art Farmer, trumpet.**

Horace . . . is that "Soulville"? I've heard that—I think I have the record. Horace gave me that piece of music some time ago . . . I asked him to give me some things that I might like to record and that was one of them. I've never got around to recording it yet, though. I like the piece tremendously—the composition is great. It has more in it than just "play the figure and then we all blow." It has a lot of imagination. The solos are all good . . . I think it's Hank Mobley and Art Farmer. I'll give that $4\frac{1}{2}$ stars.

4. Coleman Hawkins. "Chant" (Riverside). Idrees Sulieman, trumpet; J. J. Johnson, trombone; Hank Jones, piano; Oscar Pettiford, bass.

Well, the record had a genuine jazz feeling. It sounded like Coleman Hawkins . . . I think it was Clark Terry on trumpet, but I don't know. The 'bone was good, but I don't know who it was. I think the piano was very good . . . I'll venture one guess: Hank Jones. It sounded like Oscar Pettiford and was a very good bass solo. And Bean—he's one of the kind of guys—he played well, but I wanted to hear some more from him . . . I was expecting some more.

When I first started listening to jazz, I heard Lester Young before I heard Bean. When I *did* hear Hawkins, I appreciated him, but I didn't hear him as much as I did Lester . . . Maybe it was because all we were getting then was the Basie band.

I went through Lester Young and on to Charlie Parker, but after that I started listening to others—I listened to Bean and realized what a great influence *he* was on the people I'd been listening to. Three and a half.

5. Ben Webster–Art Tatum. "Have You Met Miss Jones?" (Verve).

That must be Ben Webster, and the piano—I don't know. I thought it was Art Tatum . . . I don't know anybody else who plays like that, but still I was waiting for that thunderous thing from him, and it didn't come. Maybe he just didn't feel like it then.

The sound of that tenor . . . I wish he'd show *me* how to make a sound like that. I've got to call him up and talk to him! I'll give that four stars . . . I like the atmosphere of the record—the whole thing I got from it. What they do for the song is artistic, and it's a good tune.

6. Toshiko. "Broadway" (Metrojazz). Bobby Jaspar, tenor; Rene Thomas, guitar.

You've got me guessing all the way down on this one, but it's a good swinging side and lively. I thought at first the tenor was Zoot, and then I thought, no. If it isn't Zoot, I don't know who it could be. All the solos were good . . . The guitar player was pretty good. I'd give the record three stars on its liveliness and for the solos.

7. Chet Baker. "Fair Weather" (Riverside). Johnny Griffin, tenor; Benny Golson, composer.

That was Johnny Griffin, and I didn't recognize anybody else. The writing sounded something like Benny Golson . . . I like the figure and that melody. The solos were good, but I don't know . . . Sometimes it's hard to interpret changes. I don't know whether it was taken from another song or if it was a song itself.

Maybe the guys could have worked it over a little longer and interpreted it a little truer. What I heard on the line as it was written, I didn't hear after the solos started. . . . It was good, though—I would give it three stars, on the strength of the composition mostly, and the solos secondly . . . I didn't recognize the trumpeter.

JOHN COLTRANE AND DON DEMICHEAL
COLTRANE ON COLTRANE
Down Beat, *September 29, 1960*

By 1960, many words of praise and criticism had been written about John Coltrane's music. It is to Don DeMicheal's credit that for clarification about the saxophonist's art, he went straight to the source: John Coltrane.—CW

The first occasion I had to speak with John Coltrane at length was during his recent engagement at the Sutherland Hotel. In our initial conversation I was struck by his lack of pretentiousness or false pride. The honesty with which he answered questions—questions that other musicians would have evaded or talked around—impressed me deeply. We discussed my doing an article about him. But when I saw how really interested he was in setting the record straight, I suggested that we do the piece together.

As it turned out, Coltrane did the vast majority of the work, struggling as most writers do with just the right way of saying something, deciding whether he should include this or that, making sure such and such was clear. The results of his labor is the article appearing on these pages. The words and ideas are John's—I merely suggested, typed, and arranged.
—*DeMicheal*

I've been listening to jazzmen, especially saxophonists, since the time of the early Count Basie records, which featured Lester Young. Pres was my first real influence, but the first horn I got was an alto, not a tenor. I wanted a tenor, but some friends of my mother advised her to buy me an alto because it was a smaller horn and easier for a youngster to handle. This was 1943.

Johnny Hodges became my first main influence on alto, and he still kills me. I stayed with alto through 1947, and by then I'd come under the influence of Charlie Parker. The first time I heard Bird play, it hit me right between the eyes. Before I switched from alto in that year, it had been strictly a Bird thing with me, but when I bought a tenor to go with Eddie Vinson's band, a wider area of listening opened up for me.

I found I was able to be more varied in my musical interests. On alto, Bird had been my whole influence, but on tenor I found there was no one man whose ideas were so dominant as Charlie's were on alto. Therefore, I drew from all the men I heard during this period. I have listened to about all the good tenor men, beginning with Lester, and, believe me, I've picked up something from them all, including several who have never recorded.

The reason I liked Lester so was that I could feel that line, that simplicity. My phrasing was very much in Lester's vein at this time.

I found out about Coleman Hawkins after I learned of Lester. There were a lot of things that Hawkins was doing that I knew I'd have to learn somewhere along the line. I felt the same way about Ben Webster. There were many things that people like Hawk, Ben, and Tab Smith were doing in the '40s that I didn't understand but that I felt emotionally.

The first time I heard Hawk, I was fascinated by his arpeggios and the way he played. I got a copy of his *Body and Soul* and listened real hard to what he was doing. And even though I dug Pres, as I grew musically, I appreciated Hawk more and more.

As far as musical influences, aside from saxophonists, are concerned, I think I was first awakened to musical exploration by Dizzy Gillespie and Bird. It was through their work that I began to learn about musical structures and the more theoretical aspects of music.

Also, I had met Jimmy Heath, who, besides being a wonderful saxophonist, understood a lot about musical construction. I joined his group in Philadelphia in 1948. We were very much alike in our feeling, phrasing, and a whole lot of ways. Our musical appetites were the same. We used to practice together, and he would write out some of the things we were interested in. We would take things from records and digest them. In this way we learned about the techniques being used by writers and arrangers.

Another friend and I learned together in Philly—Calvin Massey, a trumpeter and composer who now lives in Brooklyn. His musical ideas and mine often run parallel, and we've collaborated quite often. We helped each other advance musically by exchanging knowledge and ideas.

I first met Miles Davis about 1947 and played a few jobs with him and Sonny Rollins at the Audubon Ballroom in Manhattan. During this period he was coming into his own, and I could see him extending the boundaries of jazz even further. I felt I wanted to work with him. But for the time being, we went our separate ways.

I went with Dizzy's big band in 1949. I stayed with Diz through the breakup of the big band and played in the small group he organized later.

Afterwards, I went with Earl Bostic, who I consider a very gifted musician. He showed me a lot of things on my horn. He has fabulous technical facilities on his instrument and knows many a trick.

Then I worked with one of my first loves, Johnny Hodges. I really enjoyed that job. I liked every tune in the book. Nothing was superficial. It all had meaning, and it all swung. And the confidence with which Rabbit plays! I wish I could play with the confidence that he does.

But besides enjoying my stay with Johnny musically, I also enjoyed it because I was getting firsthand information about things that happened way before my time. I'm very interested in the past, and even though there's a lot I don't know about it, I intend to go back and find out. I'm back to Sidney Bechet already.

Take Art Tatum, for instance. When I was coming up, the musicians I ran around with were listening to Bud Powell, and I didn't listen too much to Tatum. That is, until one night I happened to run into him in Cleveland. There were Art and Slam Stewart and Oscar Peterson and Ray Brown at a private session in some lady's attic. They played from 2:30 in the morning to 8:30—just whatever they felt like playing. I've never heard so much music.

In 1955, I joined Miles on a regular basis and worked with him till the middle of 1957. I went with Thelonious Monk for the remainder of that year.

Working with Monk brought me close to a musical architect of the highest order. I felt I learned from him in every way—through the senses, theoretically, technically. I would talk to Monk about musical problems, and he would sit at the piano and show me the answers just by playing them. I could watch him play and find out the things I wanted to know. Also, I could see a lot of things that I didn't know about at all.

Monk was one of the first to show me how to make two or three notes at one time on tenor. (John Glenn, a tenor man in Philly, also showed me how to do this. He can play a triad and move notes inside it—like passing tones!) It's done by false fingering and adjusting your lip. If everything goes right, you can get triads. Monk just looked at my horn and "felt" the mechanics of what had to be done to get this effect.

I think Monk is one of the true greats of all time. He's a real musical thinker—there's not many like him. I feel myself fortunate to have had the opportunity to work with him. If a guy needs a little spark, a boost, he can just be around Monk, and Monk will give it to him.

After leaving Monk, I went back to another great musical artist, Miles.

On returning, this time to stay until I formed my own group a few months ago, I found Miles in the midst of another stage of his musical development. There was one time in his past that he devoted to multi-chorded structures. He was interested in chords for their own sake. But now it seemed that he was moving in the opposite direction to the use of fewer and fewer chord changes in songs. He used tunes with free-flowing lines and chordal direction. This approach allowed the soloist the choice of playing chordally (vertically) or melodically (horizontally).

In fact, due to the direct and free-flowing lines in this music, I found it easy to apply the harmonic ideas that I had. I could stack up chords— say, on a C7, I sometimes superimposed an E♭7, up to an F♯7, down to an F. That way I could play three chords on one. But on the other hand, if I wanted to, I could play melodically, Miles' music gave me plenty of freedom. It's a beautiful approach.

About this time, I was trying for a sweeping sound. I started experimenting because I was striving for more individual development. I even tried long, rapid lines that Ira Gitler termed "sheets of sound" at that time. But actually, I was beginning to apply the three-on-one chord approach, and at that time the tendency was to play the entire scale of each chord. Therefore, they were usually played fast and sometimes sounded like glisses.

I found there were a certain number of chord progressions to play in a given time, and sometimes what I played didn't work out in eighth notes, 16th notes, or triplets. I had to put the notes in uneven groups like fives and sevens in order to get them all in.

I thought in groups of notes, not of one note at a time. I tried to place these groups on the accents and emphasize the strong beats—maybe on 2 here and on 4 over at the end. I would set up the line and drop groups of notes—a long line with accents dropped as I moved along. Sometimes what I was doing clashed harmonically with the piano—especially if the pianist wasn't familiar with what I was doing—so a lot of time I just strolled with bass and drums.

I haven't completely abandoned this approach, but it wasn't broad enough. I'm trying to play these progressions in a more flexible manner now.

Last February, I bought a soprano saxophone. I like the sound of it, but I'm not playing with the body, the bigness of tone, that I want yet. I haven't had too much trouble playing it in tune, but I've had a lot of trouble getting a good quality of tone in the upper register. It comes out sort of puny sometimes. I've had to adopt a slight different approach than the one I use for tenor, but it helps me get away—lets me take another look at improvisation. It's like having another hand.

I'm using it with my present group, McCoy Tyner, piano; Steve Davis, bass; and Pete LaRoca, drums. The quartet is coming along nicely. We know basically what we're trying for, and we leave room for individual development. Individual contributions are put in night by night.

One of my aims is to build as good a repertoire as I can for a band. What size, I couldn't say, but it'll probably be a quartet or quintet. I want to get the material first. Right now, I'm on a material search.

From a technical viewpoint, I have certain things I'd like to present in my solos. To do this, I have to get the right material. It has to swing, and it has to be varied. (I'm inclined not to be too varied.) I want it to cover as many forms of music as I can put into a jazz context and play on my instruments. I like Eastern music; Yusef Lateef has been using this in his playing for some time. And Ornette Coleman sometimes plays music with a Spanish content as well as other exotic-flavored music. In these approaches there's something I can draw on and use in the way I like to play.

I've been writing some things for the quartet—if you call lines and sketches writing. I'd like to write more after I learn more—after I find out what kind of material I can present best, what kind will carry my musical techniques best. Then I'll know better what kind of writing is best for me.

I've been devoting quite a bit of my time to harmonic studies on my own, in libraries and places like that. I've found you've got to look back at the old things and see them in a new light. I'm not finished with these studies because I haven't assimilated everything into my playing. I want to progress, but I don't want to go so far out that I can't see what others are doing.

I want to broaden my outlook in order to come out with a fuller means of expression. I want to be more flexible where rhythm is concerned. I feel I have to study rhythm some more. I haven't experimented too much with time; most of my experimenting has been in a harmonic form. I put time and rhythms to one side, in the past.

But I've got to keep experimenting. I feel that I'm just beginning. I have part of what I'm looking for in my grasp but not all.

I'm very happy devoting all my time to music, and I'm glad to be one of the many who are striving for fuller development as musicians. Considering the great heritage in music that we have, the work of giants of the past, the present, and the promise of those who are to come, I feel that we have every reason to face the future optimistically.

VALERIE WILMER
CONVERSATION WITH COLTRANE
Jazz Journal, *January, 1962*

Valerie Wilmer is a British writer and photographer who has been documenting music and musicians for many years. From Sister Rosetta Tharpe and Harry Carney to Eric Dolphy and the Art Ensemble of Chicago, she has specialized in recording oral history. Listening to the voices of African-American musicians as well as their notes, she has demonstrated the way that the music and its community sustain each other. Her publications include Jazz People *(1970), a collection of interviews with fourteen American musicians;* Mama Said There'd Be Days like This *(1989), an autobiography;* The Face of Black Music *(1976), a photo-documentary; and* As Serious As Your Life *(1977), a major "free jazz" resource. Her book* Snakehips Swing, *a look at the little-known Black British musicians who influenced the music in the war years and the period immediately preceding them, is to be published in 1998.—CW*

Wilmer's 1996 introduction to this piece sets the scene:

When John Coltrane came to England in November 1961, an enviable reputation preceded him. His concerts, with guest artist Eric Dolphy, had an enormous impact, particularly on local musicians, but for those accustomed to more traditional sounds—and I was one of them then—what he was playing went a little too far beyond *Giant Steps*. Despite my reservations, I wanted to talk to him. I had been writing about jazz for a couple of years and recognised what could be learnt from conversations with diverse musicians. His stamina amazed me, anyway, and the sheer length of "My Favourite Things," so I dutifully sought him out for an interview. The musicians were staying at a newly modernised hotel on Half Moon Street in London's elegant Mayfair, and it was there that I found him on a day off from the tour, quiet but exhausted. He was dressed in a light yellow shirt and buttoned cardigan under his jacket and wore a rather rakish bowtie. He answered my questions carefully, pausing to allow me to write down his answers in longhand, and although he was anxious to phone his wife before having an early night, never hurried me or made me feel uncomfortable. When the interview was over, I asked if I could shoot off a roll of film on my Rolleiflex. With the hotel's state-of-the-art curtains as a backdrop, he blew quietly on both his horns, enabling me to make a dozen photographs which have since become classics. *Jazz Journal*, a British monthly, published the interview and paid me with a couple of albums: probably Duke Ellington and Buddy Tate, if I remember my taste at the time. All that was soon to change.—*Val Wilmer, 1996*

"Melodically and harmonically their improvisation struck my ear as gobbledegook," wrote John Tynan in the November 23rd *Down Beat.* He was speaking of the recent musical experiments of John Coltrane and Eric Dolphy, experiments which confounded even ardent Coltrane supporters when he toured England last year.

The in-person sound of Coltrane was so different from his recorded work that most people wondered whether their auditory processes were in order. It seems they were, for Coltrane himself confirmed that his music had radically altered over the last twelve months or so.

Meeting the man himself, it is hard to believe that such a quiet, calm, and serious individual could be responsible for the frantic "sheets of sound" which emanate from his tenor saxophone, or that such a sensitive person could think of some of his uglier wailings on soprano as beautiful.

"The sound you get on any instrument depends on the conception of sound you hear in your mind," he told me. "It also depends on your physical properties, such as the shape and structure of the inside of your mouth and throat. I only tried to find the sound that I hear in my mind, a sound any artist hears and hopes to be able to produce. I suppose I did strive to get it with using different reeds and things as any artist does, but now I've settled on a reed at least, and I use a hard one."

I mentioned that everyone had remarked on how different he sounded in the flesh as opposed to on records. "I've discussed this fault with the engineers because the play-backs haven't sounded right," he said. "They get too close to the horn with the mikes and don't give the sound time to travel as they should. Consequently, they don't get enough of the real timbre and they miss the *whole* body of the sound. They get the inside of it but not the outside as well.

"I've heard one or two albums with this fault and I've tried to clear it up, even suggested that I play away from the mike as I'd do in a club, which makes a much more pleasing sound. And of course the loudness also varies according to the reed you have. If you have a good one you don't change it—my good ones usually last about two weeks."

Whatever one thought of the actual *sound* of John's soprano, it was good to know that a leading modernist had taken up the instrument seemingly doomed to oblivion with the passing of Sidney Bechet. He has, in fact, been playing it for about three years, and as so often happens, took it up quite accidentally. "A friend of mine had one and as I hadn't seen one too often before, I looked at it, tried it, and liked the sound. I thought I'd like to use it a little but I'd only just formed my own group and didn't think I'd actually use it in public.

"I don't consider my work on it a success, because I'm at the same place on it as I am on the tenor. Of course the tenor has more body to it, but the soprano lends itself to more lyrical playing. There are times when I feel the need for one and sometimes I feel the need for the other. I try to use either one according to what the tune feels like."

It is also interesting to note that he has recently started playing the harp because "I like the sound. It's one of the most beautiful things and just for the fact that it's different, that's what I like about it. I got interested in it around 1958 when I was interested in playing arpeggios instead of just straight lines, and so naturally I looked at the harp. It's just pure sound, it's not even like a piano where you've got to hit the keys to make the hammers hit the strings. A harpist friend of mine showed me some fingering but I don't have time to sit down and make much out of it. Right now I don't see any chance of making jazz out of it."

Another of John Coltrane's innovations was his recent use of two basses—well, not quite an innovation because Duke had the idea twenty years ago—but his regular bassist Reggie Workman has been playing the rhythm parts, while the group was augmented with the excellent Art Davis. It was through the latter that the idea came about:

"I'd heard some Indian records and liked the effect of the water-drum," said 'Trane, "and I thought another bass would add that certain rhythmic sound. We were playing a lot of stuff with a sort of suspended rhythm, with one bass playing a series of notes around one point, and it seemed that another bass could fill in the spaces in the straight 4/4 line.

"Art and I had been working quite a bit together before the band started and I was interested in bass lines and sequences and he could help me. I actually wanted Art to join me as a regular bassist, but he was all tied up with Dizzy and so I had to get in Steve Davis and when he left Art still couldn't make it, so I got Reggie.

"Once I was in town and I said to Art to come on down because I liked him so much and I figured that he and Reggie could exchange sets. But instead of that they started playing some together and I got something from it. Reggie played as usual and Art countered it and it was very good. I only wish I could have brought Art over with me."

One night, according to Eric Dolphy, "Wilbur Ware came in and up on the stand so they had three basses going. John and I got off the stand and listened and Art Davis was really playing some kind of bass. Mingus has some 'know-how' of bass that he won't tell anyone," said Eric. "But Art sure does have some 'know-how' of bass like Mingus. John made a date with two basses, one called 'Africa' on the Impulse label, and another called 'Olé' on Atlantic, and Art plays fantastic."

There certainly seems no chance of Coltrane's group becoming stagnant, a thing which he fears more than any other, with the constant change of personnel combinations. "We had Wes Montgomery out on the Coast," he said, "and I wanted very much to have him here in England. He's really something else because he made everything sound that much fuller."

As for Eric Dolphy, whose playing disappointed so many people when heard in person, John said: "He just came in and sat in with us for about three nights and everybody enjoyed it, because his presence added some fire to the band. He and I have known each other a long time, and I guess you'd say we were students of the jazz scene," he smiled. "We'd exchange ideas and so we just decided to go ahead and see if we could do something within this group. Eric is really gifted and I feel he's going to produce something inspired, but although we've been talking about music for years, I don't know where he's going, and I don't know where I'm going. He's interested in trying to progress, however, and so am I, so we have quite a bit in common."

Apart from the epic performance of "My Favourite Things" which lasted for half-an-hour at all the London concerts, the majority of Coltrane's material is original. Of his writing he said: "I think playing and writing go hand in hand. I don't feel that at this stage of the game I can actually sit down and say I'm going to write a piece that will do this or that for the people—a thing which some artists can do—but I'm trying to tune myself so I can look to myself and to nature and to other sounds in music and interpret things that I feel there and present them to people. Eventually I hope to reach a stage where I have a vast warehouse of study and knowledge to be able to produce any certain thing.

"Duke Ellington is one person who can do this—that's really *heavy* musicianship and I haven't reached that stage yet. I've been predominately a soloist all my natural life, and now I'm a soloist with my own band, and this has led me into this other thing: what am I going to play and why?

"My material is mainly my own, and I find some of my best work comes from the most challenging material. Sometimes we write things to be easy, sometimes to be hard, it depends on what we want to do.

"A year ago we had quite a few standards which made up a third of the book, but now a number of people, certainly Ornette and Eric, have been responsible for other influences.

"At the time I left Miles I was trying to add a lot of sequences to my solo work, putting chords to the things I was playing, and using things I could play a little more music on.

"It was before I formed my own group that I had the rhythm section playing these sequences forward, and I made 'Giant Steps' with some other guys and carried the idea on into my band. But it was hard to make some things swing with the rhythm section playing these chords, and Miles advised me to abandon the idea of the rhythm section playing these sequences, and to do it only myself. But around this time I heard Ornette who had abandoned chords completely and that helped me to think clearly about what I wanted to do.

"It was Miles who made me want to be a much better musician. He gave me some of the most listenable moments I've had in music, and he also gave me an appreciation for simplicity. He influenced me quite a bit in music in every way. I used to want to play tenor the way he played trumpet when I used to listen to his records. But when I joined him I realized I could never play like that, and I think that's what made me go the opposite way.

"Recently I've been doing songs with the rhythm section having more freedom and not being bound to chordal structures, but still giving the soloist just as much freedom. Sometimes we start with one chord and drop it later, and improvise on the bass line or the piano, and this I find much easier to do on original material. I haven't done it on a 'standard' yet, but maybe I will soon. But unless I find a simple one, there are no more breakthroughs on those standards for me.

"There are some great songs that have been played in this music and only need a new approach to revive them. Faced with this fact, I couldn't revise my musical approach drastically, and so I said well, maybe I'm really doing something with this harmonic approach and should stick with it for a while.

"There are going to be songs with one chord and songs with no chords, which in my case means freedom to see if I can develop more in a melodic fashion through these unlimited harmonies."

Although he himself is not certain of the exact directions in which his music is going, this highly intelligent musician is striving for a music that will doubtless be entirely different to any we have heard before. He has been called the only important jazzman since Bird, and I asked him what he thought of his own contribution to jazz.

"Basically I am trying not to stagnate. I go this way and I go that way and I don't know where I'm going next. But if I should get stagnant, I'd lose my interest.

"There are so many things to be considered in making music. The whole question of life itself; *my* life in which there are many things on which I don't think I've reached a final conclusion; there are matters I don't think I've covered completely, and all these things have to be covered before you make your music sound any way. You have to grow to know.

"When I was younger, I didn't think this would happen, but now I know that I've still got a long way to go. Maybe when I'm sixty I'll be satisfied with what I'm doing, but I don't know . . . I'm sure that later on my ideas will carry more conviction.

"I know that I want to produce beautiful music, music that does things to people that they need. Music that will uplift, and make them happy—those are the qualities I'd like to produce.

"Some people say 'your music sounds angry,' or 'tortured,' or 'spiritual,' or 'overpowering' or something; you get all kinds of things, you know. Some say they feel elated, and so you never know where it's going to go. All a musician can do is to get closer to the sources of nature, and so feel that he is in communion with the natural laws. Then he can feel that he is interpreting them to the best of his ability, and can try to convey that to others.

"As to the music itself and its future, it won't lessen any in its ability to move people, I feel certain of that. It will be just as great or greater.

"But as to how it's going to do that, I don't know. It's left to the men who're going to do it—they would know!"

DON DEMICHEAL

JOHN COLTRANE AND ERIC DOLPHY ANSWER THE JAZZ CRITICS

Down Beat, *April 12, 1962*

Although John Coltrane's music had been criticized many times, only a few articles or reviews had attempted to characterize Coltrane's motivation, sincerity, or state of mind. Then in 1960, Down Beat *published a review of a Los Angeles engagement of the Miles Davis group with John Coltrane. The writer, John Tynan, went further than other critics had in characterizing Coltrane's mental health and in second-guessing his attitude toward his audience. Tynan wrote of "the dark corridors of his [Coltrane's] personal psyche," and that the saxophonist's performance had "overtones of neurotic compulsion and contempt for an audience."*

When Coltrane brought his own group, featuring Eric Dolphy, to Los Angeles in 1961, Tynan was again the reviewer for Down Beat. *Once again the writer went beyond discussion of the music and his opinion of it. He wrote that Coltrane and Dolphy seemed "intent on deliberately destroying" swing and that they seemed "bent on pursuing an anarchistic course in their music that can but be termed anti-jazz."*

Readers quickly wrote in responses to the review, and their opinions were both pro and con. Coltrane's characteristic public response is found in this article—to invite jazz critics to speak to him so that he could understand their criticism and they could understand his goals. Coltrane later said that none of his detractors among the critics ever contacted him (see "John Coltrane: An Interview," on pages 128–156 of this anthology for that statement and for Coltrane's more private responses to the controversy attached to his music).—CW

John Coltrane has been the center of critical controversy ever since he unfurled his sheets of sound in his days with Miles Davis. At first disparaged for his sometimes involved, multinoted solos, Coltrane paid little heed and continued exploring music. In time, his harmonic approach—for the sheets were really rapid chord running, in the main—was accepted, even praised, by most jazz critics.

By the time critics had caught up with Coltrane, the tenor saxophonist had gone on to another way of playing. Coltrane II, if you will, was much concerned with linear theme development that seemed sculptured or torn from great blocks of granite. Little critical carping was heard of this second, architectural, Coltrane.

But Coltrane, an inquisitive-minded, probing musician, seemingly has left architecture for less concrete, more abstract means of expression. This third and present Coltrane has encountered an ever-growing block of criticism, much of it marked by a holy-war fervor.

Criticism of Coltrane III is almost always tied in with Coltrane's cohort Eric Dolphy, a member of that group of musicians who play what has been dubbed the "new thing."

Dolphy's playing has been praised and damned since his national-jazz-scene arrival about two years ago. Last summer Dolphy joined Coltrane's group for a tour. It was on this tour that Coltrane and Dolphy came under the withering fire of *Down Beat* associate editor John Tynan, the first critic to take a strong—and public—stand against what Coltrane and Dolphy were playing.

In the Nov. 23, 1961, *Down Beat* Tynan wrote, "At Hollywood's Renaissance Club recently, I listened to a horrifying demonstration of what appears to be a growing anti-jazz trend exemplified by these foremost proponents [Coltrane and Dolphy] of what is termed avant-garde music.

"I heard a good rhythm section . . . go to waste behind the nihilistic exercises of the two horns. . . . Coltrane and Dolphy seem intent on deliberately destroying [swing]. . . . They seem bent on pursuing an anarchistic course in their music that can but be termed anti-jazz."

The anti-jazz term was picked up by Leonard Feather and used as a basis for critical essays of Coltrane, Dolphy, Ornette Coleman, and the "new thing" in general in *Down Beat* and *Show.*

The reaction from readers to both Tynan's and Feather's remarks was immediate, heated, and about evenly divided.

Recently, Coltrane and Dolphy agreed to sit down and discuss their music and the criticism leveled at it.

One of the recurring charges is that their performances are stretched out over too long a time, that Coltrane and Dolphy play on and on, past inspiration and into monotony.

Coltrane answered, "They're long because all the soloists try to explore all the avenues that the tune offers. They try to use all their resources in their solos. Everybody has quite a bit to work on. Like when I'm playing, there are certain things I try to get done and so does Eric and McCoy Tyner [Coltrane's pianist]. By the time we finish, the song is spread out over a pretty long time.

"It's not planned that way; it just happens. The performances get longer and longer. It's sort of growing that way."

But, goes the criticism, there must be editing, just as a writer must edit his work so that it keeps to the point and does not ramble and become boring.

Coltrane agreed that editing must be done—but for essentially a different reason from what might be expected.

"There are times," he said, "when we play places opposite another group, and in order to play a certain number of sets a night, you can't play an hour and a half at one time. You've got to play 45 or 55 minutes and rotate sets with the other band. And for those reasons, for a necessity such as that, I think it's quite in order that you edit and shorten things.

"But when your set is unlimited, timewise, and everything is really together musically—if there's continuity—it really doesn't make any difference how long you play.

"On the other hand, if there're dead spots, then it's really not good to play anything too long."

One of the tunes that Coltrane's group plays at length is "My Favorite Things," a song, as played by the group, that can exert an intriguingly hypnotic effect, though sometimes it seems too long.

Upon listening closely to him play "Things" on the night before the interview, it seemed that he actually played two solos. He finished one, went back to the theme a bit, and then went into another improvisation.

"That's the way the song is constructed," Coltrane said. "It's divided into parts. We play both parts. There's a minor and a major part. We improvise in the minor, and we improvise in the major modes."

Is there a certain length to the two modes?

"It's entirely up to the artist—his choice," he answered. "We were playing it at one time with minor, then major, then minor modes, but it was *really* getting too long—it was about the only tune we had time to play in an average-length set."

But in playing extended solos, isn't there ever present the risk of running out of ideas? What happens when you've played all your ideas?

"It's easy to stop then," Coltrane said, grinning. "If I feel like I'm just playing notes . . . maybe I don't feel the rhythm or I'm not in the best shape that I should be in when this happens. When I become aware of it in the middle of a solo, I'll try to build things to the point where this inspiration is happening again, where things are spontaneous and not contrived. If it reaches that point again, I feel it can continue—it's alive again. But if it doesn't happen, I'll just quit, bow out."

Dolphy, who had been sitting pixie-like as Coltrane spoke, was in complete agreement about stopping when inspiration had flown.

Last fall at the Monterey Jazz Festival, the Coltrane-Dolphy group was featured opening night. In his playing that night Dolphy at times sounded as if he were imitating birds. On the night before the interview some of Dolphy's flute solos brought Monterey to mind. Did he do this on purpose?

Dolphy smiled and said it was purposeful and that he had always liked birds.

Is bird imitation valid in jazz?

"I don't know if it's valid in jazz," he said, "but I enjoy it. It somehow comes in as part of the development of what I'm doing. Sometimes I can't do it.

"At home [in California] I used to play, and the birds always used to whistle with me. I would stop what I was working on and play with the birds."

He described how bird calls had been recorded and then slowed down in playback; the bird calls had a timbre similar to that of a flute. Conversely, he said, a symphony flutist recorded these bird calls, and when the recording was played at a fast speed, it sounded like birds.

Having made his point about the connection of bird whistles and flute playing, Dolphy explained his use of quarter tones when playing flute.

"That's the way birds do," he said. "Birds have notes in between our notes—you try to imitate something they do and, like, maybe it's between F and F♯, and you'll have to go up or come down on the pitch. It's really something! And so, when you get playing, this comes. You try to do some things on it. Indian music has something of the same quality—different scales and quarter tones. I don't know how you label it, but it's pretty."

The question in many critics' minds, though they don't often verbalize it, is: What are John Coltrane and Eric Dolphy trying to do? Or: What *are* they doing?

Following the question, a 30-second silence was unbroken except by Dolphy's, "That's a good question." Dolphy was first to try to voice his aims in music:

"What I'm trying to do I find enjoyable. Inspiring—what it makes me do. It helps me play, this feel. It's like you have no idea what you're going to do next. You have an idea, but there's always that spontaneous thing that happens. This feeling, to me, leads the whole group. When John plays, it might lead into something you had no idea could be done. Or McCoy does something. Or the way Elvin [Jones, drummer with the group] or Jimmy [Garrison, the bassist] play; they solo, they do something. Or when the rhythm section is sitting on something a different way. I feel that is what it does for me."

Coltrane, who had sat in frowned contemplation while Dolphy elaborated, dug into the past for his answer:

"Eric and I have been talking music for quite a few years, since about 1954. We've been close for quite a while. We watched music. We always talked about it, discussed what was being done down through the years, because we love music. What we're doing now was started a few years ago.

"A few months ago Eric was in New York, where the group was working, and he felt like playing, wanted to come down and sit in. So I told him to come on down and play, and he did—and turned us all around. I'd felt at ease with just a quartet till then, but he came in, and it was like having another member of the family. He'd found another way to express the same thing we had found one way to do.

"After he sat in, we decided to see what it would grow into. We began to play some of the things we had only talked about before. Since he's been in the band, he's had a broadening effect on us. There are a lot of things we try now that we never tried before. This helped me, because I've started to write—it's necessary that we have things written so that we can play together. We're playing things that are freer than before.

"I would like for him to feel at home in the group and find a place to develop what he wants to do as an individualist and as a soloist—just as I hope everybody in the band will. And while we are doing this, I would also like the listener to be able to receive some of these good things—some of this beauty."

Coltrane paused, deep in thought. No one said anything. Finally he went on:

"It's more than beauty that I feel in music—that I think musicians feel in music. What we know we feel we'd like to convey to the listener. We hope that this can be shared by all. I think, basically, that's about what it is we're trying to do. We never talked about just what we were trying to do. If you ask me that question, I might say this today and tomorrow say something entirely different, because there are many things to do in music.

"But, over-all, I think the main thing a musician would like to do is to give a picture to the listener of the many wonderful things he knows of and senses in the universe. That's what music is to me—it's just another way of saying this is a big, beautiful universe we live in, that's been given to us, and here's an example of just how magnificent and encompassing it is. That's what I would like to do. I think that's one of the greatest things you can do in life, and we all try to do it in some way. The musician's is through his music."

This philosophy about music, life, and the universe, Coltrane said, is "so important to music, and music is so important. Some realize it young and early in their careers. I didn't realize it as early as I should have, as early as I wish I had. Sometimes you have to take a thing when it comes and be glad."

When did he first begin to feel this way?

"I guess I was on my way in '57, when I started to get myself together musically, although at the time I was working academically and technically. It's just recently that I've tried to become even more aware of this other side—the life side of music. I feel I'm just beginning again. Which goes back to the group and what we're trying to do. I'm fortunate to be in the company I'm in now, because anything I'd like to do, I have a place to try. They respond so well that it's very easy to try new things."

Dolphy broke in with, "Music is a reflection of everything. And it's universal. Like, you can hear somebody from across the world, another country. You don't even know them, but they're in your back yard, you know?"

"It's a reflection of the universe," Coltrane said. "Like having life in miniature. You just take a situation in life or an emotion you know and put it into music. You take a scene you've seen, for instance, and put it to music."

Had he ever succeeded in re-creating a situation or scene?

"I was getting into it," he said, "but I haven't made it yet. But I'm beginning to see how to do it. I know a lot of musicians who have done it. It's just happening to me now. Actually, while a guy is soloing, there are many things that happen. Probably he himself doesn't know how many moods or themes he's created. But I think it really ends up with the listener. You know, you hear different people say, 'Man, I felt this while he was playing,' or 'I thought about this.' There's no telling what people are thinking. They take in what they have experienced. It's a sharing process—playing—for people."

"You can feel vibrations from the people," Dolphy added.

"The people can give you something too," Coltrane said. "If you play in a place where they really like you, like your group, they can make you play like you've *never* felt like playing before."

Anyone who has heard the Coltrane group in person in such a situation knows the almost hypnotic effect the group can have on the audience and the audience's almost surging involvement in the music. But sometimes, it is said, the striving for excitement *per se* within the group leads to nonmusical effects. It was effects such as these that have led to the "anti-jazz" term.

Such a term is bound to arouse reaction in musicians like Coltrane and Dolphy.

Without a smile—or rancor—Coltrane said he would like the critics who have used the term in connection with him to tell him exactly what they mean. Then, he said, he could answer them.

One of the charges is that what Coltrane and Dolphy play doesn't swing.

"I don't know what to say about that," Dolphy said.

"Maybe it doesn't swing," Coltrane offered.

"I can't say that they're wrong," Dolphy said. "But I'm still playing."

Well, don't *you* feel that it swings? he was asked.

"Of course I do," Dolphy answered. "In fact, it swings so much I don't know what to do—it moves me so much. I'm with John; I'd like to know how they explain 'anti-jazz.' Maybe they can tell us something."

"There are various types of swing," Coltrane said. "There's straight 4/4, with heavy bass drum accents. Then there's the kind of thing that goes on in Count Basie's band. In fact, every group of individuals assembled has a different feeling—a different swing. It's the same with this band. It's a different feeling than in any other band. It's hard to answer a man who says it doesn't swing."

Later, when the first flush of defense had subsided, Coltrane allowed:

"Quite possibly a lot of things about the band need to be done. But everything has to be done in its own time. There are some things that you just grow into. Back to speaking about editing—things like that. I've felt a need for this, and I've felt a need for ensemble work—throughout the songs, a little cement between this block, a pillar here, some more cement there, etc. But as yet I don't know just how I would like to do it. So rather than make a move just because I know it needs to be done, a move that I've not arrived at through work, from what I naturally feel, I won't do it.

"There may be a lot of things missing from the music that are coming, if we stay together that long. When they come, they'll be things that will be built out of just what the group is. They will be unique to the group and *of* the group."

Coltrane said he felt that what he had said still did not answer his critics adequately, that in order to do so he would have to meet them and discuss what has been said so that he could see just what they mean.

Dolphy interjected that the critic should consult the musician when there is something the critic does not fully understand. "It's kind of alarming to the musician," he said, "when someone has written something bad about what the musician plays but never asks the musician anything about it. At least, the musician feels bad. But he doesn't feel so bad that he quits playing. The critic influences a lot of people. If something new has happened, something nobody knows what the musician is doing, he should ask the musician about it. Because somebody may like it; they might want to know something about it. Sometimes it really hurts, because a musician not only loves his work but depends on it for a living. If somebody writes something bad about musicians, people stay away. Not because the guys don't sound good but because somebody said something that has influence over a lot of people. They say, 'I read this, and I don't think he's so hot because so-and-so said so.'"

Dolphy had brought up a point that bothers most jazz critics: readers sometimes forget that criticism is what *one* man thinks. A critic is telling how he feels about, how he reacts to, what he hears in, a performance or a piece of music.

"The best thing a critic can do," Coltrane said, "is to thoroughly understand what he is writing about and then jump in. That's all he can do. I have even seen favorable criticism which revealed a lack of profound analysis, causing it to be little more than superficial.

"Understanding is what is needed. That is *all* you can do. Get all the understanding for what you're speaking of that you can get. That way you have done your best. It's the same with a musician who is trying to understand music as well as he can. Undoubtedly, none of us are going to be 100 percent—in either criticism or music. No percent near that, but we've all got to try.

"Understanding is the whole thing. In talking to a critic try to understand him, and he can try to understand the part of the game you are in. With this understanding, there's no telling what could be accomplished. Everybody would benefit."

Though he said he failed to answer his critics, John Coltrane perhaps had succeeded more than he thought.

BENOÎT QUERSIN

LA PASSE DANGEREUSE

Jazz Magazine (France), January 1963

Belgian jazz enthusiast Benoît Quersin interviewed John Coltrane twice—once in the United States and once later in Paris. Quersin transcribed and translated into French the two interviews, and he edited parts of both into a single article which appeared in the French Jazz Magazine. *Quersin has since died and it has been thought that tape recordings of the original interviews were lost. Quersin's friend and colleague Michel Delorme found taped copies of both interviews and passed them on to Coltrane scholar Lewis Porter for use in his book* John Coltrane: His Life and Music *(see the Bibliography). Porter was very generous in giving me a copy of the tape for transcription and publication. This is the first publication of the complete Benoît Quersin interviews.*

For this version of Quersin's article, I have transcribed both interviews in their entirety and presented them in the order in which they were made rather than intertwined, as in the original. Thank you to Philippe Carles of Jazz Magazine *of France for allowing republication of this interview.*

The Paris interview took place on November 17, 1962, but the earlier American interview has not been firmly dated. In the first interview, Coltrane speaks of having in his band Eric Dolphy, who was regularly performing with Coltrane by July of 1961. Indeed, Dolphy can be heard on the tape warming up. Quersin and Coltrane speak of an upcoming trip to France and England for Coltrane and his group. The quintet toured both England and France just once: from November 11 to December 2, 1961.

Therefore the U.S. interview below most likely occurred in the summer or autumn of 1961.—CW

United States, probably 1961

Benoît Quersin: I've been listening to your music since nineteen-forty [Quersin misspeaks] —*Fifty-seven, or something, and I—*

John Coltrane: Oh, yeah?

Benoît Quersin: —*love it, you know. I've been very fond of it since then. You've been—well there is—there has been an evolution in your music. Like, you've been exploring new ways of playing jazz. Well, it's kind of hard for me [speaking English]. You know what I mean? I mean, the conception of jazz music, following new patterns, or something.*

John Coltrane: So, you think it's changing?

Benoît Quersin: It has *been changing.*

John Coltrane: Yeah.

Benoît Quersin: Well, it changed a lot *in the last few years. It has been improving. Also, new patterns.*

John Coltrane: Patterns.

Benoît Quersin: Patterns.

John Coltrane: Yeah. Yeah, there have been some new things introduced. And, it's good for jazz that they have been introduced, because [unintelligible] breathe new life into the whole field. And, I think young men now, they have quite a bit to listen to, and all the men that they listen to, they can take things from what they're doing, and add into their own conceptions, and go their own way and maybe produce something themselves, which might help promote this extension in the music.

Benoît Quersin: "Extension" in what way?

John Coltrane: Well, in rhythmic and melodic and possibly harmonic directions.

Benoît Quersin: So, you're trying to get out of the standard harmonic structures and all that? Well, that's where you started from.

John Coltrane: Yeah. I tried to get out of it, because I worked—I went in it in a harmonic [unintelligible], trying to work through harmonic structures because that was—I was—that was my strongest point. I mean I was better equipped to work that way than I was rhythmically or melodically. And, that's been about the extent of my work. In what I've done, I've tried to add things to my playing harmonically which I hadn't been playing over the years. And, I started [unintelligible] 1957, doing this for myself. Well, almost all of the guys who are out here now are doing so many things that are help—helping to expand the music, it's going, like I said, in other directions. It's going in rhythmic directions and also melodic *and* harmonic, too. [unintelligible]

Benoît Quersin: Well, the music [unintelligible].

John Coltrane: It's getting a little larger. There's more—there's more that a guy will attempt to play now than he would in—whatever—1955. And things that guys are doing now that's—in '55, they would say, "well, man, I don't know. It's a little too daring," maybe. But now it doesn't seem that anything can be too daring for a musician nowadays in jazz.

Benoît Quersin: So, well, there was an extension in the language—trying to extend the language the—I mean the vocabulary.

John Coltrane: How's that?

Benoît Quersin: Extend the vocabulary, and—

John Coltrane: Oh, yeah.

Benoît Quersin: —broaden.

John Coltrane: Yeah.

Benoît Quersin: *Well, the freedom, but organized freedom, as far as you are concerned.*

John Coltrane: Well, I don't—maybe it is, I don't know. I have to—I'm kind of—actually, I'm groping, I'm trying to find my way. I can only try to work out of what I've been *in*. Work my way forward, so I just try to set one stone upon another as I go.

Benoît Quersin: *Maybe [the]* Giant Steps *album was the first step, or the first definite step toward original music of yours.*

John Coltrane: Well, that album—that album represented a few things that I'd been thinking of for about five or six months before it was made. The things that I was—the harmonic structures that I was working on there, I hadn't fully developed them and I didn't understand them. Actually, "Giant Steps" was, in quite a few respects, I don't know, an experiment. And the things—some things I could have used in there—in "Giant Steps" that I made a whole song out of, I could have probably taken—taken them and applied to something else and they might have taken up a few bars and that have been it. But at that time, I was obsessed with the thing and it was all I had in my mind, because it was my first step into playing some extended chord structures, as I was trying to do, and that was those songs that were on there. Some of them had these particular structures in them. That was the first one—record that I made with them in there. And since then, I've done it, but it hasn't been so obvious because I've learned to use it as a part of something and not as a whole.

Benoît Quersin: *And then, the next step was—because it sounds—the music I hear in* Giant Steps *seems to—well, it's a wide exploration in harmony, because the harmonic structures are kind of uncommon, really new. But now, in your latest, in the latest things I heard, like* [My] Favorite Things *album and* Africa/Brass *and* Olé, *it's something else.*

John Coltrane: Well, I'm trying to learn, I'm trying to broaden myself melodically and rhythmically, too. These things that are coming along now are the culmination of—whatever—the things that I'm thinking of in these aspects, rhythmic or melodic. I haven't forgotten about harmony altogether, but I'm not as interested in it as I was two years ago.

Benoît Quersin: Harmonic structures, you say.

John Coltrane: Hm?

Benoît Quersin: Harmonic structures.

John Coltrane: Harmony structures?

Benoît Quersin: No, the latest album. Yeah, what you just said, related [unintelligible] two years ago. What's that?

John Coltrane: Well, I was more interested two years ago in harmony than I am now, that's what I'm saying. Then it was solely—I was only interested in harmony. Now, I'm trying to learn about melody and rhythm.

Benoît Quersin: And so, [you] get more freedom melodically with simpler—one seems to—you seem to play—I don't know if I'm right, but you seem to play a kind of mode, a kind of scale, modified scale.

John Coltrane: Yeah, well, I've gone into that now. I've followed Miles's lead in that, I think. He was doing that, that kind of work, when I was with him. And, at that time, I was working on the chords, but he was in the modal thing then. So, since I've had my own group, it has become necessary to use the modal concept because it *does* free the rhythm section in it. They don't have to keep their strict chordal structure. And the soloist can play any structure he wants to. But the rhythm section is basically unhindered or uncluttered. So, most of the things we're doing now are in modes for parts, in sections, then there are sections when there there are no harmonies at all, underlying, that is.

Benoît Quersin: How do you like George Russell's music?

John Coltrane: He has some good music. He has what is the type of music that seems to be coming in to the fore nowadays. I've heard a few records of his, one that Eric Dolphy was on, that I heard, that I—several things on there I like very well. And he [Russell] understands quite a few of the problems that musicians are running across today and he's probably going to do a great deal to contribute to solving of such things.

Benoît Quersin: And, what's the reason for adding Eric to the—to your quintet? To your band?

John Coltrane: Well, he just came in and started playing! [both laugh] Yeah, he just came in and started playing. He played, I forget where the job was, he brought his horn down and sat in. And, it was on a weekend, so he just played the whole weekend. And the next job we worked, he came down, I think it was in Philadelphia, he said, "Man, I don't have nothing to do." He was bored, just sitting, just sitting around New York, so he said, "I'll just come on over." And, after a while I just said, "You're in the band." [both laugh] And, that's fine, I really—we've always—I was always calling him on the phone and he was calling me, and we'd discuss things, musically, so we might as well be together. Maybe we can help each other some. I know he helps me a lot.

Benoît Quersin: Yeah, he worked on the album Africa/Brass *with you, didn't he?*

John Coltrane: Yeah, he was—he did quite a bit of work on that album. Quite a bit.

Benoît Quersin: How do you like Ornette Coleman?

John Coltrane: I love him. [laughs] Yeah, I love him. I'm following his lead. He's done a lot to open my eyes to what can be done.

Benoît Quersin: Very [unintelligible] subjective.

John Coltrane: Huh?

Benoît Quersin: Very subjective, he is—

John Coltrane: Ornette?

Benoît Quersin: Ornette. Very intelligent, fresh and sincere, but—

John Coltrane: He's beautiful.

Benoît Quersin: He's a beautiful cat. And I think he thinks a lot about his music, but isn't it kind of an intellectual approach to music? And it's good, I feel it's good.

John Coltrane: Yeah, well, I feel indebted to him, myself. Because, actually, when he came along, I was so far in this thing [the "harmonic structures"], I didn't know where I was going to go next. And, I didn't know if I would have thought about just abandoning the chord system or not. I probably wouldn't have thought of that at all. And he came along *doing* it, and I heard it, I said, "Well, that—that must be the answer." And I'm of the opinion that it is, now. That's the way I feel now. The way we do, we play, we do—right, since I have a piano, I still have to consider it, and that accounts for the modes that we play, but after all, you can't—we only—we only got a few, and after a while, that's going to get a little monotonous to do it on every song, so it might—there probably will be some songs in the future that we're going to play, just as Ornette does, with no accompaniment from the piano at all. Except on maybe the melody, but as far as the solo, no accompaniment.

Benoît Quersin: Yeah, just to set the climate and then go.

John Coltrane: Hm?

Benoît Quersin: Just set the climate and then go.

John Coltrane: Yeah.

Benoît Quersin: Yeah, it's really close to some aspects of the modern music, the so-called "classical" modern music.

John Coltrane: Hm?

Benoît Quersin: So, it's more or less close to the modern classical music. That kind of freedom.

John Coltrane: You mean the movement now in jazz?

Benoît Quersin: Mm hm. But jazz was something more.

John Coltrane: Well, it still retains its—that thing, whatever it is, that it has. And, that's what keeps it going, that—that feeling. Whatever it is, it's hard to define.

Benoît Quersin: I've heard you're going to Europe soon.

John Coltrane: Yeah.

Benoît Quersin: France? You know where?

John Coltrane: No, I don't—I don't know where, yet. I know, well, France is there, London is there. And, what else, I'm not sure.

Benoît Quersin: Because, I sure hope you come to Brussels, I'll be there.

John Coltrane: Huh? [both laugh]

Benoît Quersin: Well, if they don't hire you, I will.

John Coltrane: Well, thank you.

Benoît Quersin: I'll try to—

John Coltrane: Thank you.

Benoît Quersin: —anyway. OK, thank you.

John Coltrane: Thank you.

Paris, November 17, 1962

Benoît Quersin: Did anything new happen for you in the meantime?

John Coltrane: Well, no, just—I'm continuing to—*trying* to evolve, [laughs] I'll say. There's nothing new happening. We're trying to bring some of the things that we started to a conclusion, and hoping that there will be something else waiting after that.

Benoît Quersin: Some extensions. [unintelligible]

John Coltrane: Yeah. I hope so, yeah.

Benoît Quersin: And professionally, it has been improving a lot, yes?

John Coltrane: Well, we have been trying to extend our scope a little bit as far as the places that we work. We've worked in a few different clubs up in New York State. We've widened our circuit a little. It's a problem we've had; our circuit is small, we've played the same clubs over and over now. It kind of tires the listener, so we've been trying to broaden our—get around more to more distant places and—

Benoît Quersin: Have you been trying to get some new material together?

John Coltrane: I have. I've been trying, but I haven't—it hasn't come in a rush, yet. I've had a few things here and there but I haven't done any—I haven't gotten a—I think I need a new approach to the tunes that we get, and then I can use a whole lot of things that have been done before. But they'll be different, have a different approach.

Benoît Quersin: Have you been thinking of expanding your group, I mean the instrumentation?

John Coltrane: Well, I'm always thinking of that, but I can't do it until I better my writing ability. That's something that has to be done before I can use another horn. Yeah.

Benoît Quersin: Yeah, because—

John Coltrane: Unless I have somebody like Eric Dolphy, you see. Yeah, he can fit in, he can—a lot of time, makes his own parts, or he just—[pause]

Benoît Quersin: What happened—

John Coltrane: —fills in so well.

Benoît Quersin: What happened to him, man?

John Coltrane: He has a quintet. He has his own group.

Benoît Quersin: Africa/Brass was the first experience in some new orchestra sounds. Are you going to try something again in that field?

John Coltrane: Maybe for recording, but as far as actual roadwork, I'm quite certain that I couldn't ever be—it costs too much to employ a group of musicians like that. But for recording, I may try something with maybe nine, or eight or nine pieces. There were some things which are—we started in that *Africa/Brass,* which I'd like to maybe take a lit- tle further, but I have to work on it a little bit more 'til I see clearly.

Benoît Quersin: With what instruments? What kind of colors?

John Coltrane: Hm?

Benoît Quersin: What instruments? What colors?

John Coltrane: On *Africa?*

Benoît Quersin: No, I mean in your [unintelligible]—

John Coltrane: Oh.

Benoît Quersin: —you're thinking about.

John Coltrane: Oh, well I don't know yet. Because I'm—

Benoît Quersin: Oh, just thinking about it.

John Coltrane: I don't know. Well, just thinking about it. It would prob- ably be something like that. Probably heavy on the lower brass instru- ments and woodwinds. Not too many of the higher brass like trumpets or cornets. Few, very few, but more of the lower brasses and wood- winds. I think something like that I might—might be able to get the sound of the thing that I want.

Benoît Quersin: *Are you interested in contemporary music [unintelligible]?*

John Coltrane: Of what nature?

Benoît Quersin: *Well [the] so-called "classical" field.*

John Coltrane: Well, I've—I'm beginning now to listen to it more than I have in the past. I'm going to study some of the twelve-tone things. In fact, I have a few of them, but I haven't really studied them yet. Actually, if I hear the sound, I usually—if there's—if I hear a sound or something that I like, it doesn't matter what era it's from, I just like *that*. So, I don't know, I haven't—like I say, I haven't studied much of the contemporary music, but I do intend to do [an] exhaustive study of the twelve-tone works.

Benoît Quersin: *Do you think it can be integrated into jazz, the twelve-tone technique?*

John Coltrane: Well, it is being—I would say that Ornette Coleman is doing it. Well, he's not—

Benoît Quersin: *Consciously?*

John Coltrane: —actually doing it, he's not doing it, like, say, "I want to do this because someone else is doing it," he's doing it because he *feels* this, see? So, he's doing it in what I consider the right way, the natural way, in other words, the way which is—one arrives at through his own natural evolution. And not just because he just consciously wants to *do* something like that. That's why I, I mean, I haven't actually studied this so much, because I haven't actually evolved, myself, to the point where I'm—I want to play consistently just in a manner of twelve tones. I still like to play over chord-based, although I do like to play passages which do contain twelve tones, but I build them in my own way of structure, sequential structure.

Benoît Quersin: *Well, it's kind of a very slow technique, I mean, it takes a lot of work to follow.*

[Unknown voice] *Let's go, John.*

John Coltrane: Yeah, well it has to—

[Unknown voice] John.

John Coltrane: Yeah, OK. [continues to Quersin] It has to come naturally. And then this, because you've got to do it just like you talk and
walk, where you have to do it instantly. It's not—you don't want it to
be a thing that you've got to think out at home and work out like that,
or sit down and work out, you want it so you just do it, you know, in a
moment. That's the way it's got to happen. So you have to [laughs]—it
has to happen that way. You have to work through it. Well, I guess we
better run.

Benoît Quersin: Thank you.

FRANK KOFSKY
JOHN COLTRANE: AN INTERVIEW
Black Nationalism and the Revolution in Music, *1970*

*The late Frank Kofsky was one of the few interviewers to ask John
Coltrane about current political and social events. When asked
about Malcolm X and Vietnam, Coltrane is characteristically cau-
tious in his replies, but we get a sense of his general feelings on
these subjects. In the course of the interview, the names of many
fellow musicians come up, and Coltrane's comments are always
interesting. In this article Coltrane gets the chance to refute two
provocative statements attributed to Sun Ra, but Coltrane's
responses are sincere and generous.*

*Among younger musicians, Coltrane praises saxophonists Albert
Ayler and John Gilmore. Coltrane states that around the time he
recorded the blues "Chasin' the Trane," he was influenced by the
work of Gilmore. This statement not only compliments Gilmore,
it also shows how open and modest Coltrane was about revealing
his broad sphere of listening and his musical influences. Near the
end of the interview Coltrane talks candidly about his frustrations*

with the controversy over the playing he'd done with Eric Dolphy.
(See "John Coltrane and Eric Dolphy Answer the Jazz Critics," on
pages 109–117 of this volume.) Although he was very constructive
in that article, Coltrane here is more direct and reveals more of his
frustrations of that earlier time. —CW

I am not a religious person, but John Coltrane was the one man whom I worshipped as a saint or even a god. I could never have written that when he was alive—if nothing else, it would have been too embarrassing for him had he read it. But since he is gone, no cause remains for denying it; and I feel that that tribute is the smallest gesture I can make toward acknowledging how much beauty and happiness he has brought into my life.

My veneration of John began, I think in the winter of 1958, when I first heard him on Miles Davis's *'Round About Midnight* LP. I was immediately hypnotized and entranced by his sound. If familiarity is supposed to lead to contempt, the process worked just the opposite way in my love affair with Coltrane's music: the more I heard, the heavier was I hooked. Especially so with his later, post-1961 periods. Indeed, there have been times recently when one of the few things I could consistently rely on to convince me that life was worth the effort was the indomitably affirmative spirit that could be heard even in Coltrane's recordings. I'm sorry if that sentence reads like something by Nat Hentoff, but that is the way I felt, and Nat and everyone else will just have to bear with me for the resemblance.

Meeting John in the flesh not only did not tarnish his appeal for me, it enhanced it. I do not pretend I knew him well. I met him shortly after he formed his own quartet in 1961 to the best of my recollection, when he played his first West Coast engagement at San Francisco's Jazz Workshop. It had been arranged that he would do a benefit concert sponsored by the Students for Racial Equality at the University of California, the proceeds to go to the Student Nonviolent Coordinating Committee. The concert itself was never held—the then Chancellor Clark Kerr would not allow us to raise funds on campus for the use of organizations like SNCC, which meant that there was no point putting on the concert. (Later, the Free Speech Movement was able to mobilize the Berkeley campus around this issue; but in 1961 there was not that much concern.) Nonetheless, it had been a very real thrill for me (as liaison with Coltrane) to carry on even those few fragmentary and truncated conversations we had in the cubbyhole that passed for a dressing room in the Workshop.

I did my best to keep up the acquaintanceship in the years that followed. I moved to Los Angeles later in 1961, and whenever Coltrane played there—which wasn't often, due to the backwardness of the Los Angeles jazz audience—I made it a point to seek him out and exchange a few words with him. Poor man! How I now regret robbing him of those precious minutes that he liked to use for cat-napping between sets. But then I thought only of how I could manage to bask for a few extra moments in the presence of the Great Man himself.

In the summer of 1966 I was able to arrange for a two-week stay in New York to interview the leading musicians of the Jazz Revolution. The name that topped my list, of course, was that of John Coltrane. In spite of his crowded schedule, I was able to persuade John to allow me to question him, a triumph that left me glowing. The circumstances of that interview may help explain the affection I felt for John and why the closer one got to the man, the more one loved and respected him.

There was no earthly reason why he should have consented to be interviewed, especially since it involved a certain amount of inconvenience for him. First off, he had to drive thirty or forty minutes from his house to pick me up at the Deer Park station of the Long Island Railroad. Then, since there wasn't time for us to return to his home if I were to be on the afternoon train returning to New York, he sat with me in his station wagon for over an hour, sweltering in the August heat and humidity while we tape-recorded an interview in the parking lot of a local supermarket (part of our conversation is inaudible on the tape, owing to the rattling of the shopping carts). After the interview was over and John had returned me to the station, he insisted on waiting with me on the sunny platform, until the next train back arrived. As we waited, he asked me about my political philosophy (we had talked during the interview about changing the world for the better). He was thoughtful and attentive, when I told him I was a socialist and tried as best I could, given my nervous state, to explain the reason why. And then the train came.

That, however, was not the last of John's kindnesses to me. The next day I received a telephone call from Pharoah Sanders, saying that John had told him I was searching for him (as indeed I had been, fruitlessly, ever since my arrival in New York) to interview. And so an appointment with Pharoah was thus set up through the agency of John Coltrane.

I have never understood to this day why John went so far out of his way to assist a complete nonentity like myself. I can only surmise that, however much he may have had reservations about or outright disagreements with some of my ideas, he was convinced of my sincerity in working for a radical improvement in the human condition; and for that reason, if I am not mistaken he put himself at my disposal. To say that his actions touched me would be the greatest understatement imaginable. But by then I appreciated that John Coltrane was unlike other men: his humility seemed to grow in proportion to his greatness, and I believe him the most *genuinely* modest man I have ever met. (Those younger followers who are so anxious to try and fill his shoes with their own considerably lesser talents would do well to emulate the master in this regard.) It was the combination of modesty and human warmth that overwhelmed me in talking to John and lent another whole dimension to my understanding of what he was saying in his music.

In the 1964 election, I wrote the names of Malcolm X and John Coltrane for President and Vice-president. I mention this now only because I have been musing about it frequently in the days since John's passing. Then, I made that choice because those were the two greatest Americans I could think of. But now, I've begun to wonder if there isn't some hidden but nonetheless real connection between them. I think that there is. Both men perceived the ultimate reality about this country—the reality that you could know only if were black and you were exposed at close quarters to the jazz club–narcotics–alcohol–mobster–ghetto milieu. Both men escaped being trapped in that milieu; both sought to use the lessons they had learned from it to show us not just the necessity for creating a society without ghettos of any sort, but also how to go about it; both, that is, exhorted us to make maximum use of our *human* potentialities, our reason and emotions. Neither was ever content with a static description of reality. Instead, both continually brought their most treasured concepts, assumptions, and definitions under relentless scrutiny. When these proved inadequate or outmoded, so much the worse for them: once their shortcomings became apparent, they were discarded like yesterday's newspapers. Such was the compulsive honesty of these two giants, the total dedication to truth at any cost, that made Malcolm X and John Coltrane the charismatic figures they were and won for them their large following of young people, black and white alike. Though cut down in the prime of life with their work far from finished and their best years perhaps still in front of them, it is surely safe to say that their influence is just beginning to be felt.

I was not close enough to John Coltrane to expound on "what he would have liked us to do"; it would be a cheap trick unworthy of the reverence in which I hold him were I even to try. Possibly there are others who have this knowledge, I cannot say. What I can do is to tell you what he stands for in my mind and how I feel we can make use of his life to guide us, now that he is gone. More than anything else, I think of John as a man who could never sacrifice what he perceived as truth for mere expediency, no matter how advantageous this might have proved. He refused to accept a single set of ideas as final for all time: for him there was no orthodoxy or dogma that could not be challenged. He was ever trying to probe deeper inside himself, convinced that if he could reveal the essence of himself to his listeners, they would be moved to do the same, thus developing their creative faculties to the maximum. He therefore required absolute and total honesty of himself at all times; and though he sometimes worried about the unfavorable consequences that such a course would inevitably bring in its wake, the hesitations were momentary, the decision to push ahead, unalterable. If we are to be worthy of the music that he has left us I do not see how we can do less than try to be as skeptical of what we are indoctrinated with as Truth and as demanding of ourselves as he was while he lived.

Kofsky: The first thing I want to ask about is a story that somebody told me. The first night I came here, the people I was staying with have a friend, a young lady, and she was downtown at one of Malcolm X's speeches—and lo and behold, who should pop in on the seat next to her, but John Coltrane. [Laughter.] Right away, that whetted my curiosity, and I wanted to know how many times you have seen him, what you thought of him, and so forth.

Coltrane: That was the only time.

Kofsky: Were you impressed by him?

Coltrane: Definitely. That was the only time. I thought I had to see the man, you know. I was living downtown, I was in the hotel, I saw the posters, and I realized that he was going to be over there so I said, well, I'm going over there and see this cat, because I had never seen him. I was quite impressed.

Kofsky: That was one of his last speeches, wasn't it?

Coltrane: Well, it was toward the end of his career.

Kofsky: Some musicians have said that there's a relationship between some of Malcolm's ideas and the music, especially the new music. Do you think there's anything in that?

Coltrane: Well, I think that music, being an expression of the human heart, or of the human being itself, does express just what *is* happening. I feel it expresses the whole thing—the whole of human experience at the particular time that it is being expressed.

Kofsky: *What do you think about the phrase the new black music as a description of some of the newer styles in jazz?*

Coltrane: Phrases, I don't know. They don't mean much to me, because usually I don't make the phrases, so I don't react too much. It makes no difference to me one way or the other what it's called.

Kofsky: *If you did make the phrases, could you think of one?*

Coltrane: I don't think there's a phrase for it, that I could make.

Kofsky: *The people who use that phrase argue that jazz is particularly closely related to the black community and it's an expression of what's happening there. That's why I asked you about your reaction to Malcolm X.*

Coltrane: Well, I think it's up to the individual musician, call it what you may, for any reason you may. Myself, I recognize the artist. I recognize an individual when I see his contribution; and when I know a man's sound, well, to me that's him, that's this man. That's the way I look at it. Labels, I don't bother with.

Kofsky: *But it does seem to be a fact that most of the changes in the music—the innovations—have come from black musicians.*

Coltrane: Yes, well this is how it is.

Kofsky: *Have you ever noticed—since you've played all over the United States and in all kinds of circumstances—have you ever noticed that the reaction of an audience varies or changes if it's a black audience or a white audience or a mixed audience? Have you ever noticed that the racial composition of the audience seems to determine how the people respond?*

Coltrane: Well, sometimes, yes, and sometimes, no.

Kofsky: *Any examples?*

Coltrane: Sometimes it might appear to be one; you might say . . . it's hard to say, man. Sometimes people like it or don't like it, no matter what color they are.

Kofsky: *You don't have any preferences yourself about what kind of an audience you play for?*

Coltrane: Well, to me, it doesn't matter. I only hope that whoever is out there listening, they enjoy it; and if they're not enjoying it, I'd rather not hear.

Kofsky: *If people do enjoy the music, how would you like them to demonstrate it? Do you like an audience that's perfectly still and unresponsive, or do you like an audience that reacts more visibly to the music?*

Coltrane: Well, I guess I like an audience that does show what they feel; to respond.

Kofsky: *I remember when you played at the Jazz Workshop in San Francisco, you sometimes got that kind of an audience, which you didn't get when you played at Shelly's Manne-Hole in Los Angeles; and it seemed to me that that had some effect on the music.*

Coltrane: Yes, because it seems to me that the audience, in listening, is in an act of participation, you know. And when you know that somebody is maybe moved the same way you are, to such a degree or approaching the degree, it's just like having another member in the group.

Kofsky: *Is that what happened at the* Ascension *date? The people that were there—did they get that involved?*

Coltrane: I don't know. I was so doggone busy; I was worried to death. I couldn't really enjoy the date. If it hadn't been a date then, I would have really enjoyed it. You know, I was trying to get the time and everything, and I was busy. I hope they felt something. To hear the record, I enjoyed it; I enjoyed all of the individual contributions.

Kofsky: What do you think, then, about playing concerts? Does that seem to inhibit the interaction between yourself, your group, and the audience?

Coltrane: Well, on concerts, the only thing that bugs me might be a hall with poor acoustics, where we can't quite get the unit sound. But as far as the audience goes, it's about the same.

Kofsky: Another reason I asked you about Malcolm was because I've interviewed a number of musicians and the consensus seems to be that the younger musicians talk about the political issues and social issues that Malcolm talked about, when they're with each other. And some of them say that they try to express this in the music. Do you find in your own groups or among musicians you're friendly with that these issues are important and that you do talk about them?

Coltrane: Oh, they're definitely important; and as I said, the issues are part of what *is* at this time. So naturally, as musicians, we express whatever is.

Kofsky: Do you make a conscious attempt to express these things?

Coltrane: Well, I tell you for myself, I make a conscious attempt, I think I can truthfully say that in music I make or I have tried to make a conscious attempt to change what I've found, in music. In other words, I've tried to say, "Well, *this,* I feel, could be better, in my opinion, so I will try to do this to make it better." This is what I feel that we feel in any situation that we find in our lives, when there's something we think could be better, we must make an effort to try and make it better. So it's the same socially, musically, politically, and in any department of our lives.

Kofsky: Most of the musicians I have talked to are very concerned about changing society and they do see their music as an instrument by which society can be changed.

Coltrane: Well, I think so. I think music is an instrument. It can create the initial thought patterns that can change the thinking of the people.

Kofsky: In particular, some of the people have said that jazz is opposed to poverty, to suffering, and to oppression; and therefore, that jazz is opposed to what the United States is doing in Vietnam. Do you have any comments on that subject?

Coltrane: On the Vietnam situation?

Kofsky: Well, you can divide it into two parts. The first part was whether you think jazz is opposed to poverty and suffering and oppression; and the second part is whether you think, if so, jazz is therefore opposed to the United States's involvement in Vietnam?

Coltrane: In my opinion I would say yes, because jazz—if you want to call it that; we'll talk about that later—to me, it is an expression of music; and this music is an expression of higher ideals, to me. So therefore, brotherhood is there; and I believe with brotherhood, there would be no poverty. And also, with brotherhood, there would be no war.

Kofsky: That also seems to be what most of the musicians feel. David Izenson, for example, said almost the same thing when I talked with him. He said, well, we're saying in our music we want a society without classes, without these frictions, without the wastes, and without the warfare.

Would you care to comment on working conditions for "jazz" musicians? Do you think that jazz artists are treated as they deserve to be treated; and if not, can you see any reason why they wouldn't be?

Coltrane: I don't know. It's according to the individual. Well, you find many times that a man may feel that the situation is all right with him, where another man might say, that situation is no good for you. So it's a matter of a man knowing himself, just what he wants, and that way, it's according to his value. If he doesn't mind a certain sort of treatment, I'm sure he can find it elsewhere. If he does mind it, then he doesn't have to put up with it. In my opinion, at this stage of the game, I don't care too much for playing clubs, particularly. Now there was a time when it felt all right to play clubs, because with my music, I felt I had to play a lot to work it out, you see. But now I don't think that that was absolutely where it was at; but I had to find it out myself. It is a matter of being able to be at home and be able to go into yourself. In other words, I don't feel the situation in clubs is ideal for me.

Kofsky: What is it about clubs that you don't like?

Coltrane: Well, actually, we don't play the set forty-minute kind of thing anymore, and it's difficult to always do this kind of thing now. The music, changing as it is, there are a lot of times when it doesn't make sense, man, to have somebody drop a glass, or somebody ask for some money right in the middle of Jimmy Garrison's solo. Do you know what I mean?

Kofsky: I know exactly.

Coltrane: And these kind of things are calling for some other kind of presentation.

Kofsky: In other words, these really are artists who are playing, yet they're really not being treated as artists, but as part of the cash register.

Coltrane: Yes, I think the music is rising, in my estimation, it's rising into something else, and so we'll have to find this kind of place to be played in.

Kofsky: Why do you think conditions have been so bad for producing art by the musicians? What do you think causes these poor conditions that you've spoken of?

Coltrane: Well, I don't know; I don't really know how it came about. Because I do know there was one time when the musicians played more dances, and they used to play theaters and all; and this took away one element, you know, but still it was hard work. I remember some of those one-nighters, it was pretty difficult.

But it just seems that the music has been directed by businessmen, I would suppose, who know how to arrange the making of a dollar, and so forth. And maybe often the artist hasn't really taken the time himself to figure out just what he wants. Or if he does feel it should be in some other way. I think these are the things which are being thought about more now.

Kofsky: Do you think the fact that almost all of the original jazz musicians were black men and have continued to be throughout the generations, do you think this has encouraged the businessmen to take advantage of them and to treat their art with this contempt—ringing up of the cash register in the middle of a bass solo?

Coltrane: Well, I don't know.

Kofsky: Most of the owners, I've noticed, are white.

Coltrane: Well, it could be, Frank, it could be.

Kofsky: How do you think conditions are going to be improved for the musicians?

Coltrane: There has to be a lot of self-help, I believe. They have to work out their own problems in this area.

Kofsky: You mean, for example, what the Jazz Composers Guild was trying to do?

Coltrane: Yes, I *do* think that was a good idea, I really do; and I don't think it's dead. It was just something that couldn't be born at that time, but I still think it's a good idea.

Kofsky: This is true in the history of all kinds of organizations in this country—they're not always successful the first time. But I think it's inevitable that musicians are going to try and organize to protect themselves.

Coltrane: Yes.

Kofsky: For example, I was at the Five Spot Monday night, and I figure that there are about a hundred tables in there; and with two people at a table, it comes to about $7.50 a set, at three drinks a set. That means the owner's making $750, say, a set and he has five sets. And I know *the musicians for that night aren't getting anywhere near five times $750, or even two times $750. So actually it turns out that these businessmen are not only damaging the art, but they're even keeping people away.*

Coltrane: Yes, it's putting them uptight, lots of people, man. I feel so *bad* sometimes about people coming to the club and I can't play long enough for them, because, you know, they're hustling you. They come to hear you play and you get up, you have to play a little bit, then split. Something has to be done about it.

Kofsky: Do the musicians who play in these newer styles look to Africa and Asia for some of their musical inspiration?

Coltrane: I think so; I think they look all over. And inside.

Kofsky: Do they look some places more than others? I heard you, for example, talking about making a trip to Africa, to gather musical sources. Is that the idea?

Coltrane: Well, I intend to make a trip to Africa to gather whatever I can find, particularly the musical sources.

Kofsky: Do you think that the musicians are more interested in Africa and Asia than in Europe, as far as the music goes?

Coltrane: Well, the musicians have been exposed to Europe, you see. So it's the other parts that they haven't been exposed to. Speaking for myself, at least, I'm trying to have a rounded education.

Kofsky: Is that the significance of those rhythmic instruments that you've incorporated into your group—to give it a sort of Middle Eastern or African flavor?

Coltrane: Maybe so, it's just something I feel.

Kofsky: Why do you think that the interest in Africa and Asia is growing at this particular time?

Coltrane: Well, it's just time for this to come about, that's all. It's a thing of the times.

Kofsky: Bill Dixon suggested to me that it might have something to do with the fact that many African nations became independent in the 1950s and changed the way Negroes in this country looked at themselves; it made them more aware of the African heritage and made them more interested in going back and looking for it. Do you think there's anything to that line of thought?

Coltrane: Yes, yes, that's part of it.

Kofsky: Another question along the same lines is: it seems that group improvisation is growing in importance—for example, what you do with Pharoah [Sanders] when you're playing simultaneously. And also, of course, Ascension. Do you think that is a new trend now, or not a new trend, but do you think this is growing in importance now?

Coltrane: Well, maybe. It seems to be happening at this time; I don't know how long it's going to last.

Kofsky: Why do you think that's taking place now?

Coltrane: I don't know *why*; it just *is*, that's all.

Kofsky: But it is there—I'm not making something up when I say that?

Coltrane: No, no, I feel it, it's there, but I don't know why.

Kofsky: And another question about the new music: I've noticed that a lot of the new groups are pianoless; or even in your case, where you have a piano, sometimes you'll have the piano lay out during a solo, or during parts of a solo. Why is this coming about at this particular time? Why the desire to de-emphasize the piano or to give it another kind of role in the group?

Coltrane: I still use the piano, and I haven't reached the point where I feel I don't need it. I might, but . . . maybe it's because . . . well, when you're not playing on a given progression, you don't really need it to state these things. And it would get in your way to have somebody going in another direction and you trying to go in another, there it would be better for you not to have it.

Kofsky: It seems that the direction the horns are going in, too, is to get away from the twelve-tone scale—to play notes that really aren't on the piano: the high-pitched notes, the shrieks and screams. I don't know what words you use to describe those sounds, but I think you know what I mean. Sounds that were considered "wrong"—well, still are considered wrong by some people.

Now if you play those notes that really aren't on the piano, and you have the piano there stating notes, do you feel that this gives some kind of a clash that you'd rather avoid?

Coltrane: I suppose that's the way some men feel about it. As I say, I still use the piano. I haven't reached the point yet, where the piano is a drag to me. The only thing is, I don't, we don't *follow* what the piano does any more, because we all move in our own directions. I like it for a backdrop, you know, for its sound.

Kofsky: You do have the piano, though, lay out for a fairly large part of the time.

Coltrane: Well, I always instruct the piano players that whenever they wish they can just lay out and let it go on as it is. Because after a while, lots of times, the pianists, well, they get tired. If you can't think of anything else to play—stroll!

Kofsky: When I talked to you a couple of years ago in Los Angeles and I asked you if you would ever consider adding another horn to the group, you said probably the thing you would do is, if you added anything you would add drums. [Laughter.] Did you have in mind then these kind of things that . . . ?

Coltrane: I don't even know, man, but I guess so. I still feel so strongly about drums, I really do. I feel very strongly about these drums. I experimented in it, but we didn't have too much success. I believe it would have worked, but, Elvin and McCoy [unintelligible].

Kofsky: It doesn't necessarily have to be two drums. It could be drums and another rhythm instrument. That's what I was really referring to.

Coltrane: I think so too. It could come in different forms, shapes; I just don't know how to do it, though.

Kofsky: After all, the things that you're using in the group now—shakers, bells, maracas—are rhythm instruments too. Not all rhythm instruments are drums.

Coltrane: Oh, that's true.

Kofsky: That's what I meant, when I asked you if that's what you had in mind.

Coltrane: Yes.

Kofsky: Speaking of Elvin and McCoy reminds me of something Sun Ra said, and I'll repeat it. I'll make it clear that I don't put any faith in it, but since he said it, and he told me to tell you, I'll pass it along.
    He says that you hired Rashied Ali as a means of driving Elvin and McCoy out of the band, because you didn't want them in the band in the first place, and that was your way of doing it. Do you want to answer that?

Coltrane: No, I don't. I was trying to do something. . . . There was a thing I wanted to do in music, see, and I figured I could do *two* things: I could have a band that played like the way we used to play, and a band that was going in the direction that the one I have now is going in—I could combine these two, with these two concepts going. And it could have been done.

Kofsky: Yes. Sun Ra is quite bitter, and claims that you've stolen all of your ideas from him, and in fact that everybody has stolen all of their ideas from him. [Laughter.]

Coltrane: There may be something to that. I've heard him and I know that he's doing some of the things that I've wanted to do.

Kofsky: How do you feel about having another horn in the group, another saxophone? Do you feel that it in any way competes with you or that it enhances what you're doing?

Coltrane: Well, it helps me. It helps me stay alive sometimes, because physically, man, the pace I've been leading has been so hard and I've gained so much weight, that sometimes it's been a little hard physically. I feel that I like to have somebody there in case I can't get that strength. I like to have that strength in that band, somewhere. And Pharoah is very strong in spirit and will, see, and these are the things that I like to have up there.

Kofsky: Do you feel that spurs you on, the presence especially of a man as powerful as Pharoah?

Coltrane: Yes, all the time, there's always got to be somebody with a lot of power. In the old band, Elvin had this power. I always have to have somebody there, with it, you know?

Rashied has it, but it hasn't quite unfolded completely; all he needs to do is play.

Kofsky: That was my impression, too, that he really was feeling his way ahead in the music and didn't have the confidence Elvin had. But then, of course, look how long Elvin was with you before—

Coltrane: He was there, Elvin was there for a couple of years—although Elvin was ready from the first time I heard him, you know, I could hear the genius there—but he had to start playing steadily, steadily, every night . . . With Miles [Davis] it took me around two and a half years, I think, before it started developing, taking the shape that it was going to take.

Kofsky: That's what's so tragic about the situation of the younger musicians now: they don't have that opportunity to play together.

Coltrane: Yes, it certainly needs to be done. It should be happening all the time and the men would develop sooner.

Kofsky: Don Cherry has a record out, Complete Communion. *I think it's a beautiful record, and one of the reasons I think it's so good is because here he has a group that's worked together for a few months.*

Coltrane: Yeah!

Kofsky: And so he knows how to put something together for all the men—it isn't just a "date."
    Have you listened to many of the other younger saxophonists besides Pharoah?

Coltrane: Yes, Albert Ayler first. I've listened very closely to him. He's something else.

Kofsky: Could you see any relationship between what you were doing and what he was doing? In other words, do you think he has developed out of some of your ideas?

Coltrane: Not necessarily; I think what he's doing, it seems to be moving music into even higher frequencies. Maybe where I left off, maybe where he started, or something.

Kofsky: Well, in a sense, that's what I meant.

Coltrane: Yes. Not to say that he would copy bits and that, but just that he filled an area that it seems I hadn't gotten to.

Kofsky: It seems to me, that your solo on "Chasin' the Trane," that Albert developed some of the ideas that you had put out there and he had expressed some of them in his own ways, and that this was one of the points from which he had begun. Had you ever thought of it in that light?

Coltrane: No. I hadn't.

Kofsky: Did you ever listen to that selection much?

Coltrane: Only at the time it came out, I used to listen to it and wonder what happened to me.

Kofsky: What do you mean?

Coltrane: Well, it's a sort of surprising thing to hear this back because—I don't know, it came back another way.

It was a little longer than I thought it was and it had a fairly good amount of intensity in it, which I hadn't quite gotten into a recording before.

Kofsky: You were pleased with it?

Coltrane: To a degree, not that I could sit there with it and love it forever.

Kofsky: Well, no, you'd never be pleased with anything that you did for longer than a week!

Coltrane: I realized that I'd have to do that or better, you see, and then I—

Kofsky: I think it's a remarkable record and I also think you ought to go back and listen to it.

Coltrane: Maybe so.

Kofsky: Because I don't see any saxophonist now who isn't playing something that you haven't at least sketched out before. But maybe you would rather not think about that.

Coltrane: No, because like it's a big reservoir, that we all dip out of. And a lot of times, you'll find that a lot of those things . . . I listened to John Gilmore kind of closely before I made "Chasin' the Trane," too. So some of those things on there are really direct influences of listening to this cat, you see. But then I don't know who he'd been listening to, so . . .

Kofsky: After "Chasin' the Trane" and then Impressions *came out, you did a sort of change of pace. You remember; you did the album with Duke Ellington and* Ballads, *and the Johnny Hartman album. Whose ideas were these albums? Were they yours, or Bob Thiele's?*

Coltrane: Well, I tell you, I had some trouble at that time. I did a foolish thing. I got dissatisfied with my mouthpiece and I had some work done on this thing, and instead of making it better, it ruined it. It really discouraged me a little bit, because there were certain aspects of playing—that certain fast thing that I was reaching for—that I couldn't get because I had damaged this thing, so I just had to curtail it. Actually, I never found another [mouthpiece], but after so much of this laying around and making these kind of things, I said, well what the hell, I might as well go ahead and do the best I can. But at that moment, it was so vivid in my mind—the difference in what I was getting on the horn—it was so vivid that I couldn't do it. Because as soon as I did, I'd hear it; and it just discouraged me. But after a year or so passed, well, I'd forgotten.

Kofsky: That's funny, because I think I know your music as thoroughly as any nonmusician, yet that wouldn't have been apparent to me.

Coltrane: That's a funny thing. That's one of the mysteries. And to me, as soon as I put that horn in my mouth, I could hear it. It feels, you know . . . I just stopped and went into other things.

Kofsky: The reason I asked that was because I recall that was the time you had Eric [Dolphy] in and out of the band.

Coltrane: Yes.

Kofsky: And there was a whole wave of really hostile criticism.

Coltrane: Yes, and all of this was at the same time, so you see how it was. I needed all the strength I could have at that time; and maybe some of these things might have caused me to feel, "Well, man, I can't get what I want out of this mouthpiece, so I'll work on it."

Kofsky: You think this might have undermined your self-confidence?

Coltrane: It could have, it certainly could have.

Kofsky: Why do you think there's been all this hostility to the new music, especially in your case?

Coltrane: Oh, man, I never could figure it out! I couldn't even venture to answer it now. Because as I told them then, I just felt that they didn't understand.

Kofsky: *Do you think they were making as conscientious and thorough an attempt to understand as they could have?*

Coltrane: At the time I didn't feel they were, because I did offer them, in an article in *Down Beat,* that if any of you men were interested in trying to understand, let's get together and let's talk about it, you know? I thought if they were really genuinely interested or felt there was something here, that instead of just condemning what you don't know about, if you want to discuss it, let's talk about it. But no one ever came forth, so I don't think they wanted to know what I had to say about it. [Laughter.]

Kofsky: *I think it frightened them. Bill Dixon and I talked about this at great length; and he said: "Well, these guys, it's taken them years to pick out 'I Got Rhythm' on the piano." And now the new music comes along and undermines their entire career, which is built around understanding things based on those patterns.*

Coltrane: Yes, I dug it like that too. I said, "Well, this could be a real drag to a cat if he figures this is something that he won't be able to cope with and he won't be able to write about." If he can't write about it he can't make a living at this; and then I realized that, so I quieted down. I wouldn't allow myself to become too hostile in return. Although there was a time I kind of froze up on those people at *Down Beat.* I felt that there was something there that wasn't—I felt that they were letting their weakness direct their actions, which I didn't feel they should have. The test, was for me. They could do what they wanted to do. The thing was for me to remain firm in what I was doing. That was a funny period in my life, because I went through quite a few changes, you know, like home life—everything, man, I just went through so many . . . everything I was doing.

Kofsky: *The perfect wrong time to hit you!*

Coltrane: Everything I was doing was like that, it was a hell of a test for me, and it was coming out of it, it was just like I always said, man:

when you go through these crises and you come out of them, you're definitely stronger, in a great sense.

Kofsky: Did the reaction of Impulse to these adverse criticisms have anything to do with those records that we talked about?

Coltrane: The ballads and that?

Kofsky: Yes.

Coltrane: Well, I don't know. I think Impulse was interested in having what they might call a balanced sort of thing, a diversified sort of catalog, and I find nothing wrong with this myself. You see, I like—in fact most of the songs that I even write now, the ones that I even consider songs, are ballads. So there's something there, that I mean I really love these things.

And these ballads that came out were definitely ones which I felt at this time. I chose them; it seemed to be something that was laying around in my mind—from my youth, or somewhere—and I just had to do them. They came at this time, when the confidence in what I was doing on the horn had flagged, it seemed to the time to clean that out. And Johnny Hartman—a man that I had stuck up in my mind somewhere—I just felt something about him, I don't know what it was. I liked his sound, I thought there was something there I had to hear, so I looked him up and did that album. Really, I don't regret doing those things at all.

The only thing I regret was not having kept that same attitude, which was: I'm going to do, no matter what. That was the attitude in the beginning, but as I say, there were a whole lot of reasons why these things happened.

Kofsky: Do you think that learning how to play the soprano changed your style?

Coltrane: Definitely, definitely. It certainly did.

Kofsky: How so? Could you spell it out?

Coltrane: Well, the soprano, by being this small instrument, I found that playing the lowest note on it was like playing one of the middle notes on the tenor—so therefore, after I got so that my embouchure would allow me to make the upper notes, I found that I would play *all over* this instrument. On tenor, I hadn't always played all over it, because I was playing certain ideas which just went in certain ranges, octaves. But by playing on the soprano and becoming accustomed to playing on tenor from that low B-flat on up, it soon got so that when I went to tenor, I found myself doing the same thing. It caused the change or the willingness to change and just try to play as much of the instrument as possible.

Kofsky: Did it give you a new rhythmic conception too?

Coltrane: I think so, I think so. A new shape came out of this thing and patterns—the way the patterns—would fall.

Kofsky: It seemed to me that after you started playing soprano, and particularly after My Favorite Things, *then you started feeling that same kind of a pulse on the tenor that hadn't been there in your work before.*

Coltrane: I think that's quite possible. In fact, the patterns started—the patterns were one of the things I started getting dissatisfied with on the tenor mouthpiece, because the sound of the soprano was actually so much closer to me in my ear. There's something about the presence of that sound, that to me—I didn't want to admit it—but to me it would seem like it was better than the tenor—I liked it more. I didn't want to admit this damn thing, because I said the tenor's my horn, it is my favorite. But this soprano, maybe it's just the fact that it's a higher instrument, it started pulling my conception.

Kofsky: How do you feel about the two horns now?

Coltrane: Well, the tenor is the power horn, definitely; but soprano, there's still something there in just the voice of it that's really beautiful, something that I really like.

Kofsky: Do you regard the soprano as an extension of the tenor?

Coltrane: Well, at first I did, but now, it's another voice, it's another sound.

Kofsky: Did you ever use the two horns on the same piece, as you did on "Spiritual"?

Coltrane: I think that's the only time I've done that. Sometimes in clubs, if I feel good, I might do something like this—start on one and end on another—but I think that's the only one on record.

Kofsky: What prompted Pharoah to take up the alto? Was that to get away from—two tenors?

Coltrane: I don't know. This is something he wanted to do, and about the same time I decided I wanted to get one, so we both got one.

Kofsky: I haven't heard you play the alto. Do you play it much?

Coltrane: I played it in Japan. I played it in Frisco a little bit, but I've had a little trouble with the intonation of it. It's a Japanese make, it's a new thing they're trying out, so they gave us these horns to try, and mine has to be adjusted at certain points where it's not quite in tune, so I don't play it, but I like it.

Kofsky: I saw a picture of you with a flute! Are you playing that too now?

Coltrane: I'm learning.

Kofsky: You're always learning, aren't you?

Coltrane: I hope so. Always trying to learn.

Kofsky: I looked at the Down Beat *and* Jazz Critics Polls *two years in a row, and both years, this and last year, I noticed that European critics are much more in favor of the new music than the Americans. Almost 50 percent or 60 percent of them would vote for new musicians, whereas, say only about a quarter of the Americans. Is this what you found in Europe?—or in general, have you found outside the United States that your music is more favorably received by the critics, the power structure, shall we say, than in the U.S.?*

Coltrane: I'd say in the new music—and when I say new music, I mean most of the younger musicians that are starting out—I know that they definitely have found a quicker acceptance in Europe than they have here. When I started, it was a little different, because I started through Miles Davis, who was an accepted musician, and they got used to me here in the States. Now when they first heard me with Miles here, they did not like it.

Kofsky: I remember.

Coltrane: So it's just one of those things: everything that they haven't heard yet and that's a little different, they are going to reject it at first. But the time will roll around, the time when they will like it. Now, by being here with Miles and running around the country with him, they heard more of me here, and consequently they began to accept it before they did in Europe, because they hadn't heard me in Europe. When we went to Europe the first time, it was a shock to them there. They booed me and everything in Paris, because they just weren't with it. But now I find, the last time I was in Europe, it seems that the new music—they've really opened up. They can hear it there better than they do here.

Kofsky: I think that part of this is because what's happening in the new music is analogous to what's happened in painting, say, and sculpture and literature; and the people who appreciate jazz in Europe are much more aware of this. What do you think of this?

Coltrane: Well, I don't know.

Kofsky: In Europe jazz is regarded as a serious art, whereas here, it's regarded as, well . . .

Coltrane: Whatever it is.

Kofsky: As part of the nightclub business. Otherwise, you couldn't have a magazine like Down Beat.
    I know Albert [Ayler] is going back to Europe, and I know that there are many of the younger musicians who want to get away from the States because they just don't feel there's any hope for them here.

Do you remember Third Stream Music, what was called Third Stream Music?

Coltrane: Yes.

Kofsky: Did you ever feel much of an inner urge to play that kind of music?

Coltrane: No.

Kofsky: Why do you think it didn't catch on with the musicians? Was there anything about it that suggests why it was never popular with them?

Coltrane: I think it was an attempt to create something, I think, more with labels, you see than true evolution.

Kofsky: You mean, it didn't evolve naturally out of the desires of the musicians?

Coltrane: Maybe it did; I can't say that. It was an attempt to do something, and evolution is about trying too. But there's something in evolution—it just happens when it's ready, but this thing wasn't really where it was coming from. What was it—an attempt to blend, to wed two musics? That's what it really was.

Kofsky: You said, talking about saxophone players, that there was a common pool that everybody dipped into. Maybe here, there wasn't enough of that pool for the musicians to dip in to.

Coltrane: Well, I just think it wasn't time. It was an attempt to do something at a time when it wasn't time for this to happen, and therefore it wasn't lasting. But there may have been some things that came out of this that have been beneficial in promoting the final change, which is coming. So nothing is really wasted, although it might appear to fail or not succeed the way that men would have desired it to.

Kofsky: Even the mistakes can be instructive if you try to use them.
Do you make any attempt, or do you feel that you should make any

attempt, to educate your audience in ways that aren't strictly musical? That is, it's obvious that you want your audience to understand what you're doing musically. But do you feel that you want them to understand other things, too, and that you have some kind of responsibility for it?

Coltrane: Sure, I feel this, and this is one of the things I am concerned about now. I just don't know how to go about this. I want to find out just how I should do it. I think it's going to have to be very subtle; you can't ram philosophies down anybody's throat, and the music is enough! That's philosophy. I think the best thing I can do at this time is to try to get myself in shape and know myself. If I can do that, then I'll just play, you see, and leave it at that. I believe that will do it, if I really can get to myself and be just as I feel I should be and play it. And I think they'll get it, because music goes a long way—it can influence.

Kofsky: That's how I got interested in those things I was talking about earlier, Malcolm X. I might not have come to it, or come to it as fast, if it hadn't been for the music. That was my first introduction to something beyond my own horizons, that would make me think about the world I was living in.

Coltrane: Yes. That's what I'm sure of, man, I'm really sure of this thing. As I say, there are things which as far as spirituality is concerned, which is very important to me at this time, I've got to grow through certain phases of this to other understanding and more consciousness and awareness of just what it is that I'm supposed to understand about it; and I'm sure others will be part of the music. To me, you know, I feel I want to be a force for good.

Kofsky: And the music too?

Coltrane: Everywhere. You know, I want to be a force for real good. In other words, I know that there are bad forces, forces put here that bring suffering to others and misery to the world, but I want to be the force which is truly for good.

Kofsky: I don't have any more of my prepared questions to ask you—or my improvised questions to ask you. [Laughter.] I had a lot of questions here that were related just to you. Many of those questions about music

I don't ask of the other musicians; but I've always had a very special interest in your work, so I took this opportunity, since I don't know when I'll ever get the chance to get you down on tape again.

Do you have anything else that you'd like to get on here?

Coltrane: I think we just about covered it, I believe, just about covered it.

[As John drove me back to the station, the tape recorder was left on and we continued to talk. After some humorous exchanges, the conversation turned to the proper function of a jazz writer or critic.]

Kofsky: If you can't play the music, and if you're going to write about it, you have, I think, an obligation to do it as conscientiously as possible.

Coltrane: Yes, I believe it, man.

Kofsky: And always when it's a question of your opinion versus the musician's opinion, to give the benefit of the doubt to the musician, because he knows the music far better than you'll ever know it. In other words, you have to be humble. A lot of writers aren't humble; they get arrogant because they think they have some kind of power.

Coltrane: Well, that's one of the main causes of this arrogance—the idea of power. Then you lose your true power, which is to be part of all, and the only way you can be part of all is to understand it. And when there's something you don't understand, you have to go humbly to it. You don't go to school and sit down and say, "I know what you're getting ready to teach me." You sit there and you learn. You open your mind. You absorb. But you have to be quiet, you have to be still to do all of this.

Kofsky: That's what so annoyed me about all of that stuff they were saying about you in '61.

Coltrane: Oh, that was terrible. I couldn't believe it, you know, it just seemed so preposterous. It was so ridiculous, man, that's what bugs me. It was absolutely ridiculous, because they made it appear that we didn't even know the first thing about music—the first thing. And there we were really trying to push things off.

Kofsky: Because they never stand still.

Coltrane: Eric [Dolphy], man, as sweet as this cat was and the musician that he was—it hurt me to see him get hurt in this thing.

Kofsky: Do you think that this possibly contributed to the fact that he died so young?

Coltrane: I don't know, but Eric was a strong cat. Nobody knows what caused it. The way he passed, there was a mystery about it.

Kofsky: I didn't mean that it was directly the cause, but—

Coltrane: Indirectly?

Kofsky: Yes.

Coltrane: Yes. The whole scene, man. He couldn't work . . .

Kofsky: That's what I meant, really.

Coltrane: He always seemed to be a very cheerful young man, so I don't *think* that would put him . . . I don't think so, because he had an outlook on life which was very, very good—optimistic, and he had this sort of thing, friendliness, you know, a real friend to everyone. He was the type of man who could be as much a friend to a guy he'd just met today as he was to one he'd known for ten years. This kind of person, I don't think it would really hurt him to the point where he would do something to hurt himself consciously or unconsciously.

Kofsky: Yes. That friendliness was one of the things that has impressed me about the musicians here. I really didn't expect to be greeted with open arms, because I am an outsider, after all. And yet I have been amazed constantly at how eager the musicians were to cooperate when they decided that I was sincere and that this wasn't a joke or a con or something of that nature.

Coltrane: I think all we need is sincerity, empathy. . . . I think I want to get closer to town. Maybe there's something I can do in music. Get a place, a little room to play in. I don't want a loft, but maybe there's something I can get to play in, just some place to be able to work in.

Kofsky: Where do you play at home?

Coltrane: Anywhere. There's a room over the garage that I'm getting fixed now and I think it's going to be my practice room. You never know. Sometimes you build a little room and it ends up you're still going in the toilet. I hope I like it, but . . . I keep a horn on the piano and I have a horn in my bedroom—a flute usually back there, because when I go there I'm tired and I lay down and practice.

Kofsky: About how many hours a day do you play?

Coltrane: Not too much at this time. I find that it's only when something is trying to come through that I really practice. And then I don't even know how many hours—it's all day, on and off. But at this time there's nothing coming out now.

Kofsky: I was very surprised to hear you practicing at all, because I just couldn't conceive of what you could find to practice! But I know it isn't like that.

Coltrane: I *need* to practice. It's just that I want something to practice, and I'm trying to find out what it is that I want, an area that I want to get into.

PART THREE

Coltrane's Recording Career

John Coltrane recorded for many labels between 1949 and 1967, but the great majority of his work was made for three labels—Prestige, Atlantic, and Impulse. Early in his career Coltrane recorded for Prestige in large part because the label was ready and willing to record him frequently under the leadership of others and as a leader himself. As he discontinued his freelance work and turned to recording only as a leader, Coltrane signed with Atlantic and later with Impulse, labels that benefited artistically from Coltrane's desire to record more of his own compositions than he had been willing to do with Prestige. Impulse producer Bob Thiele was willing to record Coltrane projects quite often, far exceeding Impulse's typical pace of two albums per year. Many of these sessions were released after Coltrane's death, and indeed, previously unreleased material is still being issued today.

CARL WOIDECK
THE PRESTIGE COLTRANE SESSIONS
Adapted from John Coltrane: The Prestige Recordings, *Prestige Records, 1991*

Prestige was the first company to record John Coltrane extensively and the first to record him as a leader. He came to the company as part of Miles Davis's quintet, which recorded for Prestige from 1955 to 1956. Soon, Coltrane was recording for Prestige under the leadership of others, and this employment proved very important to Coltrane and his family. Most of his freelance recording was done for Prestige, and signing with that label to also record as a leader made it easy for him to continue a very active recording schedule.—CW

Between 1955 when he joined the Miles Davis quintet and 1960 when he formed his "classic" quartet, John Coltrane recorded for at least fourteen companies. Of all these, Prestige holds by far the largest share of his work during this period. Because Coltrane recorded so often for Prestige (at one point even daily) and in so many settings (as a so-called "sideman," co-leader and leader), these recordings constitute the most substantial document of the evolution of Coltrane's art during this pivotal stage. John Coltrane was available for virtually any recording session, and found himself in ensembles ranging from sympathetic and appropriate to indifferent and unlikely. In each case, Coltrane soloed with conviction and seriousness whether the musical material was challenging or undistinguished, well-planned or put together at the actual session.

Prestige owner Bob Weinstock wished to produce as much material as possible from each recording date. Since musicians were commonly paid by the session (not by the LP), Weinstock requested that valuable time not be wasted in recording alternate takes when that time could be used in recording additional selections. The material thus produced could be spread over several LPs, instead of just one. Unlike the Blue Note label (which paid for rehearsals before recording dates) and the Riverside label (which often took two days to record an LP), the Prestige system led to uneven results. Material simple enough to be learned on the spot tended to be commonplace or simplified (e.g., many versions of the blues and "I Got Rhythm" variants). To address this problem, a musician (such as Mal Waldron) was often designated as musical director for a date and assigned to write original compositions (often based on "standards" and the blues) and dress them up in simple arrangements for the varied and sometimes baffling instrumental combinations found on Prestige sessions. Ironically, the more interesting the arrangement and chord changes, the more likely a composition needed the unavailable extra time for the musicians to become familiar with it.

1955

On November 11th, 1955, Miles Davis first brought his group with John Coltrane to Rudy Van Gelder's studio to record for Prestige an album to be titled *The New Miles Davis Quintet*. (Columbia records had already clandestinely recorded the group, but since Davis was still under contract to Prestige, those earlier recordings could not be issued right away.) Although the group is now legendary, it was not universally appreciated at first and Coltrane took the lion's share of criticism. [See the introduction and actual review of *The New Miles Davis Quintet* on page 225 of this anthology.]

This first Davis-Coltrane Prestige session is quite relaxed in mood and tempo. On some tracks, such as "How Am I to Know?," Coltrane has problems maintaining improvisational continuity; sometimes his intonation varies from register to register. Coltrane's timbre (tone color), already personal, is not as warm as it would become and is sometimes a bit brittle (although not nearly as much as in the earlier Columbia recordings which seem to suffer from poor recording techniques). Despite these inconsistencies, Coltrane already shows considerable individuality in his approach to melodic line. From a continuity standpoint, one of Coltrane's best solos is on "Just Squeeze Me," which includes some relaxed and swinging improvisation. The rapid lines in his solo on "The Theme" (based on the chord progression of "I Got Rhythm") occasionally give a preview of Coltrane's growing tendency to double-time when possible.

1956

John Coltrane recorded a total of eleven sessions (including four with Miles Davis) for various labels during 1956, up from only two in 1955 (both with Davis). Clearly, his work with Miles was bringing him recognition and the beginnings of demand for his already individual style. Coltrane's first non–Miles Davis session for Prestige was Elmo Hope's May 7th *Informal Jazz* date.

A few days later, on May 11th, the Miles Davis quintet returned to the Van Gelder studio for the first of two marathon sessions for Prestige. Columbia definitely wanted to sign Davis, but Davis first had to fulfill the terms of his Prestige contract by giving them material to fill several more LPs. (The second extended Prestige session was on October 26th, 1956; both sessions will be discussed here together.) The idea was to record their repertoire as if they were in a nightclub, with no second takes. Most of the material recorded on those two dates was released on the LPs *Workin'*, *Steamin'*, *Relaxin'*, and *Cookin'*. Coltrane's timbre seems to have broadened, and, by Coltrane's own statement, working regularly with the Davis group had helped Coltrane develop his improvisational art. Coltrane's solo on Dizzy Gillespie's "Woody 'n' You" from *Relaxin'* is a good example of how Coltrane was both finding his artistic voice and was becoming more articulate at getting his message across. Although there are some moments of discontinuity (after all, Coltrane is trying for new things), Coltrane's approach to melody and harmony is coming into focus and is clearly distinct from his modern jazz influences Charlie Parker, Dexter Gordon, and Sonny Stitt. "Trane's Blues" (aka "John Paul Jones") from *Workin'* was possibly the first example of Coltrane's blues playing to be released. Charlie Parker's influence was becoming more diffuse, and Coltrane was finding his own way to play the blues. "You're My Everything" from *Relaxin'* likewise was probably the first-released example of Coltrane's ballad playing to be heard by the public. His tenderness and lyricism contrasts with his growing reputation as a hard-blowing saxophonist.

Historically significant was tenor saxophonist Sonny Rollins's May 24th *Tenor Madness* session which included Coltrane on the LP's title composition. This performance presents in bold relief the distinctions between the younger Rollins whose influence was at an early peak and the slightly older Coltrane whose style was just then coalescing. The two were not strangers, having both worked with Miles Davis around 1949 or 1950. In J. C. Thomas's *Chasin' the Trane*, saxophonist Paul Jeffrey remembered a two-tenor encounter later in 1956:

> I saw Coltrane and Rollins at the Bohemia in late 1956, and this was one of the times Sonny Rollins and Trane both played with Miles. I knew Sonny's style, but Trane really surprised me. . . . Coltrane more than held his own. He followed Sonny's melodic solos with some of the strangest, most convoluted harmonies and chord progressions I'd ever heard.

Rollins borrowed Miles's rhythm section for the date, and brought along Coltrane to the Rudy Van Gelder studios as a guest. Coltrane's opening notes contain some of the Dexter Gordon–influenced darkness that was apparent in his 1951 work with Dizzy Gillespie, but most of his solo features the brighter and more streamlined sound of his mature work. In contrast with Coltrane, Rollins has a much grittier sound and attacks his notes more aggressively. While equally capable, Rollins double-times less than Coltrane and in general does not turn this into a fierce "cutting contest." Although this track is now considered a classic, Nat Hentoff in a 1956 *Down Beat* review called it "the least effective in the album" and suggested it "mars what would have been an interestingly balanced all-

Rollins LP." Hentoff, it should be noted, became over time a strong adherent of Coltrane's playing.

Tenor Conclave from September 7th was one of Prestige's many leaderless all-star dates, and brought together four very different saxophonists (Al Cohn, Coltrane, Hank Mobley, and Zoot Sims) of approximately the same generation. The session consists of two pop songs and two original melodies based on common chord progressions, all arranged simply and with a minimum of frills. Hank Mobley's "F" blues "Bob's Boys" (based on the chords to Charlie Parker's "Blues for Alice") is a good example of both how different the saxophonists' styles were and also how cooperative they could be. Coltrane leads off with five blues choruses, followed by four each from Cohn, Mobley, and Sims in that order.

Composer-arranger Tadd Dameron's November 30th quartet recording *Mating Call* was John Coltrane's last studio date of 1956. Unencumbered by other horn soloists, Coltrane rose to the challenge of five Dameron original compositions and a themeless blues. "Soultrane" is a ballad that shows off Coltrane's luscious upper register. During his solo, Coltrane follows drummer Philly Joe Jones's lead into some tasty double-timing. This session marks the first recording of Dameron's "On a Misty Night." From the first note of the introduction, Coltrane makes the song his own, again using his silky high notes to great effect.

1957

This was to be a pivotal year for John Coltrane. After leaving the Miles Davis quintet, Coltrane went home to Philadelphia, stopped taking heroin, stopped drinking alcohol, and re-dedicated himself to music, as he recalled in the liner notes to his record *A Love Supreme:* "During the year 1957, I experienced, by the grace of God, a spiritual awakening which was to lead me to a richer, fuller, more productive life." He returned to New York City not only more in demand for recordings, but also more able to execute the ideas he was hearing. 1957 was also the year that Coltrane worked extensively with pianist-composer Thelonious Monk. Coltrane called Monk "a musical architect of the highest order" and spoke of his great influence. After returning to the studios in March, Coltrane would record at least once in every remaining month of the year, twenty-two separate dates in all. Significantly, he also recorded his first LPs as a leader in 1957.

John Coltrane's overdue first date as sole leader took place on May 31st, and produced an LP titled simply *Coltrane*. Reportedly, Miles Davis had urged Coltrane to sign with a label other than Prestige, preferably Blue Note. With his Prestige contract, Coltrane got adequate terms and had to publish his compositions with the in-house publishing company, but was able to continue his steady Prestige freelance schedule without any contractual conflicts. After his being hamstrung in so many weak or ill-conceived sessions as a Prestige sideman, it's interesting to see just how Coltrane conceived of and executed his own session. This was to be a split date with one basic sextet instrumentation (with three horns) for the first half, and a quartet for the second. Up to this point, Coltrane had recorded only three of his own compositions, and how much writing he had been doing is unknown.

Coltrane's "Straight Street" (not to be confused with the gospel song of the same title and similar sentiment by the Pilgrim Travelers) is a well-developed composition in twelve-bar sections with a straightforward arrangement. It comes as no surprise that Coltrane of all the soloists is most at home with its chromatic chord progression. During this period, Coltrane often quoted the melody of Bronislaw (Bronislav) Kaper's "While My Lady Sleeps," and on this album the saxophonist finally recorded the actual composition. This is the first of three Kaper compositions that Coltrane would record in the next fourteen months ("On Green Dolphin Street," recorded with Miles Davis and "Invitation," discussed below, being the other two). Coltrane finishes the performance with his first recorded multiphonic (the playing of several notes at once on a wind instrument). Coltrane credited saxophonist John Glenn and pianist Thelonious Monk for showing him the technique. "Chronic Blues" is a riff-based Coltrane minor blues in which the composer solos in a driving manner with some fresh moments.

At this point in the session, the other two wind players sat out and pianist Mal Waldron was replaced by Red Garland, Coltrane's once and future band-mate in the Miles Davis group. This combination marked the beginning of a series of successful recordings that Garland and Coltrane would make together for Prestige. "Violets for Your Furs" is a Tom Adair song much favored by singers. Coltrane's approach to ballad playing seems to derive in part from Charlie Parker's (such as the 1947 Dial recordings of "Embraceable You" and "My Old Flame"). Both "Time Was" and "I Hear a Rhapsody" are played as medium swingers with stop-time breaks leading into Coltrane's solos. In each case, he sounds relaxed and improvises inventively chorus after chorus.

After the above session, Coltrane joined Thelonious Monk's quartet for a summer residence at the Five Spot Café in New York City. (This group's three studio recordings may be found on the Riverside CD *Thelonious Monk with John Coltrane*. Their live recordings are on the Blue Note CD *Live at the Five Spot Discovery!*) In nightclubs, Monk regularly "strolled" (temporarily stopped accompanying), leaving Coltrane to solo with only bass and drums for support. That experience served Coltrane well on his next session as a leader.

Coltrane's August 16th date (most of which was eventually included on his LP *Lush Life*) was planned as a quartet session, but Coltrane, Earl May, and Art Taylor were left with studio time when the pianist didn't show up. They evidently took the change of plan in stride; the excellence of the few pieces recorded that day makes one wish for more from this trio. In 1957, Coltrane was the most explicitly "vertical" saxophonist in all of jazz, and his almost compulsive arpeggiation of chords during improvisation nearly usurped the role of a pianist when one was present. This underrated trio session gives us a chance to grasp the state of his harmonic art, especially in terms of outlining substitute changes and passing chords. In a few years, Coltrane's pianist McCoy Tyner would regularly stroll with the saxophonist's blessing in live performances.

Although they have different titles, "Trane's Slo Blues" and "Slowtrane" are that rare Prestige item: alternate takes of the same piece. Both share the same riff melody, follow the same sequence of events and stand on their own as performances. The former was issued first (on *Lush Life*) and is taken at a slightly faster tempo. It is notable for its alternation of double-time runs and funkier passages, and contains particularly striking stop-time sections after Art Taylor's solo. The latter title is taken at an even more leisurely clip, and when Taylor implies double-time on his hi-hat cymbal, Coltrane responds with some passages that are in effect in quadruple-time. From its unaccompanied introduction to its final cadenza, "Like Someone in Love" is nothing short of a Coltrane masterpiece. Coltrane treats the melody statement tenderly even when he's indulging in rapid arpeggiated asides, and his solo outlines a wonderful arc of tension-and-release. Like many of his ballad performances, this one reveals new facets over many repeated listenings. Cole Porter's "I Love You" is given a Latin-and-swing arrangement and includes some furious Coltrane passages.

John Coltrane's second album to be released (*Traneing In*) was recorded on the 23rd of August, and paired him once again with Red Garland. A versatile soloist and accompanist, Red could play boppish lines, soulful blues licks, block chords, or lush harmonies. He was also a great section player who was always looking for rhythmic back-up patterns to play in unison with the drums. As would be the norm, Coltrane and Garland chose drummer Art Taylor over their Miles Davis bandmate Philly Joe Jones, whether due to personal preference or due to Jones's conflict with Bob Weinstock.

The session began unusually with a ballad, "You Leave Me Breathless" that has Coltrane stating the melody and improvising later for a half-chorus. "Bass Blues" is a riff head in "A♭" played by sax and bass. Its key even makes the versatile Coltrane think twice. There's nothing soft about the breakneck tempo of "Soft Lights and Sweet Music." Even if the speed is at Garland's limit, Coltrane, of course, excels. The two also engage in a couple of choruses of stimulating eight-bar trades. "Traneing In" is a "blues with a bridge" in a 12-12-8-12 form. After Red sets up the groove à la Count Basie, Coltrane begins his solo with restraint, then builds wonderfully. "Slow Dance" is another in the series of Prestige Coltrane ballads, with Chambers and Garland getting most of the solo space.

Between *Traneing In* and his next Prestige session, Coltrane recorded an LP that would become a milestone both in his career and in jazz history. The record featured four outstanding and imaginatively-arranged Coltrane compositions played by an exceptional and well-rehearsed sextet. The LP was titled *Blue Train*, and, significantly, it was recorded for the Blue Note label, not for Prestige. [Coltrane's work on this session is discussed by Zita Carno in "The Style of John Coltrane" on page 7 of this anthology.] Stories differ slightly as to how and why Coltrane was able to record as a leader for another label, but in essence, he obtained a release and appeared "courtesy of Prestige Records." The quality and uniqueness of the Coltrane compositions on *Blue Train* make one wonder how many such pieces he had ready that were too challenging to be quickly recorded under Prestige's no-rehearsal policy. Coltrane continued to make fine records for Prestige, of course, but they tended to be straightforward "head arrangement" dates, and no more true Coltrane compositions would be heard among them (he would record two themeless improvisations and credit himself as composer).

Red Garland soon launched into a pair of November-December quintet dates with identical personnel. The fifteen titles that were produced (found primarily on the Garland LPs *All Mornin' Long, Soul Junction,* and *High Pressure*) were of very high quality. Garland and Coltrane were joined by trumpeter Donald Byrd, bassist George Joyner (now Jamil Nasser), and drummer Art Taylor. The repertoire chosen by Red was quite traditional and therefore ideal for the informal nature of these dates. Four of the selections were by jazz writers of the Swing era, and three were tried-and-true pop standards. Five compositions were of the still-current bebop style (after all, Charlie Parker had only been dead about two years), although none of these had been written after 1951. The only "original" selections were riff and themeless blues by Garland. (A total of five blues of various types were recorded during the November 15th and December 13th sessions.)

Space allows only a few of the highlights of this well-knit and democratic session to be discussed here. Red's brilliant re-arrangement of Gershwin's "They Can't Take That Away from Me" features a head with rhythm section accents and some re-harmonization, with fine solos all around. "All Morning Long" is a twenty-minute-long drink of the blues with a memorable stop-time opening to Coltrane's solo. On "Undecided," the ensemble thins out briefly to only Coltrane and Joyner who together produce some of the most intensely swinging passages. Garland the soloist develops a steamroller-like momentum before setting up Coltrane's entrance with strong block-chords on "Soft Winds" (much like McCoy Tyner would a few years later).

1958

John Coltrane had re-joined the Miles Davis group in late 1957, and Coltrane entered 1958 still busy as a free-lance artist. He recorded more sessions than ever under his own name, however, and was perhaps more selective about the sideman gigs he accepted: only one of these involved a large "all-star" blowing date. Of his twenty officially-recorded sessions of 1958, five were with Miles Davis, and six were under Coltrane's name. The first session of 1958 was a January 3rd Gene Ammons octet date (originally issued as *The Big Sound* and *Groove Blues*) with Mal Waldron serving as pianist, composer, and musical director. Reportedly, the original instrumentation was to include only three saxophones: Ammons, Coltrane, and Adams. When Gene's arrival from out of town was in doubt, Quinichette was booked to replace Ammons. Ammons did get to the studio in time, though, and Quinichette stayed on for three numbers. This date is unique because it is the only commercially-recorded session with Coltrane soloing on alto saxophone. Coltrane may have been originally slated to play tenor (Ira Gitler believes Coltrane's tenor was in the shop), or Waldron may have an alto-tenor-baritone front line in mind from the beginning. At any rate, Ira Gitler loaned Coltrane his horn—an alto—and the session proceeded.

Coltrane's approach to alto is not very different from his tenor style; in fact, there are times when it sounds like his tenor just keeps going up higher and higher. He plays the alto with something between abandon and mania, and occasionally seems to overshoot some of his upper target notes. Jazz historian Lewis Porter recently followed a lead from Phil Schaap and located privately-recorded sides of John Coltrane playing alto sax in 1946 while in the Navy (one selection, "Hot House," has been released on the Coltrane CD set *The Last Giant*.) It's interesting to compare these two groups of solos recorded twelve years apart. On the early sides, the nineteen-year-old Coltrane is caught between his Johnny Hodges and Charlie Parker influences, and is still learning the basics of saxophone technique and harmony. The thirty-one-year-old Coltrane shows few Parker influences and is both virtuosic in technique and encyclopedic in harmonic knowledge. Although Parker had been dead only about three years, Coltrane had built upon Parker's approach until it was transformed into a recognizably new way of looking at melody and harmony.

A week later (January 10th), Coltrane was reunited with Red Garland and Donald Byrd for a Quintet session under Coltrane's name. Material from the date was issued on three LPs. The bassist was John's and Red's bandmate from the Miles Davis band, Paul Chambers. As usual, the repertoire consisted of pop music standards and original jazz compositions. Billy Strayhorn's "Lush Life" (found on the album *Lush Life*) was at the time seldom performed by modern jazz musicians, perhaps because it was not easily molded into a vehicle for improvisation. Its chromatic chord progression demanded study, and its form suggested that the verse be played before launching into the chorus. Coltrane and company explore the ballad sympathetically and at length. This recording, and Coltrane's later version with singer Johnny Hartman, helped to keep the song current for the next generation of musicians and listeners. John Coltrane had met fellow Philadelphian McCoy Tyner in 1956, and the two had become friends. Pianist Tyner's blues waltz "The Believer" (found on the LP *The Believer*) has a chromatic set of changes that really come alive when Coltrane works out on them. Red Garland gets clearly lost during his solo, a problem that could have been avoided by more rehearsal or a re-take, both unlikely under the Prestige system.

Coltrane, Garland, and Chambers entered the Van Gelder studios again on February 7th for a quartet date that produced the Coltrane LP *Soultrane*. It was a well-conceived and well-executed session that produced exactly enough material for one LP. The selection of compositions was balanced and included two ballads, two medium swingers and one up-tempo wailer. The only lullaby feeling left in this arrangement of Irving Berlin's "Russian Lullaby" is found in Garland's solo introduction and Coltrane's brief coda. In between is an exhilarating sprint reminding one of how Coltrane did some of his freshest and least formulaic work in minor keys. This was, by the way, the performance that inspired Ira Gitler's first use of the term "sheets of sound" to describe Coltrane's approach to melodic line. "Theme for Ernie" was dedicated by Philadelphian Fred Lacey to the recently deceased alto saxophonist Ernie Henry. Coltrane embraces the melody in a respectful way perhaps derived from his former bandleader, Johnny Hodges. (In *Jazz Styles*, Mark Gridley compared the two: "Coltrane's scale-wise lead-in to a dramatically placed high note is analogous to the long, drawn-out smear [portamento] that was a trademark of the Hodges approach.") Early versions of Coltrane playing Tadd Dameron's "Good Bait" may be heard in bootleg recordings of 1951 Dizzy Gillespie broadcasts. On those, Coltrane reveals much of his Dexter Gordon influence in tone and attack. Seven years later, however, Coltrane is his own artist on this version of "Good Bait" displaying a brighter sound, more legato phrasing and a faster internal rhythmic "clock." Billy Eckstine's "I Want to Talk About You" is perhaps the masterpiece of the session, and one of Coltrane's finest ballad performances of all time. Coltrane liked Eckstine's song so much that he kept it in his repertoire until the mid-1960s, lengthening the cadenza to breathtaking proportions. Coltrane placed the piece in concert "E♭," (up from the original "D♭") which required him to begin the melody on the highest note of his saxophone and eventually take it a half-step into his altissimo range. Not to be missed are the wonderful tension-building tremolos that Garland plays behind Coltrane's first sixteen solo measures.

Kenny Burrell's March 7th session for New Jazz (*Kenny Burrell and John Coltrane*) marked Coltrane's last session as a "sideman" for the Prestige company. It was a reunion for Coltrane, Flanagan, and Burrell, who had recorded together for the same label in April of 1957. No big egos are evident in this easy-going record date that includes three original compositions and two standard popular songs.

On March 26th, John Coltrane led a quartet featuring Red Garland into the Van Gelder studios. He chose to record three standards, one original jazz composition and one improvisation on the blues. Coltrane's love of American popular song can be seen in his regularly finding excellent and under-recorded pop songs that lent themselves to jazz. Most of this session appeared on Coltrane's *Settin' the Pace* LP. Session-opener "Rise and Shine" by Vincent Youmans is taken at a speed sure to make any listener sit up and take notice. At one point, Garland lays out for a chorus (as Monk had, and as McCoy Tyner would), allowing Coltrane to improvise more abstractly with only a bass line to ground him. "I See Your Face Before Me" not only features typically romantic Coltrane ballad work, but also has great block-chording from Garland who sounds like a miniature Count Basie orchestra (à la "Li'l Darlin'"). Coltrane's interest in more abstract improvisation perhaps led him to return to Jackie McLean's "Little Melonae" (Coltrane had recorded it with Miles Davis in 1955) with its unusual melody and ambiguous "A" section harmonies. Coltrane's rapid, slashing improvisation on this track once again illustrates why the phrase "sheets of sound" was coined.

Coltrane, Garland, and Donald Byrd recorded the last of their series of quintet dates on May 23rd. The rhythm section had Paul Chambers on bass and Jimmy Cobb on drums. Red was already out of the Miles Davis group (replaced by Bill Evans), and Jimmy Cobb was around this time taking over for Philly Joe Jones with Davis. The three selections taped that day constituted just enough for an LP (*Black Pearls*), but were not issued right away. Given the amount of free-lance recording that these musicians did, it's not surprising that some sessions have a routine air to them. To the credit of these musicians, they always show a high level of craft and look for ways to challenge themselves artistically. Coltrane's work on Bill Graham's composition "Black Pearls" illustrates a crux point Coltrane was beginning to reach. Fairly quickly, he settles into long stretches of sixteenth-note runs that few saxophonists of the time could have sustained (Johnny Griffin was one of the few). At this tempo, Coltrane's harmonically-explicit "vertical" lines are exhilarating at best and yet sometimes have a frantic quality to them. (Traces of this compulsiveness are evident in Coltrane's live recordings with the Miles Davis sextet from 1958.) Coltrane was running into the limits of his rigorously-vertical approach; an alternative (modal organization) was at hand and would be pursued by Coltrane starting in 1960. "Lover Come Back to Me" is the burner of the date, and finds Byrd, Coltrane, and Garland eating up the changes of this simply yet effectively-arranged standard. The LP-side-long "Sweet Sapphire Blues" is credited to Prestige owner Bob Weinstock perhaps by default or out of wishful thinking. This is, in fact, a themeless blues improvisation that begins with Red dipping into his bag of tricks before setting up Coltrane with some tasty block-chords. Coltrane's former balance between tuneful bluesy lines and eager double-timing has fundamentally changed; most of his space is devoted to aggressively getting every last harmonic ounce out of the blues chord progression.

A marathon session on July 11th (which was originally spread over three LPs, *Standard Coltrane, Bahia,* and *Stardust*) brought together Coltrane and the above rhythm section, with Wilbur Harden on trumpet and fluegelhorn in place of Byrd. Harden was a sympathetic musician who lacked the personal voice of a Lee Morgan or the relative dexterity of a Donald Byrd. Coltrane had recently recorded three albums as sideman with Harden on the Savoy label, and perhaps hired Harden as a friendly gesture. Harden's technical abilities may explain the absence of a really fast selection on this date, and the great number of slow selections. The ballads are taken very slowly, and one becomes aware that only players with the surest "time" can maintain the forward motion of a slow ballad without rushing or dragging. Coltrane does double-time extensively on the swingers, but does not seem as frantic as in the last session. All in all, the date has a relaxed feeling to it.

"Invitation" is the last of three Bronislaw (Bronislav) Kaper compositions that Coltrane recorded, and his version is probably responsible for keeping the song in the jazz repertoire until today. At this tempo, it takes him over three minutes to state the melody, but his reading of it and the solo work that follows never flag. "Stardust" is, unfortunately, played without the verse that is an integral part of the composition. Although Coltrane does not solo upon the song, his playing of the melody is again in the Charlie Parker school of embellishment and flights of fancy. The third ballad "Don't Take Your Love from Me" and the swingers "I'm a Dreamer, Aren't We All" and "Love Thy Neighbor" have never been common vehicles for jazz improvisation; Coltrane and Garland went to great lengths to find unusual material to keep their many Prestige dates from getting stale. Interesting little arrangements like that on "Spring Is Here" also maintained interest.

Coltrane's last recording session for Prestige (December 26th) was a rather varied affair. Three of the selections featured a quintet and three a quartet. Two trumpeters (Wilbur Harden and a young Freddie Hubbard) took turns, and two drummers took turns. Again, the selections were released on three different LPs (*The Believer, Stardust,* and *Bahia*). None of the compositions are jazz originals (unless you count "Goldsboro Express," which is actually an improvisation), no blues were recorded, and four of the six pieces tend to be slow and gentle. Coming at a time when Coltrane's live performances with Miles tended to be intense and even compulsive, it's clear that Coltrane was a complex and multi-faceted artist who did not deserve being typecast as an "angry" saxophonist. Two pieces serve as contrast to the ballads. One is the Afro-Latin-arranged

"Bahia" which alternates between ostinato and swing sections and brings out the aggressively exploratory side of Coltrane. "Goldsboro Express" continues Coltrane's interest in pianoless trios, and finds him engaging drummer Art Taylor in intense fours almost from the beginning. Credited to Coltrane, this performance is actually an improvisation on the chord changes to "Indiana." Coltrane and Taylor would revisit their affinity the next year on the opening sections of two takes of "Countdown" on the 1959 *Giant Steps* album.

1959 and Beyond

The year 1959 marked an end and a beginning for John Coltrane. His contract with Prestige was over, and he would never record for the label again. Coltrane was shopping around for a new label, and was negotiating with both the Atlantic and Riverside companies. He viewed recording as an important part of his income, and had figured how much he wanted to earn per year from recording. According to Riverside's Orrin Keepnews, Coltrane wanted to record four albums per year, a number that Keepnews felt was not artistically practical. Eventually Coltrane signed with Atlantic, and recorded for them during 1959 and 1960. As part of his deal, he formed his own publishing company and retained those royalties. Under these circumstances, a torrent of unique well-wrought John Coltrane compositions flooded his LPs. He ceased recording as a free-lance musician, and in that period only recorded on his own LPs, with his boss Miles Davis and with Atlantic artists Milt Jackson and Don Cherry. Less than four months after his last Prestige session, Coltrane first recorded his milestone composition "Giant Steps." This timing suggests that Coltrane had been working on advanced compositional ideas for some time and that he could not see having the pieces recorded while in a hurry in the studio for Prestige.

Through 1958, Coltrane had taken the soloistic approach of implying as many passing and substitute chords as possible on the standards and blues that he played. With "Giant Steps," he began explicitly building into his compositions difficult chord progressions that represented his harmonic thinking. Chief among them was the symmetrical progression now known as "Coltrane changes" that was at least partially inspired by Nicolas Slonimsky's *Thesaurus of Scales and Melodic Patterns*. Just as he had found implying passing chords to be limiting, Coltrane soon found dense written-in chord progressions to be a dead end. His seemingly insatiable tendency to outline each chord had already been challenged by

Miles Davis's explorations into "modal" organization of harmony. From 1961, Coltrane would never again write densely-packed chord progressions, preferring other means of organization.

Soon, partially in response to "free jazz," the balance of tension and release in his already-intense music was fundamentally altered, leaving many listeners uncomfortable. Even after Coltrane largely abandoned functional harmony in his work, he satisfied his need of organization by deriving many of his improvisational ideas from intervallic patterns and synthetic scales. This approach to generating melodic lines was eventually codified by many instrumentalists and its analytical logic led many jazz educators and musicians to embrace it. In many hands, the results were often mechanical, not a quality associated with Coltrane.

Coltrane's Prestige recordings capture the saxophonist at an early stage in his development, one in which he took control of his life, honed his technique, and first developed his unique approach to timbre, harmony, melody, and rhythm. At the time that some of this music was made, critics wrote that Coltrane showed a "lack of individuality," and that his tone and attack were "freakish." A few years later, he was accused of practicing on the bandstand and of producing "anti-jazz." Looking back on the Prestige years, the perspective of time reveals that John Coltrane often found a wonderful balance between exhilaration and repose and between abstraction and soulfulness.

LEWIS PORTER

JOHN COLTRANE: THE ATLANTIC YEARS

Adapted from The Heavyweight Champion, 1995

Lewis Porter is Associate Professor of Music at Rutgers University in Newark, and he is the director of the master's degree program in Jazz History and Research there. A leading jazz scholar, he is the author of books and articles on jazz and is a consultant to record producers, publishers, and producers of jazz radio shows and films. His views on jazz history may be found in Porter et al., Jazz: From Its Origins to the Present *(Prentice Hall, 1993). His most recent books are* Jazz: A Century of Change, *an anthology of rare historical articles and his essays (Schirmer Books, 1997) and the definitive study of Coltrane,* John Coltrane: His Life and Music *(University of*

Michigan Press, 1998). Forthcoming is the first Baker's Biographical Dictionary of Jazz *(Schirmer Books, 1999). Porter would like to thank Ed Hazell for helping with this article.* —CW

I've always loved these recordings, because they have the freshness of discovery. They're full of lightness and grace, buoyant, and yet at the same time fiery, passionate and deep. And it's not only Coltrane who makes this happen. It's the joy of McCoy Tyner and Elvin Jones working with him, finding themselves and making exciting music happen. Tyner's playing is crisp, rhythmic, shining—not the dramatic style that it would become, but delightful in its own right.

These are also the recordings that placed Coltrane on the map as a composer, as a writer of music. Everybody knows that he was one of the great saxophonists of all time, one of the great improvisors. But it may not be as obvious, until one thinks about it, that he was also one of the great writers for small jazz groups, along with, say, Thelonious Monk, Wayne Shorter, and a few others. A few of Coltrane's original compositions have made it into the pantheon of most-played pieces, among them "Giant Steps," "Naima," "Cousin Mary," and "Mr. P. C." But Coltrane's approach to composition, and especially his approach to arranging the tunes of others, influenced the whole sound of the jazz small group (as did the Miles Davis group of 1963–68). His version of "My Favorite Things" is not just pretty—it's totally original and revolutionary. And his reharmonizations of such familiar melodies as "Body and Soul" and "Summertime," and his inspiration of injecting "Giant Steps" type chord sequences into "But Not for Me" and "How High the Moon" ("Satellite" is his name for it), have affected the whole field of jazz writing.

He had written originals before—among them "Nita" and "Just for the Love" for sessions with Paul Chambers in 1956, "Blue Train" and "Lazy Bird" and "Moment's Notice" for his Blue Note album in September 1957. "Nita," the first piece he wrote for his wife Juanita (Naima), is also the first recorded Coltrane original that uses chord progressions moving in thirds, at least part of the way. On "Moment's Notice," he is preoccupied with placing changing harmonies under a repeated note in the melody. That's interesting, because Dizzy Gillespie had done something like that on "Con Alma" that same year, and Coltrane spent important formative years with Gillespie. This exercise of finding different chords to harmonize the same note forces one to find some unusual chord connections, and I would suggest that they led partly to "Giant Steps," where the sequence of chords is equally unexpected but the melody does not stay on one pitch. In "Con Alma" the first two chords under each note are a major third apart, paving the way for Coltrane's exploration of roots moving by thirds in "Giant Steps."

In an article by Barbara Gardner in the *Down Beat Music 1962* yearbook, published in 1961 [and reprinted on page 15 of this anthology], Coltrane discussed composing as if it were a chore he was forced into: "I just have to write the tunes myself. And I don't really want to take the time away from my horn. Writing has always been a secondary thing for me, but I find that lately I am spending more and more time at it, because I can't find the proper tunes." Bassist Donald Garrett said in the same article, "He is a meticulous musician. He will often play a tune seven or eight different ways before he decides on just how he wants to play it."

Coltrane's early influences are well known—as a youth starting the alto sax at age 13 around 1939 or 1940, he heard Johnny Hodges and Lester Young. When he became aware of Charlie Parker he immediately became a disciple of the "Bird." The best evidence for this is the newly discovered recordings from a jam session one day in the Navy in July 1946, where four of the eight songs were copied from recently released Parker 78s. (Coltrane's "Hot House," a Tadd Dameron piece that Bird recorded, was issued on *The Last Giant*.) When Coltrane switched to tenor saxophone about two years later, he started listening to Dexter Gordon, Wardell Gray, and Sonny Stitt. He said in that Gardner article that Stitt was his favorite, although his tone quality in those days sounded more like Gordon's.

Then came the tenure with Gillespie—from 1949 into 1951. As a trumpeter, Gillespie may have had little influence on Coltrane's saxophone playing, but I believe Coltrane did learn from Gillespie's innovative compositonal ideas. There is a Gillespie item entitled "Good Groove" on *The Last Giant* that shows Coltrane navigating another of Gillespie's interesting chord progressions.

Coltrane acknowledged, and rightfully so, that he really blossomed during his tenure with Miles Davis between 1955 and 1960 and during the six months that he worked with Monk during 1957. (Live material with Monk was issued on Blue Note in 1992. I wrote the notes for that CD but have since learned that the tapes issued there were most likely recorded at a reunion of Monk and Coltrane in September 1958!) Coltrane credited Monk with providing the proper setting and stimulation for his musical improvement. He wrote: "Working with Monk brought me close to a musical architect of the highest order. I felt I learned from him in every way—through the senses, theoretically, technically. I would talk to Monk about musical problems and he would sit at the piano and show me the answers just by playing them" (from "Coltrane on Coltrane," written with the editorial assistance of Don DeMicheal, in *Down Beat*, 1960 [and reprinted on page 98 of this anthology]).

During 1957, Coltrane also quit taking narcotic drugs, which improved his health and probably helped account for his improved musicianship. Saxophonist Jackie McLean said in *Jazz Times*, October 1991, that Coltrane was already quitting while working with Miles Davis: "He was in misery for five or six nights, then suddenly he started to look like he was getting strong and better and not drinking as much and he wasn't doing any drugs and he was playing so much saxophone it was awesome."

Early in 1958, Coltrane rejoined the Miles Davis group, making his first recording with the group in April. He wrote in the article "Coltrane on Coltrane": "We found Miles in the midst of another stage of his musical development. There was one time in his past that he devoted to multichorded structures. He was interested in chords for their own sake. But now it seemed that he was moving in the opposite direction to the use of fewer and fewer chord changes in songs. He used tunes with free-flowing lines and chordal direction. This approach allowed the soloist the choice of playing chordally (vertically) or melodically (horizontally)." (The words in parentheses reflect Coltrane's having been exposed to the music and terminology of jazz composer George Russell.) "In fact, due to the direct and free-flowing lines of his music, I found it easy to apply the harmonic ideas that I had. I could stack up chords—say, on a C7, I sometimes superimposed an E♭7, up to an F♯7, down to an F. That way I could play three chords on one. But on the other hand, if I wanted to, I could play melodically. Miles' music gave me plenty of freedom. It's a beautiful approach."

"About this time, I was trying for a sweeping sound. I started experimenting because I was striving for more individual development. I even tried long, rapid lines that Ira Gitler termed 'sheets of sound' at that time. But actually, I was beginning to apply the three-on-one chord approach, and at that time the tendency was to play the entire scale of each chord. Therefore, they were usually played fast and sometimes sounded like glisses. I found there were a certain number of chord progressions to play in a given time, and sometimes what I played didn't work out in eighth notes, 16th notes, or triplets. I had to put the notes in uneven groups like fives and sevens in order to get them all in. I thought in groups of notes, not of one note at a time. I tried to place these groups on the accents and emphasize the strong beats—maybe on 2 here and on 4 over at the end. . . . Sometimes what I was doing clashed harmonically with the piano—especially if the pianist wasn't familiar with what I was doing—so a lot of times I just strolled with bass and drums."

An interesting aspect of the above quotation is the emphasis Coltrane places on harmony. He explains the sheets of sound as well as the complex rhythmic groupings from the point of view of harmony. Both, he writes, unavoidably resulted from the rapid superimposition of several scales over each chord. (The matching of scales to chords was espoused by Lennie Tristano and George Russell during the early 1950s.) This suggests an emphasis on harmony, with rhythms almost happening by accident. Another quotation from the same piece suggests that is correct: "I want to be more flexible where rhythm is concerned. I feel I have to study rhythm some more. I haven't experimented too much with time; most of my experimenting has been in a harmonic form. I put time and rhythm to one side, in the past." Yet, clearly, Coltrane was not disregarding rhythm. He speaks of placing the groups of notes on the accents and emphasizing the strong beats. Notice that he refers to 2 and 4 as the strong beats, since they are emphasized in jazz. In most kinds of music, 1 and 3 are the strongest.

Critical of his own progress, Coltrane said, "Now it [sheets of sound] is not a thing of beauty, and the only way it would be justified is if it becomes that. If I can't work it through, I will drop it." (quoted by Ira Gitler in "'Trane on the Track," *Down Beat* 1958 [and reprinted on page 3 of this anthology]).

Coltrane had mentioned that Davis was getting interested in simplifying the backgrounds over which one improvised. On March 2 and April 6, 1959, with pianist Bill Evans and the unrelated Gil Evans, Davis designed the album *Kind of Blue* as an experiment in simplicity. In most jazz pieces the chords change about once a measure. The modes (scale types) change as the chords change. But Davis's new music would stay on the same chord—and therefore mode—for as long as 16 measures at a time.

The freedom of modal jazz also posed a challenge—to make coherent and interesting music with a minimum of harmonic guidelines. On "So What?", the opening selection, Coltrane spontaneously composed a tightly unified solo notable both for the abstract quality of its melodic motives, and for the way he develops each motivic idea. The "So What?" solo indicates the direction that Coltrane's music was to take during the 1960s, more so than "Giant Steps." He became more and more concerned with structural aspects of improvisation, and, as he did so, he concentrated more exclusively on modal backgrounds, which gave him the time he needed to develop his ideas at length.

During this time period, on April 1, 1959 he recorded the first session of his own music for Atlantic. (When recording without Davis he did not have to record for Davis's label, Columbia. His association with Atlantic had begun on January 15 with the quintet session with Milt Jackson.) It went unissued until 1974, but it is very significant because it gives us the first versions of "Giant Steps," "Naima" and "Like Sonny."

With the full session reel now in hand and in the ear, we now know more about Coltrane's working habits. Every member of the rhythm section has a very specific part to play. On "Like Sonny," he instructs Cedar Walton to play in unison with the bass until the saxophone enters with the theme. Coltrane worked for several takes on the complicated Latin rhythm that underpins the theme, and on making the transition from that into a more standard jazz swing feeling. The Latin rhythm shows Coltrane's interest in African and Latin elements even this early. It is an indication of Coltrane's genius for composition that this entire piece was developed from a little turning figure that his friend Sonny Rollins liked to use—thus the title "Like Sonny." (Joe Goldberg pointed out one place that Rollins may be heard playing this lick: his solo on "My Old Flame" from Kenny Dorham's Jazz Contrasts album, May 1957.) Coltrane's own music manuscripts of this tune and others—12 pages in all—were reproduced in Coltrane: A Biography by C. O. Simpkins (1975; reprinted in 1989 by Black Classic Press). These important documents deserve to be studied closely.

"Like Sonny" was constantly developing. In its next incarnation, in December 1959, you can hear that the rhythm has become a kind of bossa nova. A third version was recorded for Roulette Records in September 1960, with Billy Higgins on drums. In this incarnation it was called "Simple Like"—perhaps short for "Simple Like Sonny"?—and the rhythm has become more free. (Once it was issued as "Simple Life," which is suggestive because that is an expression that his cousin Mary likes to use.) "Naima" is also carefully written out, the bass part in particular. The haunting, serene quality of this ballad sets in a different world from the typical romantic love song.

It is thrilling to hear the development of the historic first recording of "Giant Steps." Its sixteen-measure chord progression begins with eight measures of root movement in thirds and closes with eight measures of ii-V-I progressions. It has since become a test piece for jazz musicians, and is required fare in jazz education programs. Coltrane chose to construct his solo largely out of four-note patterns which could be easily transposed to fit each chord. One basic pattern, involving the first, second, third and fifth degree of each key, appears several times. This use of "pentatonic patterns," as they are called (because the sixth of the scale, which is omitted, would make it a pentatonic scale), is widespread today. There are entire books devoted to the application of these and other patterns to technique practice as well as to improvisation, and to slower-moving as well as fast-moving chord progressions. Coltrane alternated these pentatonic patterns with other material, most of it also derived from pentatonic scales. Another kind of four-note pattern, the simple arpeggio, appears often, particularly during the first eight measures of each chorus. These arpeggios are all related to five-note scales, with one note omitted. In some cases this may be more easily seen if the scale is rotated, or if it is built on a different root than the chord. For example, the opening C-sharp minor arpeggio (of his issued solo on the session with Tommy Flanagan) employs notes of an E pentatonic scale rotated to B. Coltrane employed contrasting upward and downward motion to add variety, especially during the first four measures of each chorus. He frequently also used a connecting scale, which may be seen as a filling in of the pentatonic scale. In short, Coltrane relies heavily on formulas, especially ones derived from pentatonic scales, to negotiate the first eight measures of this chord progression, but his repertoire of formulas is so vast that he is able to keep the solo interesting.

The earlier version of "Giant Steps" moves at a pace of 253 beats per minute, somewhat slower than the originally issued recording. At the slower tempo Coltrane sounds more relaxed and more lyrical. Still, he does not invite Cedar Walton to solo on this difficult piece. (Walton is concentrating hard just to accompany Coltrane correctly.) The little fills that Walton played during the second half of the theme were developed in the studio. Before the penultimate take, we can hear Coltrane instruct Walton to play those. On May 5, Coltrane recorded the originally issued version of "Giant Steps," the title piece of his first Atlantic album as a leader. *The Heavyweight Champion* includes a take that preceded the issued take, and the one that followed it! Tommy Flanagan is a superb musician, and it is no discredit to him that he found it difficult to solo on this daunting piece. (On the last unissued take he just soloed in chords.) Apparently, Coltrane had the sense to give a lead sheet (melody line and chords) to Flanagan before the recording session. But he did not mention the style, so Flanagan had assumed it was to be played at a slow or medium tempo! (Hal Leonard publishers has released David Demsey's book *John Coltrane Plays Giant Steps*, with transcriptions of all of Coltrane's "Giant Steps" solos, including these newly released takes.)

Fascinated by the cyclic harmonic pattern of "Giant Steps," Coltrane used similar progressions on several other pieces during 1959 and 1960, notably "Countdown," "Exotica," "Fifth House" (based on "Hot House," which is based on "What Is This Thing Called Love?"), "26-2" (based on Bird's "Confirmation," this untitled item was perhaps named for being the 2nd piece recorded on October 26), and, as I mentioned earlier, "Satellite" and "But Not for Me." (David Demsey's masterful analysis of these pieces appeared in the *Annual Review of Jazz Studies 5*, 1991.) In "Countdown," which appeared on the *Giant Steps* album, Coltrane plays at an extremely fast tempo and launches directly into a blistering improvisation, stating the theme only at the end. These recordings epitomize one major concern of Coltrane at this time, that of developing the ability to successfully negotiate the fastest moving chord progressions.

Coltrane was of course a regular member of the Miles Davis group at this time. During the spring and summer of 1959, the Davis group performed at the Apollo in Harlem—sharing the bill with Monk and Ruth Brown—for a week beginning March 13, at the Blackhawk in San Francisco, and back to Birdland in Manhattan. They played at the Randall's Island festival (off of Manhattan) on August 23; at a benefit for the N.A.A.C.P. at Hunter College on October 4; and from October 23–29 at the Brooklyn Paramount theater, sharing the bill with the Count Basie band and others. But Coltrane's bandmates were going off and becoming leaders in their own right. Bill Evans had already left, and Cannonball Adderley had left around the time of the Brooklyn concert.

For a long time, Coltrane had been considering starting his own band. When Davis wasn't working, Coltrane would perform with pickup groups, mostly in New York and Philadelphia. At some point around May or June of 1959, he brought a quartet to the New House of Jazz in Philadelphia for a week. Late in 1959, he led a quartet at Town Hall in Manhattan, on a bill with other groups. Meanwhile, Davis's group, now billed as a quintet, played a dance concert (Tito Puente's band was there too) at the St. Nicholas Arena in Manhattan on November 27. They played Christmas week of 1959 in Chicago. The quintet was back at the Apollo for a week beginning January 15, 1960. Finally, they performed all over Europe from March 21 through April 10.

Upon returning from Europe, Coltrane felt he was ready and struck out on his own. He played magnificently on this tour (as documented mostly on bootlegs) and in fact the extra time with Davis was probably of value, because during the nights of playing at length on "So What?", "On

Green Dolphin Street," and "All Blues" he developed a wild looseness and abandon. The last engagement with Davis was two shows in Stuttgart, Germany on Sunday April 10. On April 16, "Today's Top Tenor" and his "All-Star Band" were on a bill with the groups of Dizzy Gillespie, Oscar Peterson, and others at Manhattan's Town Hall. At the beginning of May, Coltrane, "formerly with Miles Davis," opened at a club called the Jazz Gallery (at 80 St. Mark's Place—8th Street near 1st Ave.) with Steve Kuhn on piano, Steve Davis on bass, and Pete LaRoca on drums. The response was enthusiastic. On Sunday, May 15, the New York Daily News reported, "Run, do not walk or otherwise loiter on your way down to the Jazz Gallery. The reason is John Coltrane, a tenor saxophonist who has the future coming out of his horn." [The full review is found on page 218 of this anthology.] The Coltrane cult had begun.

At the Jazz Gallery, Coltrane's group alternated sets with Chico Hamilton's Quintet for the first few weeks, then with singer Al Hibbler. In June he played second billing at the Gallery to two of his favorite mentors—Gillespie in early June, and Monk at the end of the month. Coltrane appeared on June 30 at the Newport Jazz Festival and then went on tour with his group. On September 24, 1960 they performed at the Monterey Jazz Festival in California.

During this summer of 1960, Coltrane had begun performing on the soprano saxophone. For years he'd been pushing the upper limits of his tenor, as if yearning for an extended range, and a thinner, more exotic, tone. He had heard the modernist Steve Lacy, who specialized in the soprano, he knew the older work of Sidney Bechet, and he found the instrument brought to mind the sounds of Middle Eastern and African reed instruments.

Coltrane first recorded on the soprano on June 28 and July 8, 1960 in a remarkable context: intrigued by the work of his fellow Atlantic artist Ornette Coleman, he recorded Coleman's tunes (and one by Don Cherry, and one by Monk) with Coleman's associates. The session was not released until 1966. It is revealing that, perhaps feeling he was not yet ready for free improvisation, Coltrane chose for that session some of Coleman's earliest compositions, which use chord progressions. Furthermore, his improvising on the session is not especially Coleman-esque, abounding as it does in typical Coltrane melodies of that period. Coltrane's own musical personality was too well established to incorporate Coleman's saxophone style. Instead, it seems to be Coleman's concepts and spirit that influenced Coltrane. And of course, during the next few years Coltrane's music did venture farther and farther from tradition.

But the session of July 8 came in the middle of all the activity with his own quartet, with which he had yet to record. After the first few weeks at the Jazz Gallery, Coltrane had replaced Steve Kuhn with McCoy Tyner, who would remain with him for the next five years. Kuhn is a marvelous and original stylist—too often lumped together with Bill Evans—but for whatever reason, he just didn't click with Coltrane. Tyner played from the beginning with a big sound, and he could sound warm, even lush, while maintaining a powerful rhythmic flow. He also knew when to fall silent, as he explained to Stanley Dance in *Down Beat* (October 24, 1963): "A rhythm section is supposed to support and inspire a soloist, and it is a very sensitive thing. . . . Sometimes when John is soloing I lay out completely. Something very important is involved here, I think. The pianist tends to play chords that the soloist knows are coming up anyway. Normally, all the pianist does is try to give him a little extra push in the accompaniment and possibly to suggest some new ideas. When the pianist isn't there, the soloist can concentrate purely on what he has in mind with fewer limitations or boundaries. Otherwise, what the pianist plays can attract his attention away from his original thought. So it is all a manner of giving the soloist more freedom to explore harmonically." However, perhaps this could be carried too far—it is said that during Tyner's last year with the group he grew frustrated of spending so much time waiting his turn.

Tyner's playing had something of the lush voicings of Red Garland and of the percussive hard swinging attack of Wynton Kelly in his playing, and little of the Bill Evans style that was just becoming influential. From his first records with Coltrane, he contributes a bright, ringing, open type of sound. (Part of this, I'm sure, is owed to the particular sound of the piano and studio at Atlantic.) Over the next two years Tyner developed a particular type of voicing in fourths that was to characterize the sound of the quartet. (A fourth is the interval taken up by four scale notes. For example, C-D-E-F are four scale notes in order, so C and F comprise a fourth, as do D and G, E and A, G and C, and so on.) He also would create rumbling pedal points and thunderous bombs with his left hand in the lower register. Chick Corea and many others emulated Tyner's approach, and he has perhaps been underestimated by the critics as an influence on modern piano style along with Evans.

Tyner was important to Coltrane's quartet. Drummer Elvin Jones, Coltrane's closest collaborator and musical kindred spirit, was its heartbeat. Elvin Jones, the youngest brother of pianist Hank and trumpeter Thad Jones, replaced Pete LaRoca. Jones shared Coltrane's amazing physical stamina. More importantly, he shared the saxophonist's powerful interest in complex rhythms. "I especially like his ability to mix and juggle rhythms," Coltrane said of Jones. "He's always aware of everything else that's happening. I guess you could say he has the ability to be in three places at the same time" (quoted by Nat Hentoff in the liner notes to *Coltrane "Live" at the Village Vanguard*, Impulse). Jones implied the basic rhythm in a highly elliptical manner, yet he always swung like mad. He seemed to anticipate the rhythms of Coltrane's and Tyner's improvisations, sometimes playing the rhythms along with them.

In one wonderful week of October 1960, the new quartet with Tyner, Jones, and bassist Steve Davis (of whom little is known) recorded all the material that would eventually be issued as *Coltrane's Sound, Coltrane Plays the Blues,* and *My Favorite Things.* The latter was the hit album of the three. Side one featured Coltrane on soprano saxophone, and he posed with it on the cover. (At that time very few jazz fans knew what it was.) The Rodgers and Hammerstein waltz, "My Favorite Things," is best known today as sung by Julie Andrews and a crew of children in the 1966 movie *The Sound of Music,* but in 1960 the show was a Broadway hit with Mary Martin in the leading role. Coltrane transformed this pretty little song into a grand symphonic statement by making several seemingly small, but telling changes. In an otherwise thoughtful article in the journal *Critical Inquiry* (Winter 1994), Ingrid Monson makes the mistake of assuming that Coltrane wanted to dress this song up because he must have thought this tune was silly. Quite the opposite, he took the song seriously and saw things in it that the composer had not.

The song's structure as written is AAAB. All of the A sections use the "raindrops and roses" tune and emphasize happy things. The B part is the first mention of negative experiences—"when the dog bites"—but its point is that the good things help us to overcome the bad. Coltrane plays two A parts at the beginning of his version. Only at the very end of the performance does he play the B part. In the meantime, he stretches out the sense of time in several ways. He has the rhythm section begin with a vamp in E minor, and he comes in at his leisure. After the first A they switch to an E major vamp, and he solos briefly over this. Then it's back to E minor for the second A. At the end of this one, the E minor vamp returns, and the solos begin. Each solo follows a plan: the soloist, Coltrane or Tyner, plays over the E minor vamp as long as he wants, and then moves on cue to the E major vamp. The cue is a return to the theme. You can hear Tyner return to the theme in the middle of his solo, which is his cue to the others, and then the vamp becomes major. Coltrane does the same during his solo. And during every live version of this piece each soloist, including Dolphy, does the same. When the B section finally enters at the end, we feel that we have been through an entire world of music.

In his first Atlantic recordings, as we've noted, Coltrane carefully worked out the parts for the rhythm section. Now he had found a way, with the help of Elvin Jones, to retain his sense of organization and yet offer spontaneity. The swaying rhythm of the piano and bass on the simplified modal structure creates a feeling of stasis, while the extremely active soprano and drums create the opposite effect, of change and a sense of searching. It is a creative tension Coltrane would use over and over again.

One of Coltrane's most important contributions to jazz was the incorporation of musical ideas from other cultures. Coltrane's personal record collection included the North Indian virtuoso Ravi Shankar, and Olatunji's versions of African music (Coltrane wrote "Tunji" for him). His notebooks contained pages of scales from different countries. (One such page is reproduced on p. 113 of the Simpkins book.) No doubt Gillespie's involvement in Latin music was an example to Coltrane, as was Monk's bassist Ahmed Abdul-Malik, who drew from Middle Eastern music on his own recordings.

In Nat Hentoff's notes to Coltrane "Live" at the Village Vanguard, Coltrane was quoted as saying, "I've really got to work and study more approaches to writing. I've already been looking into those approaches to music—as in India—in which particular sounds and scales are intended to produce specific emotional meanings. I've got to keep probing. There's so much more to do." These influences were just starting to happen during the Atlantic period and it may be that we hear their effects on "My Favorite Things." The use of a drone in the bass on this and other numbers may have been inspired by the drones used in Indian music. One might hear the Indian influence in the melodic improvising, in the use of little motives that he develops in the improvisation, which is an Indian way much more than a jazz way of improvising. Jazz artists tend to use longer, free flowing melodies. (The criticisms of Coltrane's music reflected that fact that some listeners have trouble hearing his music as lyrical, since he eschews songlike melodies in the vein of, say, Charlie Parker.) African concepts of space and of rhythmic repetition are essential here as well. In fact, West African drumming groups will repeat one section until the leader gives a cue to go on to the next, much as Coltrane does in "My Favorite Things."

Coltrane also recorded the blues "Equinox" during that first spate of studio sessions with his newly formed quartet. Coltrane was a serious blues player, and his blues pieces reflect a desire to get back to a primal type of blues, and away from the lighter, harmonically more complex blues of the boppers. The twelve-bar minor theme consists essentially of the first four scale degrees of D-flat minor. (The piece is often written in C-sharp minor but Coltrane's sketches in the Simpkins book are in D-flat.) As in traditional vocal blues, the first two four-bar phrases are based on the same rhythm and the same melody. Harmonically, the last phrase provides the greatest harmonic activity of the theme by beginning on a flat VI chord before moving to the expected V chord in measure ten. This is reminiscent of "All Blues" from the *Kind of Blue* album.

Six bars of a Latin rhythm introduce the piece, as shown in Coltrane's sketches. Then the rhythm section plays eight measures of an ostinato, which continues under the theme. The relentless ostinato underpinning of the piano and bass, contrasting with the leisurely, uncrowded melody, creates an ominous, even primitive atmosphere. Elvin Jones takes advantage of this solid base to provide rolls and cymbal crashes which contribute to the drama and intensity of the theme and solo sections. He plays with mallets and has his snares turned off, so as to achieve a softer, darker, and more legato effect. The bassist, Steve Davis, is allowed little variation from his pattern throughout the piece. The piano part, played by McCoy Tyner, begins in octaves with the bass. Maintaining the same rhythm, it opens up into chords under measures five and six of the theme, providing a counterline against Coltrane's melody. Throughout the improvised choruses, Tyner plays a chordal version of the original ostinato, with no variation. Although Tyner is tied to this rhythm, he creates great variety through his chord voicings, providing a new voicing for each chorus and building the sequence of voicings so that they beautifully support the increasing tension of Coltrane's improvisation.

Over this background, Coltrane invents an astounding improvisation that builds and builds, then winds down again before Tyner solos. He starts simply, poignantly, building to faster and faster notes with each chorus, and to higher and higher notes. Each chorus has its own characteristic motive: furthermore, there is a logical development of motives from one chorus to the next.

Most of the outtakes from these sessions are lost. But the creation of "Blues to Elvin," a slow number that was issued on *Coltrane Plays the Blues*, can be followed on a surviving session reel. Interestingly, this slow down home blues gets slower with each take, whereas the norm is to get faster. It is a very difficult feat to maintain a swing at a slow pace, but obviously Coltrane felt strongly about it. Also, he changes the key before the last take, which was the one issued.

Every piece recorded for Atlantic has its story, and its distinctive musical flavor. We already mentioned some of the items that use his "Giant Steps" approach to chords. One of them, "Central Park West," is vaguely reminiscent of "Peace," by Horace Silver, whom Coltrane said he admired. While we're on the subject of admiration, "Liberia" is clearly a tribute to Gillespie and his "A Night in Tunisia."

That week of October 1960 was the key week in Coltrane's Atlantic output. But after that he did not enter the studio again for seven months. In the beginning of 1961, he began playing with fellow saxophonist Eric Dolphy. Through 1962, Coltrane experimented with several bass players, sometimes using two at a time. (Duke Ellington had used two bassists between 1935 and 1938, but otherwise the practice was almost unknown.) Among the bass players he used after Steve Davis were Reggie Workman, Art Davis, and Donald Garrett. Garrett, a Chicago resident, explained to Barbara Gardner how the two-bass concept came up: "We have been friends since 1955, and whenever he is in town, he comes over to my house, and we go over ideas. I had this tape where I was playing with another bass player. We were doing some things rhythmically, and Coltrane became excited about the sound. We got the same kind of sound you get from the East Indian water drum. One bass remains in the lower register and is the stabilizing, pulsating thing, while the other bass is free to improvise, like the right hand would be on the drum. So Coltrane liked the idea."

They played mostly in New York and Philadelphia. They were at the Apollo for a week beginning March 17, 1961, sharing the bill with Miriam Makeba, Oscar Brown Jr., and Machito's band. During this week he guested on Davis's recording *Someday My Prince Will Come.* It was the last time they would play together. From April 25 through May 7, the Coltrane group played at the Jazz Workshop in San Francisco.

On May 23, 1961 Coltrane began recording *Africa/Brass,* his first session for Impulse Records. But he still had to fulfill obligations to Atlantic, and on May 25 he recorded the album *Olé* with his quartet plus guests Freddie Hubbard on trumpet and Eric Dolphy on alto saxophone and flute. (Ostensibly because he was under contract to Prestige Records at the time, the original issue identified Dolphy as "George Lane"!) Although Dolphy was a crucial element of Coltrane's musical life, he appeared mostly in the ensemble on the albums issued during Coltrane's lifetime. For example, there is only one Dolphy solo on the Impulse album *Live at the Village Vanguard.* (Since Coltrane's death, much live material with Dolphy soloing has been issued by Impulse, and on many bootlegs.) So

Olé is an important opportunity to hear the rapport between Dolphy and Coltrane.

Dolphy (1928–1964) was a schooled performer with exceptional technical agility, and a clear, singing, yet distinctive tone quality on each of his instruments. His melodic lines often change direction and leap unpredictably. He treated the chord progressions very freely, creating frequent moments of dissonance. Dolphy's relationship to the chord progression was often distant, to say the least, yet he preferred to work within the outline of standard chord changes and on his own recordings he was not stretching out on modal vamps as Coltrane was doing. But the unbridled freedom of his harmonic approach made a strong impact on Coltrane. No doubt Dolphy's influence helped reinforce Coltrane's own increasingly frequent excursions out of the given key. From the Gardner article again: "Eric Dolphy is a hell of a musician, and he plays a lot of horn. When he is up there searching and experimenting, I learn a lot from him, but I just haven't found exactly what I want yet."

From the opening title track, "Olé," it is evident that the group has changed a lot in the past seven months since "My Favorite Things." The basic idea of a repeated bass and piano vamp is still there, with Jones and Coltrane thrashing freely around it, but everybody is looser now. Tyner has begun reaching into the lower register of the piano, the two basses create a churning undercurrent, and there is a sense that this could go on forever without one getting bored. The improvisation sections now take place over one vamp—there is no second part and no need to cue one. Coltrane's interest had led him to Spanish music—thus the title—which is interesting since Davis had recorded the Gil Evans material entitled *Sketches of Spain* in 1959 and 1960. Spanish music had had a big impact in the classical field as well—the innovations of Debussy and Ravel had been partly inspired by Spanish folk sources. As for the other titles, "Dahomey Dance," a blues pared down to its absolute essence, reflects Coltrane's growing interest in Africa. And "Aisha" is one of only two Tyner originals that Coltrane recorded, and a gorgeous one at that. (The other Tyner tune is "The Believer," done in 1958 with Red Garland on piano.)

One could make a few general observations about Coltrane's saxophone playing from close listening to the music in this collection. His approach to the soprano saxophone differed from his tenor playing in that he played much more floridly, filling in long, rippling legato lines where an eighth-note run might have served on the tenor instrument. On either instrument, he sustained high notes for their sheer intensity, usually at the beginnings of phrases.

Coltrane preferred a choked, screaming sound at fast tempos. In the lower register, at fast tempos, he honked and overblew to obtain harsh effects. (By blowing forcefully and adjusting one's embouchure, one may obtain several simultaneous overtones in addition to the fingered note. Jazz saxophonists call this overblowing.) He sometimes used multiphonics (more than one note at a time) to obtain specific two-note intervals, as in the theme of "Harmonique." (In the *Down Beat* "Coltrane on Coltrane" piece, he credited Thelonious Monk and one John Glenn with showing him how to play multiphonics.)

Coltrane had a very different approach to ballads. On ballads he allowed the low notes to sound warmly, with much airiness and vibrato. He tended to adhere closely to the written melody line, but he would decorate that melody with his unique and graceful ornaments. It seems to me that Coltrane's paraphrasing of a ballad melody did not vary much from one performance to another of the same piece, even in the specific locations and types of ornaments added. This suggests that he tended to conceive of a definitive paraphrase of a given melody, and that he proceeded to hear the melody the same way each time he played it. Some singers, like Billie Holiday, worked this same way. Coltrane's respectful approach to ballad melodies reflects a tradition before bop; the Parker way was to improvise lots of double time lines and fills in a ballad. In fact, Johnny Hodges, the alto saxophonist with whom Coltrane performed in 1954, was famous for his sensuous ballad paraphrases, with his own distinctive set of ornaments applied the same way each time. It is extremely likely that Coltrane learned much about ballad playing from Hodges, although he certainly learned as well from recordings of Ben Webster, Lester Young, and his other cited pre-bebop favorites.

Coltrane possessed one of the greatest compositional minds in jazz, and it is a shame that his important contribution in this area has not been more widely noticed. The sense of structure comes through not only in his writing and arranging, but in his improvising. It really starts to become evident during the Atlantic years. His adoption of tonally slow-moving, or stationary, "modal jazz" pieces was related to his search for more structure in his own improvisations. In concert, he liked to improvise for a half-hour or more at a stretch, almost certainly setting a new record for jazz, as his detractors angrily noted. But there was good reason for this seemingly inordinate length. He was concerned with following his compositional ideas of the moment, and preferred not to try to curtail, edit, or predetermine this process. As he explained to one interviewer: "When some evenings, in beginning to play, we feel inspired and we foresee the possibility of realizing good things, it seems illogical and unreasonable to us to shorten our solos. . . . My ideas have to develop themselves naturally in a long solo" (my translation from an interview by J. Clouzet and Michel Delorme published in French in *Les Cahiers du Jazz,* 1963). As his colleague Julian "Cannonball" Adderley recalled, he once simply said after a solo, "It took that long to get it all in" (quoted by Ralph Gleason in his liner notes to *Coltrane's Sound*). In playing extended solos, Coltrane was aware that he risked running out of ideas, and he acknowledged in the notes to *Olé* that he sometimes played too long. He also said in "John Coltrane and Eric Dolphy Answer the Jazz Critics" (*Down Beat,* 1962 [reprinted on page 109 of this anthology]): "If I feel that I'm just playing notes . . . maybe I don't feel the rhythm or I'm not in the best shape that I should be in when this happens. When I become aware of it in the middle of a solo, I'll try to build things to the point where this inspiration is happening again, where things are spontaneous and not contrived. If it reaches that point again, I feel it can continue—it's alive again. But if it doesn't happen, I'll just quit, bow out."

The Atlantic recordings from October 1960 came out in 1961. *Down Beat* honored Coltrane as "Jazzman of the Year" in their review of 1961. In their International Critics Poll he won for tenor saxophone, miscellaneous instrument (soprano saxophone), and new star combo. In the Readers Poll he also won tenor and miscellaneous prizes. Barbara Gardner wrote, "His influence on other musicians continued to grow; many young tenorists continued slavishly to imitate him. . . . In 1961, John Coltrane came into his own."

But despite his success, Coltrane was always pushing himself, always searching for new things. He told Gardner, "I work a lot by feeling. I just have to feel it. If I don't, then I keep trying. . . . I haven't found it yet. I'm listening all the time, but I haven't found it. . . . I don't know what I'm looking for. Something that hasn't been played before. I don't know what it is. I know I'll have that feeling when I get it. I'll just keep searching."

Gardner reminded him that in 1959 or 1960 he had said that he had found something that he was afraid to play, because people (critics?) would't let him get away with it. He responded, "I don't remember what I was talking about specifically. I guess I must have tried them already. I've gone through all the things I used to want to do. Some I liked and am still working on. Others I had to set aside. . . . I just can't seem to find the right songs. I'm listening everywhere. I listen to other groups, records, the men I work with, trying to find what I'm looking for. I learn a lot from the fellows in the group."

That perfectionism, that humility, that drive for exploration, continued to define Coltrane even after his Atlantic years. In the English publication *Melody Maker* of August 14, 1965, Mike Hennessey asked him if there was anything missing in his playing. He responded, "I don't know if you can ever be a complete musician. I'm not. But I don't think I'll know what's missing from my playing until I find it." These Atlantic recordings are a vital and exciting part of that search.

DAVID WILD

JOHN COLTRANE: THE IMPULSE YEARS

Recordings 1961–1967

Author/pianist David Wild has written for Down Beat, Coda, *and other publications. Wild contributed to the* New Grove Dictionary of Jazz *and John Litweiler's* Ornette Coleman: A Harmolodic Life, *and he compiled* The Recordings of John Coltrane: A Discography *and* Ornette Coleman 1958–1978: A Discography.—CW

Prolog

Thirty years ago a cancerous liver stilled the voice of saxophonist/composer John Coltrane, drawing boundaries around the man and his work. A subset of the human equation, those two elements—death and time—taken together equal perspective. What was blurred up close is now distant, in focus. The path uncharted becomes a mapped highway; the nearby sun now a distant star framed by the telescope.

Perspective requires an object, something left behind, a body of work to view. Here jazz benefits from the relentless push of technology, with inexact music notation supplanted by the echoes of the sounds themselves. The art of recording lets us peer across the boundaries of death and time ever more clearly, see, hear and evaluate more of the music as it actually was.

Virtually all of Coltrane's recordings, his legacy, are concentrated into just twelve years. Oddly, those recordings can be meaningfully divided according to the contracts that paid for them, handy bookmarks in the welter of music. From 1955 through 1957 Coltrane was without contract, an up-and-coming freelancer. The Prestige contract (1957–1959) marks the period of the in-demand sideman, and the first of Coltrane's recordings as a leader. The Atlantic contract (1959–1961) has Coltrane, increasingly selective about how he is recorded, go from star sideman (with Miles Davis) and leader of seminal studio sessions to a leader in fact, with a working band and commercial as well as critical successes.

The intent here however is to gain perspective over the last six years of Coltrane's career, the recordings made under contract to the Impulse label (ABC-Paramount). Those recordings, spanning 1961 through 1967, reflect purely his concepts—there are no sessions with Coltrane as a sideman. He could afford to be choosier about what he recorded, but he chose to record often, and Impulse accommodated. His working group for most of the period, the so-called "classic quartet" with McCoy Tyner, Jimmy Garrison and Elvin Jones, created an instantly identifiable sound and approach whose effects were felt throughout jazz. Coltrane achieves an uncommon level of success, allowing for unusual projects, opportunities to experiment which otherwise would never have occurred. These are arguably the masterworks, the major achievements which exemplify the career.

Technology has also spawned a class of recordings without precedent. "Bootlegs," recordings of performances taped without the artist's consent, broadcasts captured from the air, private rehearsal tapes—these are now part of the collected works of artists such as John Coltrane. Such recordings provide insight, showing how ideas evolved or how the repertoire evolved over time, but they lack Coltrane's approval. We'll note them, but our focus must remain on that which the saxophonist chose to commit to tape.

One last distinction. Although many of the recordings discussed here were made as part of a specific project, often Coltrane recorded simply to preserve a particular approach or set of compositions. Even when he recorded for a specific project, Coltrane often taped more than was needed for that project, producing alternate takes and unissued titles equal in quality to that selected for release. Obviously, the decision on what to release was not Coltrane's alone, and was tempered by commercial considerations. Still, those recordings he approved for release while he lived have a special stature, "first among equals." These too will be noted, although they now form only part of the Coltrane legacy.

1961

Coltrane was one of the first to be signed by the newly created Impulse label of ABC-Paramount records, early in 1961. Evidently Coltrane saw the move to Impulse as a chance to try things he had not been able to do with his previous label. Impulse was willing, and Coltrane's initial projects (both recorded in 1961) were spectacular firsts—the two studio dates that produced the orchestral *Africa/Brass* and, a scant four months later, his first live recording under his own name, the seminal Village Vanguard Sessions. Both projects stretched beyond a single recording session, leaving us with alternate takes and titles which have appeared posthumously.

For the first project producer Creed Taylor agreed to pair the Coltrane group with a large orchestra, something new for Coltrane. Yet Coltrane had different sounds in mind, and the unusual orchestra assembled in Van Gelder's studio on May 23 was dark and brass-heavy—two trumpets, two euphoniums, four French horns and a tuba, leavened by three reeds and driven by Elvin Jones and two bassists. The conception was Coltrane's, but the execution owes much to pianist McCoy Tyner and future band-member Eric Dolphy. Dolphy was the arranger for all but one of the charts recorded during the sessions. Those arrangements however draw heavily on Tyner's accompaniments, a characteristic style of block chords which had already become a central part of the developing sound of the "classic John Coltrane Quartet." The instruments and a Coltrane composition, "Africa," gave the first LP and the sessions themselves the name *Africa/Brass*.

First on the agenda at the May 23 session was "Greensleeves." It's clearly a collaboration, with McCoy Tyner's quartet piano accompaniment scored for the orchestra by Dolphy.

Its obvious predecessor is "My Favorite Things," recorded earlier for Atlantic and Coltrane's "greatest hit." The formula they share—a modal song in 3/4 featuring the soprano saxophone—must have fascinated Coltrane, since "Greensleeves" is only the first of a number of more or less similar compositions to pass through the quartet's repertoire during the Impulse years. The arrangement is held together by Reggie Workman's strong bass pattern, which outlines the repeated two-chord pattern on which Coltrane and Tyner solo.

The group then turned to "Song of the Underground Railroad." A product of Coltrane's research on nineteenth century spirituals, this composition becomes a straightahead swinger on which Coltrane (on tenor saxophone) and Tyner cook over another minor two-chord vamp. It was released posthumously. Evidently not satisfied with the first take of "Greensleeves," the orchestra taped another version (also a posthumous release), slower and more relaxed than the first, with Workman straying further from the eighth-note figure.

Trumpeter Calvin Massey, a long-time friend of Coltrane's, contributed "The Damned Don't Cry," the only non-Dolphy arrangement. The orchestra did not spend long on the complex chart, and its eventual release owes more to Coltrane's powerful solo than to the anemic, tentative reading of the arrangement. Finally, "Africa." This masterful arrangement, with the deep anchor of the bass's E pedal, the dark brass in open fourths, Elvin Jones's characteristic Afro-Cuban rhythm and the polytonal theme, is the centerpiece of the sessions. This earliest of the three "Africas" was released in the 1970's.

Coltrane, apparently dissatisfied, convinced Impulse to schedule a second session on June 7, with a similar but slightly smaller orchestra. Although the main focus was "Africa," the first piece recorded likely was "Blues Minor." A modal blues, it was a last-minute inclusion, arranged by Dolphy using Tyner's voicings. The powerful swing generated by this simple chart won it a place on the original release. The orchestra then returned to "Africa." Dolphy had modified the chart after the May session, bringing the orchestra more to the forefront (note the whoops from the French horns), and replacing flutes with his alto saxophone. Two complete versions exist from this date, differing in tempo, in the style of Elvin Jones's solo and other key elements. The final, most adventurous take, is the original release.

Dolphy and the Coltrane quartet (Tyner, drummer Elvin Jones and bassist Reggie Workman) headed in opposite directions after these sessions, and Dolphy did not rejoin the group until September, on the West Coast. The group played in California and Chicago before arriving at New York's Village Vanguard for a two-week stay. Producer Bob Thiele, new at Impulse, had inherited a project to capture Coltrane "live." Although only one night of recording was originally planned, at the last the microphones remained for four nights (November 1, 2, 3 and 5, 1961).

The Village Vanguard Sessions, as the four nights are usually called, consist of 22 different performances. While several titles are duplicated—Coltrane obviously had a specific group of tunes in mind—the variety in the recordings is amazing. Coltrane experimented with tempos, with soloists, with the addition of unusual instruments (Ahmed Abdul-Malik's oud and Garvin Bushell's oboe and contrabassoon)—all signs of the restless experimenter, searching for the best combination for each idea. Ultimately all performances were released (or should be by the time this overview is published).

The initial release, entitled simply *Live at the Village Vanguard*, included just three selections. Coltrane recorded "Spiritual" (based on an actual spiritual) during each of the four nights preserved from the Vanguard. In the version recorded November 3 (released on that first LP), Coltrane states the theme (out of tempo) over percussion and a deep bass clarinet pedal point. Solos by Coltrane, Dolphy (on bass clarinet), Tyner (piano) and Coltrane again, now on tenor, float over a hypnotically simple chord pattern in a gentle 3/4. Of the other three versions, that from November 5, with its inclusion of Garvin Bushell's contrabassoon, is especially noteworthy.

Of the other two performances on *Live at the Village Vanguard,* one, "Softly as in a Morning Sunrise," is a quartet version of the old standard, begun by Tyner, whose solo is a sparkling gem, and ended by Coltrane on angular soprano. The other is a unique version of an unusually free, singsong-like approach to the classic 12-bar blues—a blues in F without a predefined theme, a composition caught at the point of coalescence. Recorded November 2 and featuring just Coltrane, "Chasin' the Trane" is one of the major jewels in the Vanguard collection. In its relentless intensity, its obsessive probing of the most basic of blues changes, its fearless rejection of easy virtuosity and European technique, it is unlike anything else Coltrane recorded. Two other versions of this blues were taped at the Vanguard. Earlier on November 2 Coltrane recorded a version in B-flat (with Roy Haynes on drums), which starts almost conventionally before moving into the sparse angularity of the later version; it was released posthumously under the title *Chasin' Another Trane.* A third version (in F, like the one originally released) was taped November 1. Released in 1978, this *Chasin' the Trane* features an exceptionally creative solo by Dolphy.

1963's *Impressions* LP featured two more Vanguard performances. "Impressions" (November 3) molds a new (albeit derivative) melody onto the structure of Miles Davis's modal "So What?" and is notable for Coltrane's unflagging drive and inventiveness. Alternate versions include solos by Tyner and Dolphy, as well as a Dolphy countermelody. "India" (also November 3) is a spare modal composition, with bass and piano limited to pedal points and infrequent chords; Coltrane (on soprano) and Dolphy (on bass clarinet) soar over Jones's propulsion. Alternate versions add Garvin Bushell on oboe and the drone of Ahmed Abdul Malik's oud.

Other titles from the Vanguard did not see the light of day until 1978's *The Other Village Vanguard Tapes.* There are two unusual versions of "Naima," a famous Coltrane composition first recorded in 1959 for Atlantic. Atlantic's contract prohibited Coltrane from re-recording it in 1961, so Coltrane inverted the melody in order to preserve the quintet's version. "The Red Planet" (two versions), later recorded as "Miles's Mode," features a dodecaphonic melody framing solos built around a B minor mode. "Greensleeves" was recorded twice, in a quartet version quite similar to that of the *Africa/Brass* sessions. Finally, "Brasilia," its out-of-tempo theme leading to medium tempo solos by Coltrane, Dolphy, Tyner and Reggie Workman, is a fascinating early version of a theme later reworked for a 1965 recording.

Within a week of the end of the Vanguard gig the Coltrane Quintet was in Europe, touring England and continuing through France, Holland, Scandinavia, and Germany. A number of these concerts have made their way onto bootleg releases, with a remarkable variety of performances of the same handful of tunes. The performances of "Naima" from the tour are particularly interesting.

1962

If *Chasin' the Trane* represents the foam line left by high tide, then the music of 1962 represents the flow of the waves back towards the surf, still high on the shore but closer to the common sea. It's as if even one so strong as Coltrane must stop and catch his breath. Broadcasts (with Dolphy at Birdland in February, and without Dolphy in June) show that, live, the group was still adventurous. Yet when juxtaposed to the complex weight of *Africa/Brass* or the fiery Vanguard performances, the April and June studio recordings have a decidedly conservative cast. There are more prosaic reasons—an attempt to improve his mouthpiece had ruined it, leaving him unable to play certain things, and he had separated from his first wife. Negative critical reactions probably did not help, and Impulse's natural desire to have a well-rounded catalog of Coltrane recordings fit right in.

Which does not diminish the value of the 1962 studio recordings originally released on the eponymous *Coltrane*. From the April 11/12 1962 sessions only "The Inchworm" and "Big Nick" remain, the other titles and takes having disappeared. "The Inchworm" was the soprano-waltz feature for the session, with melody and two-chord vamp alternating much as they did in "Greensleeves." "Big Nick," Coltrane's remembrance of saxophonist Big Nick Nicholas, is a dancing, at times swaggering 4/4 soprano feature. At the June 19 session Coltrane revisited Mal Waldron's "Soul Eyes," first recorded in March 1957. Coltrane's spare statement of the theme is followed by a dancing, triplet-laced Tyner solo (over Jones's double-time brushes). "Out of This World," a Harold Arlen pop tune, seems tailor-made for Coltrane, who sails high above Jones's odd mix of 3/4 swing and Afro-Cuban. It echoes the shattering intensity of "Africa." The Miles of "Miles's Mode" is of course Miles Davis; called "The Red Planet" at the Vanguard, the twelve-tone melody probably owes more to the collaboration with Dolphy. The performance builds a relentless sense of perpetual motion over Jones's complex churning drums. "Tunji," for drummer Olatunji, is a medium slow modal blues.

For Coltrane the timing was also right for an album of ballads. Most of the compositions recorded for the *Ballads* album (September 18 and November 13) were popular music standards not a regular part of the group's repertoire. The relatively short performances, which focus on thematic interpretations, are an interesting contrast to the marathon, multinoted expositions Coltrane usually turns in.

A hiatus between recording contracts had made composer Duke Ellington a temporarily free agent, and producer Bob Thiele grabbed the chance to pair Ellington the pianist with Coltrane at a session the week after the first *Ballads* date (September 26). Cross-generational pairings often flounder on differences in rhythm or in the musical language itself, but Coltrane's early apprenticeship with Johnny Hodges and Ellington's open mind made the session work. Each man brought his own rhythm section (Jimmy Garrison and Elvin Jones for Coltrane; Aaron Bell and Sam Woodyard for Ellington). The gem of the session is no doubt "In a Sentimental Mood," a perfect match of Ellington the accompanist and Coltrane the soloist. The seams do show on some of the other titles, as when Garrison and Jones take off and leave Ellington to lay out, and the Bell-Woodyard rhythm section seems almost pedestrian at times. But most of the performances work remarkably well.

In November, following the Ellington and *Ballads* sessions, Coltrane took the quartet on a European tour (mid-November through mid-December). Some of the Scandinavian performances were among the first to appear on bootlegs. These performances, like the summer's quartet recordings, seem conservative when compared to the work from 1961, although they have their moments. Coltrane closed out the year in Chicago, with Dolphy returning for the gig.

1963

Performances on two nights at Birdland in New York City were broadcast (February and March 1963); these performances show more adventurousness than those of the previous year. Shortly after the Birdland dates

Coltrane brought the group into the studio for two sessions. Most of the first (March 6) has been swallowed by time, with only the dancing "Vilia" remaining to mark what might have been. The second session (March 7) paired the group with singer Johnny Hartman. Coltrane knew Hartman from their days with Gillespie and evidently filed his dark, lyrical voice away as a future resource. "My One and Only Love" is probably the stand-out from this session, although all of the performances are excellent. Like the *Ballads* session of the previous fall, *John Coltrane and Johnny Hartman* offers a different take on the quartet, a unique chance to hear how well this fire-breathing unit could support a singer.

In early April 1963 Elvin Jones left the Coltrane group for medical treatment; during his six month absence he was replaced by drummer Roy Haynes. The sound of that quartet is preserved in a routine April 29 quartet session, from which only two performances survive. One, the out-of-tempo ballad "After the Rain," is most interesting as the first example of what would become a characteristic approach to ballads. The other, "Dear Old Stockholm," reworks a Coltrane feature from his earliest days with Miles Davis. A much better example of this edition of the quartet can be heard in the posthumously released performances from the Newport Jazz Festival (July 7), with a particularly fine version of the ballad "I Want to Talk about You."

In October Elvin Jones returned to the band, just in time for another visit to Birdland, this time with Rudy Van Gelder's microphones in the audience. Haynes had been an excellent substitute, but the drum chair belonged to Jones, and the joy at his return, on home ground, in front of the hip New York audience, is almost palpable. *Coltrane Live at Birdland* offered three of the live performances paired with two studio recordings from later in the year. "Afro-Blue," by Mongo Santamaria, is the 1963 3/4 vehicle for the soprano, with Jones's polymetric propulsion an integral factor. The obscure Billy Eckstine ballad "I Want to Talk about You" was first recorded by Coltrane in 1958; by 1963 it had become the foundation for a remarkable coda, out of tempo and unaccompanied, a showcase for his ability to combine unusual scales and patterns into coherence. Comparisons with the earlier version (from Newport) are instructive. "The Promise" is one of Coltrane's better compositions, with a freely interpreted melody and strong solos.

In October Coltrane took the quartet to Europe for another tour, lasting well into November. Much of that tour was captured, and the music is more adventurous, more "current" ("Chasin' the Trane," resurrected from the Vanguard, is balanced by "The Promise" and "Afro-Blue," both in play by the quartet). By November 18 they had returned to New York City, and were again in the studio. The evidence suggests that this was not a particularly productive session, with only two titles recorded. The lilting "Your Lady," written for Alice McLeod, is a soprano feature. The haunting composition "Alabama" exists in two versions. The more common version inadvertently combined the last two takes (the incomplete take 4 and a theme-only take 5) of the composition. In this earlier version the unfinished nature of the solo (where take 4 breaks down) adds to the drama of the piece, but the later, correct version (take 5 only) was eventually substituted.

In December, while the quartet was in San Francisco at the Jazz Workshop they recorded a half-hour segment of critic Ralph Gleason's *Jazz Casual* TV show. The performance deservedly has been released both as a recording and a video. It captures the essence of the band, its casual unpretentiousness, its seriousness, the intuitive interplay of the group. At Coltrane's request there are no interviews, just an introduction by Gleason, followed by excellent performances of "Afro-Blue," "Alabama," and "Impressions." "Alabama" is probably the standout, a powerful and complete performance that realizes what the earlier studio version barely hints at.

1964

Coltrane's 1964 recordings consist of two projects, both studio sessions containing superb music. (Coltrane did not tour Europe that fall, eliminating a potent source of bootleg recordings). The first, recorded in April and June, resulted in the album *Crescent*. The April 27 session produced enough music for the entire album, but Coltrane was evidently not satisfied, since two titles were rerecorded on June 1. *Crescent* is very much a showcase for the members of the quartet, but it also displays Coltrane the composer, and underscores the increasing maturity and depth of the group's playing. From the April session we have "Lonnie's Lament," a dirge-like melody with medium tempo swing solos, "The Drum Thing," Elvin Jones's feature, and the rich, dark "Wise One," one of Coltrane's most profound and beautiful compositions. The June session contributed "Bessie's Blues," a concise example of how the quartet handled the 12-bar format, and "Crescent," a deep, freely stated theme of considerable power.

Six months later, on December 9, the quartet recorded the suite *A Love Supreme*. This four-part suite is the first major work and the first and perhaps best complete expression of Coltrane's religious consciousness. It also begins twelve months of unparalleled creativity. Even the cover, among Coltrane's favorites, with its simple, unpretentious yet serious profile in subdued black-and-white, and a prayer in place of liner notes, contributes to the whole. Not surprisingly, this suite was both a commercial and critical success.

"Acknowledgment," the first movement, opens with Coltrane's call over a wash of cymbals, followed by the endlessly repeated, hypnotic bass line over which Coltrane and Tyner build Aztec temples out of sound. The chanting behind Tyner's solo is especially incantatory. "Resolution" offers an angular, Monk-ish theme and medium tempo swing, "Pursuance" a faster tempo, while "Psalm" ends the suite with an out-of-tempo "ballad" that builds to an almost aching level of intensity. (The second saxophone at the end of "Psalm," incidentally, is Coltrane himself, overdubbed at the session.)

1965

Scarcely two months after recording *A Love Supreme,* Coltrane brought the quartet plus bassist Art Davis back to Van Gelder's studios. They spent most of the two days of recording working on a version of Eden Ahbez's unusual, Eastern-flavored pop song "Nature Boy," in a complex 10/8 meter. In the posthumously released version from February 17 Garrison repeats an ominous bass line accented by Tyner and Jones. The version from February 18 (released on the album *The John Coltrane Quartet Plays*) is much freer, with only Jones's straight-ahead swing hinting at the unusual time signature. The quintet also recorded the ballad "Feelin' Good" on the 18th, in a version not released until the 1970's.

The quartet recorded one more version of "Nature Boy," at a benefit concert at the Village Gate in New York City on March 28, more important for its association of Coltrane with the emerging New Music scene than for the performance itself. Three broadcasts from the Half Note, in New York City, have also been issued on various bootlegs, documenting the raw power of the group. Coltrane did not return to the studio until mid-May, but from then through the end of June he seems to have lived at Rudy Van Gelder's New Jersey studio. These multiple sessions clearly document the changes the music was undergoing.

The May 17 session produced three titles, all released on *The John Coltrane Quartet Plays.* "Chim Chim Cheree" was Coltrane's soprano/jazz waltz vehicle for the year. In the group's hands any trace of its Mary Poppins origins were obliterated, as Coltrane angularizes the attractive theme over a repetitive Tyner chord pattern. "Brasilia" is a considerably different version of a composition recorded at the Vanguard in 1961 (but first released in this version). "Song of Praise" is a ballad in the out-of-tempo approach of "Psalm." At a session a week later (May 26) Jones was replaced by Roy Haynes. "After the Crescent," evidently once part of a suite with "Crescent" recorded in 1964, and "One Down, One Up" are straightahead modal screamers, showing how well Haynes adapted to that style. The airy "Dear Lord," by contrast, is almost conventional in its easy swing. It starts blandly but grows in complexity and interest, and features a dancing Tyner solo.

On June 10 the quartet was back at Van Gelder's. "Welcome" is an out-of-tempo ballad with an odd-shaped, altissimo melody, released in 1968. "Untitled 90314" gives the soloists (Coltrane and Tyner) a series of unrelated modes to explore, while "Transition" (once probably part of the suite with "Crescent" and "After the Crescent") is a medium swing outing more or less centered on a D dorian scale. The suite is a brooding collection of themes in five continuous, interlinked parts, with features for all four musicians.

Coltrane's second June session (June 16) starts with "Living Space," a soprano saxophone feature. Coltrane reinforced the already powerful melody by overdubbing the soprano saxophone (doubling the melody at the unison and octave); he and Tyner sizzle over the strange suspended scale. "Dusk Dawn" is a vehicle for a medium tempo solo by Tyner and an extended Garrison bass solo. "Vigil" by contrast is a high-power duet between Coltrane and Jones, and is the only title from the session released before Coltrane's death. The final "Untitled 90320" points clearly towards the future, with unusual multiple levels of rhythm, an almost free rhythm from Jones, and Coltrane's deep honks and shrill screeches.

That future arrived in less than two weeks, with a session on June 28. Coltrane combined seven horns (two trumpets, two alto saxophones, and three tenor saxophones) with rhythm (adding a second bassist) in a New Music summit. He brought in a simple line (a B♭-minor blues fragment that echoes "A Love Supreme") and organization (collective improvisation on a sequence of modes, loosely related to that theme, alternated with individual solos in free dialogue with the rhythm section). The result, "Ascension" (released on an LP with the same name), shows Coltrane's linkage to the younger free-music players, his willingness to experiment in the studio, to rewrite the rules. *Ascension* is distant from the controlled religious ecstasy of *A Love Supreme,* with an abandonment to the possibilities of sheer sound and a level of intensity that starts numbingly high and still manages to build. Its rhythmic freedom and collective improvisation is even further from the soloist-plus-orchestra of *Africa/Brass*. Whether this massive, major work is a success or failure is, more than Coltrane's other work, a matter of personal response. Certainly its impact, its power, the urgency of its message is unequaled in the Coltrane legacy.

After an appearance at Newport, Coltrane took the quartet to Europe. The inevitable bootlegs of concert performances are of considerable interest, since they include a live, "Ascension"-informed version of "A Love Supreme" and "Blue Valse" (the title is probably not Coltrane's), actually a quartet version of "Ascension." A Chicago Jazz Festival appearance with Archie Shepp added showed the group exploring post-*Ascension* sensibilities. *Sun Ship,* a set of performances recorded on August 26, and *First Meditations,* recorded September 2, are powerful final views of the quartet. *Sun Ship* shows how much of the change in the music was evolutionary, with Coltrane's tonal and rhythmic freedom complemented by Jones's multi-layered rhythms and Tyner's dissonant harmonies. *First Meditations* is particularly of interest as an earlier, quartet-sized performance of the last of Coltrane's major works, with a level of creative tension similar to *Sun Ship* and a suite of themes differing somewhat from the final version of *Meditations.*

For his fall tour of the West Coast, Coltrane added saxophonist Pharoah Sanders and others, producing a number of interesting recordings in the process. The augmented group was captured live at a club in Seattle, with fascinating versions of such staples as "Body and Soul" and "Out Of This World." "Om," also recorded in Seattle, surrounds a claustrophobic, mostly collective free improvisation with Eastern chanting. From October, in Los Angeles, we have "Kulu Se Mama," a free outing built around a local poet's oration.

Back in New York in November, Coltrane recorded the last of the major works. *Meditations,* a five-part suite, adds saxophonist Pharoah Sanders and drummer Rashied Ali to the original quartet. The suite offers a sense of hard-won balance, a kind of summation of all the elements of the year's music. It blends the approaches of *A Love Supreme* and *Ascension,* with the former work's compositional foundation, control and religious depth added to the latter's freedom, intensity and cathartic joining of voices. Themes are simple, evocative and explored in multiple keys.

The two saxophonists' eerie falsetto yodeling sets an otherworldly tone for "The Father and the Son and the Holy Ghost" and forms the backdrop for the major-scale theme. Compassion is given over to an extended Tyner solo, in a complex 3/4 swing. "Love" begins with Garrison, alone, joined later by Coltrane, Tyner and Jones, who state and explore the peaceful melody. The telegraphic "Consequences" is largely Sanders, who shatters tonality in a solo in which texture replaces melody. Tyner's long, mostly unaccompanied solo follows, rich and impressionistic, almost a farewell (this would be his last recording with Coltrane). It leads to the dark, spiraling theme of "Serenity," Coltrane moving from tonal center to tonal center before settling on a minor triad, the repose of the present offset by the uncertain future. *Meditations* is profound, mature, Ellingtonian in its blending of disparate individual voices; it forms a fitting close to a year of remarkable creativity.

1966–1967

By January 1966 the classic quartet was gone, Tyner replaced by Alice McLeod Coltrane, Elvin Jones by Rashied Ali. Recordings from this later period seem sparse after 1965's riches—Coltrane's health problems, the change in groups, or even the young Coltranes in Alice's care are probable contributing factors. A private Coltrane session in February 1966 yielded four titles, including a performance by Coltrane on Eric Dolphy's bass clarinet, but an Impulse studio session from April has disappeared. Coltrane's appearance at the Village Vanguard in May was captured. "My Favorite Things" and "Naima" provide familiar frameworks against which the changes in the music show clearly, most evident in Ali's multi-layered rhythmic wash in place of Elvin Jones's time-centered propulsion. Two Japanese concerts in July were recorded and released posthumously.

Coltrane's health began to fail in the fall of 1966. Although concerts were canceled and appearances were few, the music is well documented in studio sessions. "Offering" from a February 15, 1967 quartet session was released shortly after Coltrane's death; the balance of the session was only released in 1995. There are obvious changes in the music, with performances more tightly focused and a greater use of group composition and structure.

The following week Coltrane recorded a marvelous series of duets with Rashied Ali, released a decade later as *Interstellar Space*. Other sessions in March and May contributed to the final *Expression* (prepared for release just before Coltrane's death in July). Music from a concert in April (Coltrane's last live performance) also exists.

All jazz is a work in progress—single performances being individual samples of a constantly changing mix of inspiration, technique, group dynamics, material, and the rest of the performer's world and self. Technology can preserve these children of the instant, alive for the space of a breath—but truly the moment occurs only once. We have traveled through six years packed with these individual moments, seeking perspective on a work in progress left incomplete by death. What remains however is a sense of awe at the copiousness of those years, the variety, the moments of magic captured on tape, their sum the rich legacy left behind by John Coltrane.

FRANK KOFSKY

THE NEW WAVE: BOB THIELE TALKS TO FRANK KOFSKY ABOUT JOHN COLTRANE
Coda, May–June 1968

Several non-musicians were very important behind the scenes of John Coltrane's recordings. The one with the longest tenure was engineer Rudy Van Gelder, who recorded Coltrane from 1955 to 1959 and from 1961 to 1967. For a few audio samples of an interview with Van Gelder, see the "enhanced CD" release The Ultimate Blue Train, *discussed in the Discography on page 248 of this anthology.*

Bob Thiele had a long history of producing jazz and popular music before he was assigned to produce Coltrane for the Impulse label. Thiele began with Coltrane's second LP for the company and supervised nearly every subsequent recording session until the saxophonist's death in 1967. Most of these recordings united Coltrane with Van Gelder and Thiele, and they are classics of transcendent artistry, fine engineering, and sympathetic presentation.

Frank Kofsky's later works include John Coltrane and the Jazz Revolution of the 1960s *(New York: Pathfinder Press, 1997);*

Black Music, White Business: Illuminating the History and
Political Economy of Jazz *(New York: Pathfinder Press, 1997);
and* Harry S. Truman and the War Scare of 1948: A Successful
Campaign to Deceive the Nation *(New York: St. Martin's Press,
1993; paper edition, 1995).*—CW

Bob Thiele: John Coltrane was signed to Impulse when it was decided
by ABC to form a jazz label and I think that two bits of credit should
go out—number one to Creed Taylor, the A & R man—and number
two, to someone people would think never existed, Sam Clark, Vice-
President today of the American Broadcasting Company. ABC under
Creed Taylor had been making quite a few jazz records and frankly,
nothing very much was happening and I think Creed would be the first
to admit that nothing was happening as far as sales were concerned. For
some reason, everyone at the company agreed that they should sign
some good names, bigger names as far as jazz was concerned and sign
some people who would sell more records. It was Sam Clark who
decided to separate the labels; in other words, ABC for normal popular
recording and a separate jazz label called Impulse Records.

The first group of artists were Coltrane, J. J. Johnson, I think Art
Blakey and Gil Evans—they issued seven records. Coltrane's first album
was with a big band. Creed Taylor left the company just after the label
started and I went to work and made Coltrane's second album which
was a live album and was, in fact, my first meeting with Coltrane, at the
Village Vanguard.

I didn't know too much about him and I showed up to record for
one night and wound up recording four nights. It was sort of a distant
relationship, really. I was a—well—a little surprised at my own ability
to communicate with him. His attitude was that you're here to record
and here to make good records and I hope you do. I tried to do it and I
think we came up with some good records.

I had read about him and heard about him but I hadn't really listened to him. It was sort of a rough assignment for me—in a way. I
think one of the first records I made for ABC was *"Live" at the Village
Vanguard.* It was my idea to record live, but it was tough for me
because I really wasn't that familiar with his music.

I had four nights of recording and by the second or third night I
was really becoming involved in what was happening and I was just listening. I selected what I felt was the best of the four nights' recording.
Most of the listening at that time was done at Rudy Van Gelder's studio

and when we had finally selected the finished record, we called John and asked him if he would listen to it. He was very happy with the selection and said, go ahead and release it—that's fine. We didn't have a title for one piece and Rudy felt that it was such a tour de force, and it was—you know—like, chasing a train—that's how the title "Chasin' the Trane" came about.

I was grabbed by the music but I don't really think I knew exactly what was happening. I knew that I was emotionally affected, but I don't think I took the time to find out why. I knew that I enjoyed and liked what I had heard. I think right off the bat—I like to think this anyway—Coltrane and I hit it off even though there were no lengthy conversations. There were glances, and you know how things like that are—people can look at one another and in a way, may not be able to express exactly the feeling in words, but I think that there was understanding and a respect for one another.

Frank Kofsky: That album and Impressions *both got relatively poor reviews. Did that prompt you to go off into some other direction, instead of doing more of the long, semi-abstract pieces such as "Chasin' the Trane"?*

Bob Thiele: I think the reviews had an effect but I don't think they really affected what he was doing and what I wanted to do initially. I think that he was less affected by the reviews than I was. After you've been in the record business for years and years, you're always concerned about the commercial aspects, although you try to record as many artistic things as possible. You're always concerned with how well the record will sell.

I read reviews in *Down Beat* which really—I guess they were upsetting things, mainly because I knew that Coltrane was so sincere. I think the fact that Coltrane was sincere and was such an honest and genuine musician affected me and I knew that I was concerned as to why the so-called critics were not as affected as I was. In other words, I am not a critic and here am I deeply affected, but the critics of *Down Beat* were almost like demons in their attacks about what they called the new music and wrote that Coltrane was just rambling and blowing—I really don't remember the exact wordage of the reviews, but they seemed very unfair and almost irresponsible, almost as if they hadn't given any thought to what he was doing.

A very important thing about Coltrane—about anyone who listens to music is that if you are truly interested in music, and affected by music, it would seem to me that either you're immediately affected or never. Coltrane affected me and I am honest enough to admit that I didn't know why, but I knew that there was a response to his music and it would seem to me that the same response should have existed in the so-called critical fraternity and the fact that they weren't meant that maybe they are not the true critics of American jazz music.

Frank Kofsky: Of course, that's what LeRoi Jones has been maintaining all along—that these men bring a different sensibility to the music and anything that isn't in accord with their assumptions, they're simply incapable of understanding.

Bob Thiele: Through the years as I've listened to music and collected records I think it's a very simple deduction that the music is Negro music to begin with and for these guys to write about the music as though it's an American music, that everybody plays equally, and that we all love one another, and we're all brothers, to me, really, that's a lot of horseshit. I mean, I read critics even today in 1968, who say that in the old days, the Negro musicians were never unhappy and they didn't complain about the social conditions in the country, I think they forget that in those old days it just wasn't done. A Negro musician just couldn't come out and say, hey, the situation stinks. And this, to me, I think is the crux of the matter. I think that the reason the Negro can speak out, and really should speak out, is because of the white society. I don't think it's really because of their own society. I think that the Negro has, thank God, been educated, and the more educated Negroes we have, the more dragged they are at white society—and justly. There were educated Negroes 20 years ago, 50 years ago, but if they had opened their mouths I imagine there would be blood flowing. But today, anybody who wants to can speak out and I think it's great, and they should!

Frank Kofsky: Was the album with Duke Ellington, the Ballads *album and the album with Johnny Hartman all your ideas?*

Bob Thiele: Yes, they were all my ideas and John accepted them and was enthusiastic about them. *Ballads* was really my idea to try and educate more listeners. John understood it and knew what we were trying to do. I really think it's one of his great albums.

In those days, what *Down Beat* said with respect to sales of records wrongly affected record people, and now I find that most of the things they said at that time, and even the things they say now, amount to nothing.

Here I was working for a record company and concerned about how well our records would sell and we have a critic who comes along and says, John Coltrane's records are windy, flat and need editing, etc., or whatever he said. I have done my best to forget what he ever said, but at the time he registered and I figured we had better go in and see if we can get John to do some melodic things, do some standard tunes. It turned out to be a great album, so in a way, it was my idea, through Ira Gitler, if you get the message.

With *Ballads* and with *[John Coltrane and] Johnny Hartman*, the selection of tunes was sort of a joint effort. I don't really remember at this point which tunes I selected and which tunes John selected, but it was a joint thing. I selected a few and he selected a few and then we rejected a few and I came up with some more and he came up with some more. It was his idea to record Johnny Hartman. I really don't remember the original singer we were thinking about. We had both agreed on some singers but one night, John says, there's a guy that I think is great and he described the background—where he heard him and why he liked him. So I contacted Johnny and that was the Hartman-Coltrane album. I think it is a great album, too. Of course, most people who read this really don't know me. It's not hindsight when I say this (and in most things I could use a little hindsight), but with Coltrane I felt that every damned thing we were doing was just great.

With Ellington we had two great musicians existing from two different eras and I felt that they could play together. I think that most musicians can really play together so I went and asked Duke if he would want to do an album with John Coltrane with just a rhythm section. He said yes and that's how that album came about.

I've said this before. I don't know whether it was in an interview or not, but the thing that impressed me most about Coltrane and Ellington, was the fact that Coltrane, up until the Ellington album, had always spent what I would consider really too much time on his recordings. He would do a tune, maybe 12, 15 or 20 times before he was satisfied and even though we did a tune 20 times he might go back to, or agree to go back to, the second or third take or something like that. The first tune we did with Ellington was "In a Sentimental Mood." We did that in one take and I'll never forget my reaction. I figured, when the tune ended, now I've got a real problem. Ellington, I know from past experience, is going to say *that's* it, great, and Coltrane would say, I feel we should go over this a few more times. Immediately I ran out of the studio and though I didn't know how I would handle it I had to get the two guys together. I said, Duke (he was the oldest of the three of us here), what do you think, knowing he would say it was great, which it was. He said, "That's fine," and I said, John do you think we should do it again, giving him the opportunity to say something. Duke immediately interrupted and said, "Well, what for, you can't say it again that way, this is it." John said, "Yes, Duke, you're right," and from then on the album went very smoothly. Also from then on, John's recordings were really based on one and two takes. I must say that after that meeting with Ellington, Coltrane never spent that much time on a take, on a tune. He would like to get it in one or two takes and if it didn't happen we would scrap it. That would be the end of it and he would go on to something else. I think it was a very, very important point in Coltrane's recording period, the meeting with Ellington, and I think they both liked the record. Johnny Hodges told me quite emphatically that, as long as he had been playing "In a Sentimental Mood," the best reading of the tune was Coltrane's. I find that in working with an Ellington or a Coltrane or any of the great musicians, they don't seem to think about how great that we got together; they're there to play and they play and I think it's as simple as that.

Frank Kofsky: At what point did you feel you began to get inside of Coltrane's music and have more confidence in your ability to understand it? Can you pinpoint that with any accuracy, or was it too gradual a feeling for you to know?

Bob Thiele: I am sure it was a gradual thing. I think what really happened was finally, a depreciation of time and rhythm as opposed to what he was actually playing. I think once I understood what was happening with it, rhythmically, and what Elvin was doing, then I really began to appreciate Coltrane. I said this before and might as well say it again: after recording John for about a year, and reading those ridiculous reviews, I remember saying to Elvin one night that I had just read a poor review in *Down Beat* and I really couldn't understand it, because they were pressing a point as to how strange and different the music was. I said to Elvin that I don't find it that way anymore. It doesn't seem that way to me and he said, "You've become like the fifth member of the group." I don't think he meant it as a compliment. He was just trying to explain that I had become so involved. This led me to tell people as often as possible that with the new thing, you must spend time to listen to it. I don't think anything that is truly creative should be easy—to create it or appreciate it. Most people, I guess, don't have the time (musicians or listeners) to really sit down and let that music just get into you, and spend all that time listening to it.

Frank Kofsky: There has been some static in various magazines about the fact that two versions of "Ascension" have been released. Why don't we take this opportunity to clarify how that came about.

Bob Thiele: Well, we did "Ascension" in July 1965. That piece ran approximately forty minutes and there was absolutely no splicing of tapes involved in the music. What transpired that afternoon was two 40-minute takes and that was it. There were hardly any rundowns. There was just a discussion of solos, with respect to order of appearance and we made two takes.

After the first take, we listened to it and John said he felt that it was definitely the master. Then he said that he would like to try another and, for the second take, I had run a 7 ½ inch tape copy which I gave him to take home and listen to. We discussed the two takes and both agreed that the first was the one that should be issued. Well, a few months passed and we issued the first take. When the album came out, John called me and said, "That's not the master."

He had begun to enjoy the tape copy of the second one and believed it was greater than the first take. So, when the first take came out, he had become confused and couldn't understand why it was different from the tape he had at home. I reminded him that when we did the recording we both agreed that the best take was the first take. But now, he felt the second was superior and would like to see it issued.

John wanted it out as soon as possible and I agreed that it should come out right away. So, rather than delay the issue, we merely inscribed on the second master, Edition Number II. Now, I've seen it reported (for instance in the discography in *Down Beat's Yearbook*) that there were two issues put out without any explanation. I felt like writing a letter to *Down Beat* but I've written so many letters that they haven't printed, I decided against it. So in a way this is an opportunity to explain that it is clearly marked on the master. However, I must admit that the first version is not readily available now.

Frank Kofsky: *Did your work with Coltrane lead you to become involved with other, younger, newer players who played in the new style?*

Bob Thiele: Coltrane was really a fantastic individual. People have touched on this. Yet, I don't think that enough people know of it. It was certainly through Coltrane that I became aware of Archie Shepp and many of the younger players. When John heard any good player, he would call me and ask that I please give him some consideration. I think that if we had signed everyone that John recommended we'd have four hundred musicians on the label. He was very much concerned about the young musicians. I think that nobody knows this, but Coltrane, shortly before he died, wanted to move to New Jersey. He lived in Long Island and as he wasn't playing clubs, wanted to move to New Jersey to be closer to New York. He wanted a home for his children and for Alice. His mother used to visit quite a bit, but his goal, shortly before he died, was to get a loft in the Village and he wanted to set up a place where people could come in, listen to his music and listen to music being created—in other words, people could attend rehearsals, no admission, just the price of a Coca-Cola, ten cents if you wanted anything to drink, but this was definitely an ambition of his. We only talked about it briefly, but his goal was to have an area where guys could play and people could come and listen. It's unfortunate that he never really got it because he was definitely on the right track. He was earning enough money through records and through his music, his songs, that he could afford to do this. He really didn't have to work too much except for recording, and I think it's a tragedy that he died and a tragedy that young musicians didn't reap the benefit of his ideas.

Frank Kofsky: *So he was very concerned with being a patron of the younger guy?*

Bob Thiele: Oh, yes, there's no question about it. Of course, you knew him just like I did and John Coltrane really had very little to say. It was quiet action. If he heard a young musician he would call me and all of a sudden the player would be recording. He was really helping an awful lot of people.

Frank Kofsky: *You mentioned that he really didn't have to work much more. How did his record sales compare with that of other artists? The* reason I ask that is that it is often maintained, especially by nightclub owners, that there is no market for the Coltrane and post-Coltrane type of music.

Bob Thiele: You know, we all try to be realistic and the only reason you make records is to sell records and Coltrane happened to sell an awful lot of records. Most of the musicians in the new movement happened to sell records too. I don't say that they sell in the quantities that Coltrane sold, but they do sell records and there is a market for them, not only in the United States but all over the world. I think that the problem of the clubs reverts back to what I was talking about before, that it requires some concentration on the part of the listener, and you know, a little bit of intellect—it's that kind of music and when you're in a club and you're boozing it up and you have a broad with you, you really aren't there to listen. I think you're there to be involved in making the scene— "I'm here Coltrane, and all that!"

If Coltrane had lived he would have reached the point where he would be playing at Town Hall or Carnegie Hall and I think there would be full houses and I think there would be attentive audiences and big audiences. I think it's going to happen anyway with respect to jazz music—I think that's the only way jazz music can go. The reason we sell records is undoubtedly because somebody is listening and let's face it, a lot of the records that we put out require a lot of concentration.

Frank Kofsky: How much actual direction did you exert at the Coltrane record sessions?

Bob Thiele: I would say that there was less direction with Coltrane than there would be with a pop record or with a big band date or with a Duke Ellington.

I'm not looking to take credit for very much with respect to Coltrane. The only thing I felt was a contribution on my part was in the area of good recording and—encouragement. Encouragement is the word because there were many nights that we recorded when I felt that he was really into something and there was a subtle situation where I had to get him to continue. So that, to me, is the major contribution that I made with respect to Coltrane, getting him to record and, once in the studio, having him continue work when maybe he didn't want to or maybe some of the musicians didn't want to.

Frank Kofsky: Do you have any idea what Coltrane's favorite Impulse record was? Did you ever talk about that with him?

Bob Thiele: I spent a few hours with John at his house a few times and being in his home, I found that this was the only time that he completely relaxed; in other words, the only time he really was willing to talk was when he was in the confines of the four walls of his living room. I remember very definitely, I said, "Which album do you really dig the most" and he said, "Well, I like them all," but he said, "After I listen to one for a few weeks, I stop listening and I forget about it."

Frank Kofsky: Who made the final decision on what takes of a tune went into an album? Or, if you had recorded more than enough for an album, how did you finally arrive at the decision as to what was to go in?

Bob Thiele: The situations varied. If we were trying to a make a certain release date, he had enough confidence in me to let me pick the takes and put the album together. If we had the time, we would try to do it together. Naturally, I tried wherever possible and whenever possible, to give him the time to listen to the things that we had done. We have many things in the can right now that he thought were great at the time he recorded them. He would say, "let's hold up on what we've done, I've got something new." This is why there are things still to be issued. I am appreciative of the fact that he had enough faith in me that many of the albums were based on my own selections.

I'd like to point out that during the last year of his life he began to feel that there shouldn't be liner notes written. He felt basically that everyone that wrote liners was really saying the same thing over and over again. How much more can you say and how much more can you try to educate the buyer as to what he was playing? He felt that all he wanted to do is play it, record it and issue it and those that want to buy it, buy it. With no explanations. In fact, I asked Nat Hentoff to make that point in the final album, the last album he recorded.

I've had some lengthy discussions with Alice Coltrane, who is a very, very beautiful woman. Alice Coltrane still lives in Long Island where John lived and I don't think she gets to New York too often. We have agreed, not because of any legal reasons, but because of John Coltrane, and because of my own feeling about the man, that we're going to try and work together on selecting the material for maybe the next three or four albums. As I said, Alice is a very beautiful woman and she is leading a life right now, according to the wishes of John. The things that she remembers and the things he said have affected her deeply and the life that she lives is based on the things that he said. She expressed, re-expressed his desire not to have liner notes on his albums and of course, I will comply.

I feel that there should be liner notes that discuss the man and present the man as he was, not necessarily descriptions of the music. I don't think that John really disagreed with any of the notes that were written. And Alice expressed that to me, too. She said, "Say whatever you want about John Coltrane but how can you really write about or tell anyone as to what the music was about?" I think that the greatest thing he ever said was in the interview that you did, where you asked him, "What have you got to say about people that don't like your music?" He said, "That doesn't bother me at all." In other words, he never was the Dale Carnegie of the music world.

He did call every once in a while to find out if there was an acceptance to a new album. I guess I am oversimplifying his lack of interest in the public, but I really don't think he was that concerned.

Frank Kofsky: Is there any vast difference between material that has been released and that which hasn't?

Bob Thiele: No, I don't think so. The material that is unreleased is from the period of 1963. Then we have material definitely from Newport 1966 and we have material from California and we have material that was done in New York, and, as I said, it's about three or four LPs. This unreleased material is not inferior, it is just that he became quite busy in the studios. I wanted him to record more and I had a sneaky little way of getting him into the studio. He was always concerned about the welfare of the quartet. When I say welfare, I mean literally, the financial aspects. When the quartet was out of work for a few weeks I knew that this was the best time to get him to record because of two things. Number one, he wanted naturally to record music but he also wanted to get money for Elvin and Jimmy and McCoy. There's really nothing devious about it but I knew that if I said to John, "Let's get into the studio so that we can get the money for the trio," that was a motivation and that would get him right in. And yet I wish I had recorded him live more. Those live sessions— incredible!

Frank Kofsky: Did you ever get into any serious artistic disputes, where you had strong opinions on opposite sides of a question?

Bob Thiele: No. It would be interesting if I could say yes, but I can't say we ever had any disagreement. The only pressure that I brought to bear was the *Ballads* album. We never had any problems, none at all. I was really getting to know him near the end and I wish he had lived, not only to hear more music but to get to know him better. I was really getting close to him and it was a good feeling. Of course, he never had any harsh words for anybody, he never put anyone down and he never fought with his musicians and he never raised his voice.

Frank Kofsky: Do you have a favorite album, of all the albums of his that you recorded?

Bob Thiele: I don't think there is a favorite album. But I think there are favorite things, if you'll pardon the expression—a couple of tracks in the Ellington thing and I like *Ballads* and the first *Village Vanguard*.

He was probably the greatest musician in the history of popular music and I was lucky enough to be involved in his recordings and many people ask me about John Coltrane and what was he like and what was it like to record him and, of course, you're asking the same things and I don't really want to build up some sort of mystique about my relationship with John Coltrane. I think that I have expressed it honestly, as it really was and it really isn't that romantic or that glamorous. It was a very, very friendly and warm relationship and, not to sound corny, I think that he opened up a lot of things for me. I think that if I had never met Coltrane, I would be in serious trouble with respect to the real crappy economic aspects of my own career, and so I think that I owe a lot to Coltrane and I think a lot of people ought to— you know—admit it. The young kids admit it and maybe some of the old time critics won't admit it, but some critics should admit it. He was a terrific guy, he really was.

PART FOUR

Nightclub and Concert Reviews

John Coltrane's appearances were reviewed many times during his career, and many of the best reviews appeared in *Down Beat* magazine. However, because I had to be highly selective in my choices of *Down Beat* material for this anthology, I chose to reprint the lengthier articles found earlier in this volume and then survey and quote from those and other live reviews. Two complete reviews from other sources are included below in this survey.

CARL WOIDECK
EARLY CRITICAL RECEPTION
1997

Formal reviews of Coltrane playing with Miles Davis during 1955 and 1956 are scarce. In J. C. Thomas's *Chasin' the Trane*, Columbia Records producer George Avakian recalls, "I met Coltrane with Miles at the Café Bohemia late in 1955." While playing, Coltrane "seemed to grow taller in height, larger in size, with each note that he played, each chord he seemed to be pushing to its outer limits." In the same book, saxophonist Paul Jeffrey remembers hearing Davis in late 1956 with two saxophonists—the established Sonny Rollins and the up-and-coming John Coltrane: "I'd always thought of Rollins as a great tenor virtuoso, but Coltrane more than held his own. He followed Sonny's melodic solos with some of the strangest, most convoluted harmonies and chord progressions I'd ever heard."

In 1957 John Coltrane stopped taking drugs and drinking. In many ways, various aspects of his music came together that year. 1957 was also the year that Coltrane spent a summer working with Thelonious Monk's quartet at Manhattan's Five Spot Café. Reviewing Monk's group in *Down Beat*, Dom Cerulli called Coltrane "a forceful voice on tenor. On the sets caught, he blew longish lines with a fierceness that didn't impede his flow. He is achieving a distinctive sound on tenor, one with tremendous vitality."

Coltrane soon rejoined Miles Davis's group and stayed for several years. In late February, Miles Davis's group with Coltrane was heard in Los Angeles by critic John Tynan and subsequently reviewed for *Down Beat*: "Slashing at the canvas of his own creation, Coltrane erupted in a fantastic onrush of surrealism and disconnected musical thought best appreciated within the dark corridors of his personal psyche. The philosophical implications of his performance, with its overtones of neurotic compulsion and contempt for an audience, belong in another area of journalistic examination." Tynan's comments were a prelude to his extremely negative review of Coltrane's own group in 1961, a review which in part inspired Coltrane to respond to his critics in print. (See "John Coltrane and Eric Dolphy Answer the Jazz Critics," on pages 109–117 of this volume.)

DON NELSEN
'TRANE STOPS IN THE GALLERY
New York Daily News, *May 15, 1960*

As soon as Coltrane returned from a March–April European tour with Miles Davis, the saxophonist permanently left Davis's band and started his own group. His first engagement was at Manhattan's Jazz Gallery. A reviewer for Variety *wrote that "Coltrane's driving, building choruses, which might raise the dead, managed to get a living reaction out of the sober railbirds [audience members seated in a railed-off section]. The saxman's tenor solo on 'Body and Soul' is a particularly brilliant exhibition and almost a history of jazz. The range of tonal effects covers both the Colemans, Ornette and Hawkins."*

Don Nelsen reviewed the Coltrane group for New York Sunday News. *His classic and often-quoted opening sentence gives some indication of the enthusiastic response of many listeners to Coltrane's music. Interestingly, private tapes (as yet unissued) of the Coltrane quartet at the Jazz Gallery do exist. Let's hope that they will be legitimately issued soon.*

Note: Material about Chico Hamilton's group has been deleted.
—CW

Run, do not walk or otherwise loiter on your way down to the Jazz Gallery. The reason is John Coltrane, a tenor saxophonist who has the future coming out of his horn.

This musician is phenomenal. Few jazzmen possess such a thorough knowledge of their instrument plus the combined imagination and feeling to translate that knowledge into great music. Coltrane is not just a player. He is a composer, practicing his craft every moment he is on the stand. He creates huge patterns of interwoven themes united in a beautifully-knit whole. The sounds he produces are often weird, like they shouldn't be coming out of that horn at all, but somehow he makes them seem natural. It's as if these notes were hiding inside all along, just waiting for someone to appear and release them.

Every now and then, however, Coltrane lays the tenor aside and works on that rare bird of jazz, the soprano saxophone. The story here is the same. Tremendous. If I were a budding soprano saxophonist and heard Coltrane, I'd send my horn to the Salvation Army. Who can follow the boss?

Though Coltrane completely dominates the stage, he has sturdy backing from pianist Steve Kuhn, bassist Steve Davis and drummer Pete LaRoca. Kuhn is especially resourceful and Davis sounds fine. LaRoca, too, performs well, though his occasional histrionics could probably get him a card in Actors' Equity.

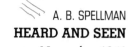 A. B. SPELLMAN
HEARD AND SEEN
Metronome, *November 1961*

In 1961 John Coltrane added alto saxophonist–bass clarinetist–flutist Eric Dolphy to the group, making it a quintet. Down Beat critic John Tynan heard the group in October and wrote, "I happen to object to the musical nonsense being peddled in the name of jazz by John Coltrane and his acolyte, Eric Dolphy." At the time of this review, the group had become a sextet with the addition of a second bassist, and A. B. Spellman finds much to like about them. In light of Tynan's reference to Dolphy as Coltrane's "acolyte," it's interesting that Spellman humorously characterizes the group as "three ogres, their priest, and his altarboys."—CW

Place: Village Gate, 185 Thompson St., NYC.

Artists: John Coltrane Sextet: Coltrane, tenor and soprano saxes; Eric Dolphy, alto sax, flute and bass clarinet; McCoy Tyner, piano; Art Davis and Reginald Workman, basses; Elvin Jones, drums.

There are times when finding yourself in front of an action makes you grateful to be there. At these times, if music is the action, if jazz is the music, there is something like a bridge but not at all a bridge between mouth and ear that puts ear inside mouth or mouth inside ear and makes experience mutual.

Here is a group consisting of three ogres, their priest, and his altarboys. Often they assault innocent little tunes, ripping their flesh apart while the renegade priest points the way to new violence with the bones of the victim. This is to say that, despite its apparent weirdness, this group's approach is harmonic, as opposed to Ornette's rhythmic experimentation. McCoy Tyner hands up the changes in big round chords that are almost predictable, which Elvin Jones, a ruthless motor, masticates into little energy units. Elvin's African energies go directly into the solos, as they should, so that you have to listen to hear what he's doing, though there are few people louder. Tyner's work appears at first to be another voice altogether, but he actually provides the harmonic reference, the canvas Trane and Eric throw those violent splashes of sound against. "My Favorite Things" isn't my favorite tune. Since it's come to be so popular, they play it so often they are liable to go by rote. But therein we find the salient methodology of the band. For this tune, Trane uses the soprano sax (as you no doubt know) and Eric plays flute, and not at all like a bird against the screaming jungle. Tyner's job is set and invariable. From git to go he plays the minor chords the song is built upon so faithfully it could be Mary Martin's wobbly contralto instead of Trane's soprano. Fortunately it isn't. The soprano sax's a difficult horn, and few men (only Bechet and Hodges that I can think of) have been able to handle its timbre and technique. Its tone is enough to put you off unless someone like Trane or Bechet (who somehow round off the edges) is playing it. Trane uses its shrillness to extend your (and his) ear to the far, far ends of harmony. He goes straight into, maybe through, Tyner's minor field and further. Dolphy too. He is the only jazz musician I can think of who doesn't make the flute sound like a whistle. Well, much, much more should be said about Eric's playing, particularly on bass clarinet and alto, and Elvin's as "My Favorite Things" is really his tune; and how the string bass went back to its more European melodic and harmonic uses in jazz by the simple addition of another string bass which may be bowed; and what a sweet pianist McCoy Tyner is, etc., etc., but there isn't that much room here and you'd probably want to go to hear all that rather than read about it anyway. So go.

CARL WOIDECK
LATER CRITICAL RECEPTION
1997

On December 31, 1963, John Coltrane's quintet with Eric Dolphy appeared in a Lincoln Center concert, which was reviewed for *Down Beat* by LeRoi Jones (Amiri Baraka). Of Coltrane's solo on the composition "Impressions," Jones wrote: "Coltrane started squatting and tooting on this number and got into that hysterically exciting thing he can do with such singular expressiveness." This was evidently the last public appearance of Coltrane and Dolphy together. The concert also included the Cecil Taylor quintet with tenor saxophonist Albert Ayler. Ten years younger than Coltrane, Ayler belonged to a younger generation of exploratory musicians who would strongly influence Coltrane in the next three years.

In 1964 (after the death of Eric Dolphy) Coltrane began inviting younger exploratory musicians (especially saxophonists) to play with his group occasionally. Tenor saxophonist Archie Shepp was among the first of these. Then in 1965, tenorist Farrell "Pharoah" Sanders and drummer Rashied Ali were gradually incorporated into the Coltrane group, making it a sextet. On November 10, 1965, this group plus saxophonists Archie Shepp and Carlos Ward were reviewed for *Down Beat* by A. B. Spellman: "I think I see what Coltrane wants—an ever evolving groundswell of energy that will make the musical environment so dangerous that he and the others will have to improvise new weapons to constantly beat back the Brontosaurs." Spellman went on to say that when drummers Jones and Ali both played, the nightclub could not contain and separate their sounds: "I had no idea what the soloists were saying, and I doubt that the players could hear each other."

Elvin Jones soon left the group for artistic reasons, and Ali became the primary drummer. Pianist McCoy Tyner also left the group eventually and was replaced by Alice McLeod, who soon became Alice Coltrane. Only bassist Jimmy Garrison remained from Coltrane's classic quartet accompanists.

The quintet with Coltrane, Sanders, McLeod-Coltrane, Garrison, and Ali were joined by alto saxophonist Carlos Ward, tenor saxophonist Albert Ayler, and trumpeter Donald Ayler for a Lincoln Center "Titans of the Tenor" concert that also included tenorists Coleman Hawkins, Sonny Rollins, Yusef Lateef, and Zoot Sims elsewhere on the program. In Dan Morgenstern's *Down Beat* review, he reported that Coltrane appeared "relaxed and happy." Morgenstern also wrote that at the end of the Coltrane group's highly intense set, "The stunned audience collected its wits sufficiently to offer mild applause and scattered booing. After this display one wonders what had happened to Coltrane. . . . Has he lost all musical judgment? Or is he putting on his audience? Whatever the answer, it was saddening to contemplate this spectacle, unworthy of a great musician."

John Coltrane's last concert took place on April 23, 1967 at New York's Olatunji Center of African Culture. Coltrane's quintet was joined by two percussionists. The master of ceremonies was Billy Taylor. In J. C. Thomas's *Chasin' the Trane*, Taylor recalls hearing Coltrane during this last period: "Coltrane played extremely technical music, then progressed to an abstraction of that, an abstraction in sound. These extra-musical sounds—honking, screaming, almost crying—seemed to be an integral part of his overall tonal structure. It was like a man who was really in control of his language; he was saying something that you absolutely understood."

PART FIVE

Record
Reviews

The history of John Coltrane's critical reception as a recording artist can be found in the pages of magazines such as *Metronome, Down Beat, The Jazz Review, High Fidelity,* and *HiFi/Stereo Review* (earlier *HiFi & Music Review* and *HiFi/Stereo*). Some excellent reviews—most from *HiFi/Stereo Review* and *High Fidelity*—are reprinted below. Quotations from other magazines are woven into the commentary to provide a broader context.

BILL COSS
THE NEW MILES DAVIS QUINTET
Metronome, *July 1956*

In this review, Bill Coss not only criticized Coltrane for being "out of tune" (which he was occasionally on this record), but the author also had mixed feelings about Garland, Chambers, and Jones. In fact, only Davis received unqualified praise, although his new maturity is characterized as "almost in spite of himself." When Nat Hentoff reviewed this recording for Down Beat, *he strongly praised Coltrane's bandmates. Miles Davis was said to be in "wonderfully cohesive form," Red Garland played "some of his best choruses on record," Paul Chambers laid down a support "that could carry an army band," and Philly Joe Jones was "pulsatingly crisp as usual." Hentoff mentioned Coltrane's influences in Dexter Gordon, Sonny Rollins, and Sonny Stitt and wrote, "But so far there's very little Coltrane. His general lack of individuality lowers the rating." Listening to this album today, Coltrane sounds well on his way to transcending his influences and finding his own voice, although, to be fair, his playing on this album is uneven. Incidentally, Nat Hentoff went on to become one of Coltrane's strongest admirers, as later reviews in this section show.*

One later Miles Davis review which could not be included here is saxophonist (and Coltrane friend) Benny Golson's classic assessment of Davis's Milestones *LP which appeared in the January, 1959, issue of* The Jazz Review *(readers can find the entire review in Gary Carner's* The Miles Davis Companion, *another anthology in this Schirmer Books series). Golson wrote, "I have heard no one, lately, who creates like Coltrane. . . . I feel that this man is definitely blazing a new musical trail. . . . In closing, I'd like to say—keep one eye on the world and the other on John Coltrane."—CW*

"Squeeze Me," "There Is No Greater Love," "How Am I to Know," "S'posin'," "The Theme," "Stablemates" (Prestige LP 7014).

The cover reads, *The New Miles Davis Quintet.* Fortunately, it has the same *old* Miles Davis because everything else is much below par. There is too much echo on all the soloists, the ensembles are generally bad; the tenor on the Rollins-Stitt kick is even more out of tune; Paul Chambers plays well though still with some intonation trouble; Philly Joe Jones is often too busy; Red Garland's piano is a nice *single* line, though the two-handed bit is too close to Garner for comfort. Miles on the ballads is worth the price of the album. "Theme" will be the track to receive the most notice. But none of it would have any real value except for Miles who seems, almost in spite of himself, to be building to a new maturity.

NAT HENTOFF
JOHN COLTRANE
HiFi & Music Review, *February 1958*

This 1957 recording was John Coltrane's first LP under his sole leadership. Since his first LP with Miles Davis, Coltrane had become a much more experienced musician. Soon before this recording, he quit taking narcotics and stopped drinking alcohol. Straightening out his life (one of the compositions on this album is titled "Straight Street") fostered a new consistency and greater individuality in Coltrane's improvisation. As he told Barbara Gardner, ". . . I got the recording contract with Prestige and I decided that if I was going to put anything on record, then it ought to be me." The result of that vow can be heard on this important recording.—CW

John Coltrane. "Bakai"; "Violets for Your Furs"; "Time Was"; "Straight Street"; "While My Lady Sleeps"; "Chronic Blues." John Coltrane (tenor sax), Paul Chambers (bass), Al Heath (drums), Red Garland & Mal Waldron (piano), Johnnie Splawn (trumpet), Sahib Shihab (baritone sax). Prestige 7105.

John Coltrane, 31, has in the past year detonated more concentrated enthusiasm among eastern modern jazzmen than any tenor since Sonny Rollins. Coltrane served a valuable apprenticeship with Miles Davis for many months and, since the summer of 1957, has learned and grown more with Thelonious Monk.

Coltrane's first album as leader sets him in four sextet tracks plus two with quartet. He is a player in what is over-loosely termed the "hard" school of modern jazz in that he plays with fierce, propulsive urgency, possessing a tone and attack that is bluntly direct. Harmonically, he is consistently adventurous, and in overall conception, he has become unusually absorbing. Among his supporters in this launching, the most notable are Mal Waldron, pianist on three of the tracks; bassist Paul Chambers; and the muscularly assertive baritone saxophonist, Sahib Shihab.

JOHN S. WILSON
BLUE TRAIN
High Fidelity, *March 1958*

Blue Train is regarded today as a classic early Coltrane recording. Coltrane was able to obtain a one-album release from his usual Prestige label to record this album for Blue Note. Unlike Prestige, Blue Note paid for rehearsals before the recording date, and the result was superior ensemble playing and greater group unity. The

Blue Note rehearsal policy also gave Coltrane the confidence to include a greater number of original compositions—and more challenging ones—than he had in the past. All four of the Coltrane originals on this record are still played today and form part of the repertoire for hard-swinging modern jazz.

For the most part, John S. Wilson was not an admirer of John Coltrane's playing. During the 1950s, Wilson found Coltrane's solos to be "strident" and his timbre to have a "harsh shallowness," although in 1958 he praised Coltrane for having "a greater sense of form than many of his blow-happy contemporaries." Here, Wilson compares Coltrane's tone to a hacksaw, while praising the young Lee Morgan's trumpet contributions.—CW

Blue Note 1577

Coltrane's hard, fierce tone slashes through this disc like an urgent hack saw, but he is completely overshadowed by young Lee Morgan's fantastic excursions on trumpet. Morgan's horn crackles and roars through the up-tempo selections which, fortunately, dominate the disc. The single ballad in the set is as tedious as these affairs usually are in the hands of such hard-toned modernists.

RALPH J. GLEASON
GIANT STEPS
HiFi/Stereo, *May 1960*

Giant Steps was the first Coltrane-led LP to feature all-original compositions by the saxophonist. Many critics recognized the record as a Coltrane landmark. In The Jazz Review, *Mait Edey wrote, "I have never heard Coltrane play so well, and think for the first time that all that roaring praise (which has seemed somewhat indiscriminate in the past) is becoming fully justified." Interestingly, earlier in 1960 Ralph Gleason had also reviewed* Giant Steps *for* Down Beat *magazine. Gleason gave the record the maximum five stars and wrote, "You can tag this LP as one of the important ones.*" Metronome's *H. A. Woodfin, however, found much of Coltrane's playing "rhythmically dull and disconcerting" and thought that Coltrane's saxophone timbre was "almost flat and colorless compared to the sound he had previously made his own." (All of Coltrane's previous recordings as a leader were made at Rudy Van Gelder's studio; this LP was made at the Atlantic Records studio.) Today, many alternate takes of "Giant Steps" are available in the seven-CD box* The Heavyweight Champion: The Complete Atlantic Recordings.—CW

Interest: First rank modern jazz
Performance: Sensitive

Tenor sax-man John Coltrane is one of the few artists in jazz whose every LP is worth owning. This one, the first devoted entirely to his own compositions, shows him to be a composer of earthy, almost folksy melodies on which he displays a very inventive improvisatory ability. Into everything he does, even when he is being more lyric than usual—as is the case in this album—Coltrane injects a high degree of personal feeling. No matter how complicated his improvisations may become, he always keeps the basic rhythm in a swinging mode, and always manages to make his soaring lines and almost breathtaking intensity sound logical. The accompaniment from bassist Paul Chambers is particularly sympathetic and Wynton Kelly, on "Naima," shows the flash of subdued fire that has made him an important member of the Miles Davis Quintet this past year. Of all the tunes on the LP, "Syeeda's Song Flute," a handsomely designed short melody named for Coltrane's daughter, sticks in the ear long after the LP has been played through. A good sign.

NAT HENTOFF
MY FAVORITE THINGS
HiFi/Stereo, *July 1961*

My Favorite Things *was the first opportunity for most listeners to hear John Coltrane play the soprano sax. The soprano was uncommon in modern jazz; its last major players were the innova-*

tor Sidney Bechet and his soprano sax protégé, Johnny Hodges. In Pete Welding's review of this disc for Down Beat, *he wrote of Coltrane's approach to the soprano, "One is tempted to say that Coltrane is already the second significant innovator on this instrument . . ." [after Bechet]. Welding gave the album the maximum of five stars, calling it "nothing short of magnificent. . . . There are no loose ends here; all the disparate elements of his style have fallen into place for Coltrane, and a synthesis has been effected."*

Hentoff's review of the LP is generally positive, but he finds the lengthy performance of "My Favorite Things" to be too long at over thirteen minutes. Coltrane had begun playing unusually long solos while he was with Miles Davis—in the years after this review Coltrane's nightclub solos sometimes ran thirty minutes in length, and one selection might continue for forty-five minutes. This was not the last time critics or listeners found a Coltrane performance to be "too long."—CW

Interest: Exploratory jazz
Performance: Stronger on tenor

This is the first full album by John Coltrane's current quartet, and it is also the first to provide a fairly extended chance to hear Coltrane on his new subsidiary instrument, the soprano saxophone, which he uses for two essays in creating moods—a sinuous, too long, but generally effective "My Favorite Things" and a softly colored "Everytime We Say Goodbye."

The second side, on which Coltrane returns to tenor saxophone, is more fiery and, to me, seems to have more interesting ideas; Coltrane's "Summertime," for example, is a brilliant, intense personalization of the tune. Steve Davis and Elvin Jones are excellent, flexible associates, but I find McCoy Tyner's piano playing a disappointment. He is much less individualistic than his leader, and his style is rather diffuse. All told, this is a satisfying disc, but not indispensable.

NAT HENTOFF
OLÉ
HiFi/Stereo, *March 1962*

Nat Hentoff devotes his review to the title composition. He expresses concern about the length of Coltrane's performances and is not alone in his reservations about this practice. In evaluating Olé *and another LP* (Africa/Brass) *for* High Fidelity, *reviewer John S. Wilson wrote of "the sameness of Coltrane's solos and of his group's general style, and the extreme length of the performances . . . which serves to emphasize the over-all monotony." Many listeners found, however, that their concerns about the length of Coltrane's performances were transcended when they experienced the evident passion and commitment of Coltrane in his nightclub performances.—CW*

> *Interest: Major but prolix jazzman*
> *Performance: Intense*

Repeated listening to the first half of this album—the eighteen-minute "Olé"—leaves this reviewer with the impression that if the emperor's clothes are not in this case entirely nonexistent, the emperor is nonetheless underdressed. Despite the title, the sinuously insistent theme is more Near Eastern than Spanish. It is true that Coltrane and his colleagues create and sustain a magnetic, broodingly passionate mood. A considerable help, incidentally, in maintaining the trance is the use of two basses—one as a drone and the other to supply supplementary rhythms. And there is a dialogue between the basses that makes for the most intriguing section of the piece.

By the fourth time around, however, one begins to look harder for melodic substance in the work of the horns and the pianist. There is very little. Coltrane can get away with suggesting more than he plays because of the emotional impact of his playing and because of his harmonic ingenuity. But the other players add rather obvious embellishments to a very slight theme. It's fine for background music to the novels of Paul Bowles, but it's decidedly wispy for jazz.

BALLADS
HiFi/Stereo Review, *May 1963*

Since his previous recording for Atlantic, Olé, John Coltrane's music continued to evolve. Coltrane had asked his friend, saxo-phonist–flutist–bass clarinetist Eric Dolphy, to join Coltrane's group and make it a quintet. Critic John Tynan heard this group in 1961 and called it a demonstration of an "anti-jazz" trend. Coltrane's new record label, Impulse, recorded the quintet and guests "live" on three nights at New York City's Village Vanguard. These recordings documented new and more intense directions in Coltrane's improvisational approach and group sound.

This album of mostly calm and slow ballads, then, was a departure for Coltrane in the early 1960s. In the interview with Frank Kofsky found on page 128 of this anthology, Coltrane says that the idea of an album of ballads definitely arose from his own feelings for the songs and was also partly inspired by Impulse's desire for musical balance in their Coltrane catalog. In Down Beat *magazine, John S. Wilson gave this LP two stars out of a possible five, call-ing it "an unimpressive set" and writing that Coltrane "rarely does anything of interest with these tunes."*

Interest: The calmer Coltrane
Performance: Introspective

As I have observed in previous appraisals of Coltrane, the man's playing is in essence lyrical—even when he is at his most demoniacally complex. In this set of ballad interpretations, the quality of that lyricism should dis-arm even the most implacable of Coltrane's critics. He indicates, first of all, that like all major jazzmen, he can stay close to the melody in a first chorus, and yet infuse it with compelling individuality. In the subsequent variations, Coltrane further reveals how disciplined, sensitive, and eco-nomical his improvisation can be. The aching cry that is always charac-teristic of Coltrane's tone becomes particularly evocative in ballad performances. His rhythm support—and McCoy Tyner's solos—are a fit-ting complement, resilient and lucid.

JOE GOLDBERG
A LOVE SUPREME
HiFi/Stereo Review, *July 1965*

A Love Supreme *is generally considered to be one of the best examples of John Coltrane's classic quartet. This suite of four sections satisfyingly combines Coltrane's intense improvisational side with his ever-changing compositional interests. The album is a milestone in Coltrane's career in that it was the first time that he so explicitly displayed his growing sense of music as spiritual expression. In the liner notes, Coltrane wrote, "During the year 1957, I experienced, by the grace of God, a spiritual awakening which was to lead me to a richer, fuller, more productive life. At that time, in gratitude, I humbly asked to be given the means and privilege to make others happy through music. I feel this has been granted through His grace." From this point on, many of Coltrane's compositions—including "Meditations," "Ascension," and "Om"—would have titles that suggested spirituality and personal growth.*

Don DeMicheal gave the LP the maximum five stars in his review for Down Beat, *writing, "This is a significant album, because Coltrane has brought together the promising but underdeveloped aspects of his previous work; has shorn, compressed, extended and tamed them; and has emerged a greater artist for it." In this review, Goldberg praises the playing on this record and finds musical continuity with Coltrane's other recent albums. At the same time, Goldberg feels that the philosophy contained in the liner notes was unnecessary for appreciation of the music.—CW*

Performance: Garrulous Coltrane

John Coltrane has made it very difficult to discuss this disc with any objectivity. In the liner notes and an accompanying poem, Coltrane tells us of a religious experience he has undergone, and dedicates himself and the album to God in a manner that is almost embarrassingly open and fervent. It is God who is the recipient of the "Love Supreme" that is the album's title.

I find little difference between the music on this record and that which Coltrane has played on the last several discs he has released. There are the modal passages, the long, garrulous statements, and (in the last section here) the suggestion of an ominous spiritual, all of which he has employed before. Elvin Jones and Jimmy Garrison both play better than I have ever heard them play before. The result is a good record, one of the better ones Coltrane has made for Impulse. And I think the listener might enjoy the music without need of the philosophy that accompanies it.

NAT HENTOFF
ASCENSION
HiFi/Stereo Review, *August 1966*

John Coltrane's Ascension *is an album-length composition/performance by an expanded group built around his classic quartet with four additional saxophones, two trumpets, and an additional bass. In* Down Beat *magazine, Bill Mathieu awarded it the maximum five stars and wrote, "This is possibly the most powerful human sound ever recorded." This work, strongly influenced by Ornette Coleman's octet composition/performance "Free Jazz" from 1960, is indeed "intense" as Hentoff calls it. Interestingly, neither Coleman nor Coltrane ever quite returned to this format on subsequent albums.*

Performance: Intense

John Coltrane is becoming increasingly interested in the manipulation of textures as the primary shaping force in his music. As Archie Shepp, quoted in the notes, says, "The idea is similar to what the action painters do, in that it creates various surfaces of color which push into each other, creating tensions and counter tensions and various fields of energy." Logically, therefore, Coltrane has been enlarging his regular group in order to have more textural possibilities with which to work. Simultaneously, he concentrates on a group concept of playing. There are still solos—often long ones—but in this album they are subordinate to the *group's* movement-by-colors. In *Ascension*, he has achieved his most absorbing success so far in this style. The record begins at a high level of intensity and continues to climb as horns play against each other in ensemble passages and as soloists engage in fierce dialogues with the rhythm section. The best advice for a listener who finds it difficult to discover a coherent direction to hang onto is that given by Shepp: "There is unity, but it is a unity of sounds and textures rather than like an A-B-A approach." Quite apart from analysis, the performance is of extraordinary emotional force. As altoist Marion Brown recalls, "We did two takes, and they both had that kind of thing in them that makes people scream. The people who were in the studio *were* screaming."

JOE GOLDBERG
MEDITATIONS
HiFi/Stereo Review, *February 1967*

Meditations *continued some of the aspects of Coltrane's previous albums. As with* A Love Supreme *and* Ascension, *the performances are quite high in energy and the compositions have titles with spiritual implications. And as with* Ascension, *Coltrane's classic quartet was expanded, in this case with a second saxophone and a second drum set. Down Beat had anticipated the potential controversy that such an intense record would produce, and assigned the LP to two writers for two reviews. Don DeMicheal gave the record the maximum five stars, and wrote that the music "opens up a part of my self that normally is tightly closed, and seldom-recognized feelings, emotions, thoughts well up from the opened door and sear my consciousness." William Russo gave the record one star and wrote that "Coltrane lacks the spirit of the idiom he attempts. He gets stuck, repeating figurations time and time again, as if such repetition could somehow improve what little they had to offer the first two or three times they occur."*

In this review, Joe Goldberg observes that Coltrane had of late pursued artistic directions that the writer could not appreciate. The writer notes that Coltrane's long-time drummer, Elvin Jones, had recently left the group for artistic reasons.—CW

John Coltrane, long one of my favorite musicians, has recently gone where I cannot follow, and his latest album is another footfall in that land. In the notes, my colleague Nat Hentoff describes the album as an exposure of "the rawness of palpable, visceral, painful, challenging, scraping, scouring self-discovery." After the *Ascension* disc, and now this, I cannot be scoured or scraped any more.

The sides are not banded; the album is practically one long work. There are two drummers, which Coltrane now prefers, but which reportedly caused the magnificent Elvin Jones to leave the group. Much of the solo space is given to Pharoah Sanders, who begins where Coltrane leaves off—shrieks and double tones are his basic vocabulary. The churning, boiling effect of the two drums and two tenors has somehow made the formerly indifferent pianist McCoy Tyner truly lyrical.

I wonder at myself for not liking this music, especially when an equally severe assault on my system in a theater, such as *Marat/Sade,* leaves me exhilarated. Perhaps it is because in the theater there is something to watch, or because I can see the craft. In this *Meditations* album, I feel only that I am being wildly assaulted, and must defend myself by not listening.

JOHN S. WILSON
KULU SE MAMA
High Fidelity, *July 1967*

John S. Wilson had expressed criticism of John Coltrane's playing since the 1950s, so it is surprising to read such a positive review of late-period Coltrane. Bill Mathieu had declined to rate the record in his review for Down Beat, *preferring to describe the music and then conclude enigmatically, "Rating: None. All."*

The issue of High Fidelity *containing Wilson's review went on sale soon before John Coltrane died on July 17, 1967.—CW*

I have found much of John Coltrane's work difficult to listen to. Even on the many occasions when I felt he had something good going, he has managed to lose me eventually by overdoing it, either in terms of length or manner. Approached with this background, *Kulu Se Mama* is a surprising collection. The title piece, which takes up one side of the disc, is an extended mood piece based on a poem by Juno Lewis. Chanted sporadically by Lewis over a rhythmic, insistent background and broken up by long instrumental passages, the piece becomes more and more possessively hypnotic. In a sense, this is the opposite side of the coin from Coltrane's *Ascension* (Impulse 95)—a half-hour extemporization by a moderately large group, also with a strong hypnotic effect but in a more flaring and arrogant manner. "Kulu Se Mama" is the better work. It is developed in a more sustained fashion with the voice creating enough variety to break up what could otherwise have become a monotonous flow of sound.

The second side of the disc is divided between two pieces by Coltrane's quartet as of a year or so ago—Tyner, Garrison, and Elvin Jones. But these are not just leftover pieces by the group. "Vigil" is a duet between Coltrane and Jones that is an exhausting listening experience—exhausting in an excellent sense since it results from the growing tension produced by Coltrane's incredible extended display of virtuosity, supported only by Jones's drumming. Not the least of Coltrane's accomplishments in this piece is the production of a nine-minute solo without resorting to any of the disparate or desperate shrieks that he usually throws into his work. The second selection, "Welcome" is the perfect balance wheel—an expression of open, flowing relaxation with Coltrane rising and actually seeming to smile, Tyner's piano drifting through the saxophone passages, a flow of cymbals and, under it all, a richly bowed bass. As a production, this is a record that has form and shape. Taken as a whole, it is a structured entity, something you can live with for a long time.

Chronology

The following material has been culled from a variety of sources. For a more detailed and highly accurate chronology of Coltrane's musical career, I recommend Lewis Porter's *John Coltrane: His Life and Music* (see the Bibliography).

1926	On September 23 John William Coltrane is born in Hamlet, North Carolina to John Robert and Alice Blair Coltrane. The family soon moves to High Point, N. C. where the elder Coltrane becomes a tailor and plays violin, ukulele, and clarinet for pleasure.
1939	On January 2 Coltrane's father dies. Later, the young Coltrane plays alto horn in a community band, eventually switching to the clarinet. In September Coltrane enters William Penn High School in High Point.
1940	Coltrane plays alto sax in a school band.
1943	Coltrane graduates from William Penn High School in June and moves to Philadelphia, where he and a friend get an apartment together. Coltrane gets a job in a sugar refinery.
1945	Coltrane begins studying briefly at the Ornstein School of Music in Philadelphia. He plays his first professional jobs. Coltrane enters the U. S. Navy in August and is stationed in Hawaii, where he plays with Navy musicians.
1946	Coltrane is informally recorded on July 13 in Hawaii playing the alto sax with fellow Navy jazz players. These are his first recordings, and a strong Charlie Parker influence is apparent in titles like "Ornithology," "Ko Ko," "Now's

the Time," and "Hot House." In August Coltrane is discharged from the Navy and he returns to Philadelphia, where he meets fellow saxophonist Benny Golson.

1947   Coltrane works with trumpeter King Kolax early in the year. On February 19, he reportedly meets and plays with Charlie Parker for the first time at the home of bassist George "Red" Callender in Los Angeles. Coltrane later returns to Philadelphia and works in Jimmy Heath's Big Band.

1948   Late in the year, Coltrane begins a lengthy tour with vocalist and saxophonist Eddie "Cleanhead" Vinson. He is asked to play tenor sax and does so briefly. Also in the band is pianist William "Red" Garland, who will play with Coltrane in the 1950s.

1949   In September, Coltrane joins Dizzy Gillespie's big band playing second alto sax to Jimmy Heath's lead alto. The group with Coltrane first records on November 11.

1950   In late summer Gillespie gives up his big band and tours with a sextet that includes both Coltrane and Heath. When Heath is fired, Coltrane stays on and is firmly established as a tenor saxophonist.

1951   During the winter, the Gillespie group works often at the New York nightclub Birdland. The band broadcasts many weekends, and informal recordings from Birdland show Coltrane playing in a Dexter Gordon–influenced style. In spring the band breaks up and Coltrane returns to Philadelphia.

1952   Coltrane tours with and is recorded with bands such as Gay Crosse and Earl Bostic. He is not heard improvising on these recordings, however.

1953   Coltrane is based in Philadelphia and works with groups such as Daisy Mae and the Hepcats.

1954   Early in the year, Coltrane joins the band of alto saxophonist Johnny Hodges. Hodges has temporarily left the Duke Ellington big band. This Hodges band is taped noncommercially in Los Angeles in June. The recordings show Coltrane finding his own saxophone style and timbre. By late summer, Coltrane leaves the band and returns to Philadelphia.

1955   Coltrane continues freelancing, including a memorable job with organist Jimmy Smith in Philadelphia. In September Coltrane joins the quintet of Miles Davis. Already in the band is pianist Red Garland, whom Coltrane knows from 1947. On October 3 Coltrane marries Juanita (Naima) Grubbs in Baltimore. On October 27 the Miles Davis quintet with Coltrane, Red Garland, Paul Chambers (bass), and "Philly" Joe Jones (drums) makes its first recordings, on the Columbia label.

1956   On May 6 Coltrane records with Elmo Hope's sextet for Prestige Records. This session is Coltrane's first of twenty-five dates for Prestige outside his work with Davis. Coltrane's increased exposure in the Miles Davis quintet generates more demand for Coltrane as a free-lance saxophonist. In June Coltrane and his wife move from Philadelphia to New York to take advantage of the city's nightclub and recording possibilities. In July Bill Coss reviews a Miles Davis album in Metronome magazine and refers to Coltrane, saying "the tenor, on a [Sonny] Rollins–[Sonny] Stitt kick is even more out of tune."

1957   In the spring Miles Davis reportedly asks Coltrane to leave the band because of narcotic addiction and drinking problems.

Coltrane returns to Philadelphia and soon gives up narcotics and alcohol. Later he writes, "During the year 1957, I experienced, by the grace of God, a spiritual awakening which was to lead me to a richer, fuller, more productive life." On April 16 Coltrane does his first recording with pianist Thelonious Monk for the Riverside label. Coltrane begins visiting Monk's apartment to learn Monk's compositions. On May 31 Coltrane records his first LP as a leader, Coltrane, for Prestige. It includes several of his compositions, including "Straight Street." In July Coltrane begins working with Thelonious Monk's quartet at Manhattan's Five Spot nightclub. Coltrane's highly articulate playing adds to his reputation as a unique improvisor. Due to conflicts between Monk and Prestige (Coltrane's recording label), the group is only recorded clandestinely. The group's three studio performances are released after Coltrane leaves Prestige. On

September 15, having obtained a temporary release from his Prestige recording contract, Coltrane records the LP Blue Train for the Blue Note label. Coltrane carefully crafts four pieces for the date and the results are a classic recording. In December Thelonious Monk's engagement at the Five Spot ends.

1958
Coltrane rejoins Miles Davis's group, which now becomes a sextet, including Julian "Cannonball" Adderley (alto sax). On February 4 the Davis sextet makes its first commercial recording for Columbia. One of the pieces, Miles Davis's "Miles" (later often called "Milestones" or "Milestones II") is organized by modes (scales) rather than by chord progression. This modal approach would eventually play an important part in Coltrane's music. On September 11 Coltrane fills in for saxophonist Johnny Griffin at New York's Five Spot club, and Coltrane's wife records at least five pieces played that night. (Originally, this session was thought to be from 1957). To this date, these are the only released live recordings of Coltrane and Monk. On December 26 Coltrane makes his last recording for Prestige. He quickly switches to the Atlantic label. Coltrane biographer Lewis Porter reports that 1958 is a likely year for the birth of Coltrane's daughter Sheila Coltrane, born out of wedlock.

1959
Around this time, Coltrane begins playing the soprano saxophone, an instrument rare in modern jazz. Coltrane said that a fellow musician had accidentally left one behind in a car; Coltrane gave it a try and liked it. On January 15 John Coltrane makes his first recording for Atlantic, Bags & Trane. Vibraharpist Milt "Bags" Jackson is the co-leader. On March 2 the Miles Davis sextet begins recording their classic LP, Kind of Blue. One of the pieces, "So What?", is modally organized. Most of the selections on the album include Coltrane, Adderley, Bill Evans (piano), Paul Chambers (bass) and Jimmy Cobb (drums).

March 26
Coltrane first records "Giant Steps" for Atlantic. Its complex and rapidly moving chord progression is in some ways the opposite of a modally organized piece such as "So What?" ("Giant Steps" is based in part on a passage

in Nicolas Slonimsky's <u>Thesaurus of Scales and Melodic Patterns</u>.) The takes of "Giant Steps" recorded on this date are not released until years later. On April 6 the Davis sextet finishes <u>Kind of Blue</u>. Another modally organized piece, "Flamenco Sketches," is recorded on this date. On May 5 Coltrane records an acceptable take of "Giant Steps," which becomes the title track of his first Atlantic release as sole leader.

1960
Early in the year, Coltrane gives Miles Davis notice that he intends to leave the group. Davis asks Coltrane to remain through the quintet's coming tour. From March 21 to April 10 Miles Davis's quintet with Coltrane, Wynton Kelly (piano), Chambers, and Cobb tours Western Europe and Scandinavia. Coltrane reportedly practices soprano sax in his free time on tour. In April John Coltrane's quartet with Steve Kuhn (piano), Steve Davis (bass), and Pete "LaRoca" Sims (drums) opens at Manhattan's Jazz Gallery. From this point on, Coltrane will lead his own band. In May pianist McCoy Tyner replaces Steve Kuhn in the quartet. He will remain in the group until 1965. In September drummer Billy Higgins replaces LaRoca, and later that month Elvin Jones replaces Higgins. Coltrane, Tyner, and Jones will form the nucleus of Coltrane's groups until 1965. In October the quartet of Coltrane, Jones, Tyner, and Davis makes its first recordings for Atlantic. Their landmark version of "My Favorite Things" is recorded on October 21.

1961
In January Coltrane's friend Eric Dolphy (alto sax, bass clarinet, and flute) is added to the group. (Dolphy sometimes does not appear with the group because of other commitments.) Bassist Reggie Workman replaces Steve Davis. On March 20 John Coltrane makes his last recordings with Miles Davis, the LP <u>Someday My Prince Will Come</u>. On May 25 Coltrane finishes his recording obligations to Atlantic. Two days before, he had made his first recordings for the Impulse label, with which he would remain for the rest of his career. From November 11 to December 2 the Coltrane quintet with Dolphy tours England and Europe. On November 24 they are filmed in Germany.

1962	Bassist Jimmy Garrison replaces Reggie Workman. This group of Coltrane, Tyner, Garrison, and Jones is often called Coltrane's "classic quartet." During 1962 Eric Dolphy continues to join the quartet for some live appearances. From November 17 to December 2 the Coltrane quartet tours Europe.
1963	In May Elvin Jones enters a drug treatment facility, where he stays until August. His replacement is usually drummer Roy Haynes. In late summer Coltrane leaves his wife Naima and soon begins living with pianist Alice McLeod. From October 22 to November 4 Coltrane's quartet tours Europe. On December 7 the Coltrane quartet is filmed in San Francisco for Ralph Gleason's television program "Jazz Casual." On December 31 Eric Dolphy makes his last appearance with the Coltrane group at New York's Lincoln Center.
1964	Eric Dolphy dies in Berlin on June 29. On August 26 John Coltrane and Alice McLeod's son John W. Coltrane, Jr., is born. On December 9 the John Coltrane quartet records a four-part suite, A Love Supreme. In the liner notes Coltrane writes that the album is an offering to God. The titles of the four parts ("Acknowledgment," "Resolution," "Pursuance," and "Psalm") reflect Coltrane's spirituality, and the titles of his subsequent compositions reflect his interest in personal growth. On December 10 Coltrane records alternate versions of three of the parts of A Love Supreme with added musicians Art Davis (bass) and Archie Shepp (tenor sax). (As of this book's publication, these tracks have not been released.) The inclusion of Shepp shows Coltrane's growing interest in the music of younger exploratory "avant-garde" players who are influenced by saxophonist Ornette Coleman.
1965	On June 28 Coltrane records his large work "Ascension." His quartet is augmented by seven players: two trumpeters, two alto saxophonists, two additional tenor saxophonists, and a second bassist. The alternation of worked-out ensembles and collective improvisation recalls the format of Ornette Coleman's 1960 composition "Free Jazz." From July 26 to August 1 the John Coltrane quartet tours Europe. On August 6 Coltrane and

McLeod's second son, Ravi John, named after Indian sitar virtuoso Ravi Shankar, is born. On August 16 the Coltrane quartet is joined by tenor saxophonist Archie Shepp at the Down Beat Jazz Festival in Chicago. In September tenor saxophonist Farrell "Pharoah" Sanders joins, making the group a quintet. From this point on, Coltrane will regularly augment his group with additional percussionists, wind players, and bassists. In November drummer Rashied Ali is added to the group. The basic band is now a sextet, with two tenor saxophonists and two drummers. In December McCoy Tyner leaves the band. Alice McLeod soon joins to play piano.

1966   In January Elvin Jones leaves the band. On February 19 Coltrane leads a nine-piece group in the "Titans of the Tenor" concert at Lincoln Center. From July 8-24 the Coltrane quintet with Sanders, McLeod, Garrison, and Ali tours Japan. In July or August Coltrane marries Alice McLeod in Mexico. In November Coltrane cancels a European tour, probably because of health problems.

1967   On February 22 Coltrane records an album of duets, Interstellar Space, with percussionist Rashied Ali. On March 19 Coltrane's third son, Oranyan Olabisi, is born. On April 23 Coltrane gives his last live performance. The occasion is a scholarship fund benefit for the Center of African Culture in New York. Aware that his health is declining, he cancels forthcoming concert and nightclub engagements. On May 17 Coltrane makes what is currently believed to be his last studio recording, "Kaleidoscope." On July 16 Coltrane is taken to Huntington Hospital in Long Island. He dies at the hospital on July 17. The cause is liver cancer. On July 21 John Coltrane's funeral takes place at St. Peter's Lutheran Church in New York City. The Ornette Coleman quartet and the Albert Ayler quartet play for the ceremony.

Discography

All recordings are released under Coltrane's name unless stated otherwise.

Recordings with Miles Davis (1955–1959)

Workin' (Fantasy OJCCD-296-2). This album by Davis's "classic quintet" includes Red Garland, Paul Chambers, and "Philly" Joe Jones. Drawn from Davis's "marathon" 1956 sessions, which also produced the excellent *Steamin'* and *Cookin.'*

Kind of Blue (Columbia CK 64935). One of Miles Davis's most important and most enjoyable recordings. Outstanding performances from 1959 by Davis, Coltrane, Julian "Cannonball" Adderley, Bill Evans, Wynton Kelly, Paul Chambers, and Jimmy Cobb. Highly recommended. This new reissue is remastered and corrected for pitch, and has an alternate take of "Flamenco Sketches."

Recordings with Thelonious Monk (1957–1958)

Thelonious Monk and John Coltrane (Fantasy OJCCD-039-2). Contains three powerful 1957 studio recordings of the legendary Monk quartet with Coltrane, plus other Monk/Coltrane material.

Live at the Five Spot (Blue Note CDP 99786). Five 1958 nonprofessionally recorded live recordings of Monk and Coltrane. Fidelity is just adequate, but the performances are frequently stunning. The tapes were transferred to CD off-pitch. It is unknown if the problem was later corrected on this CD.

Prestige Recordings (1956–1958)

Coltrane (Prestige OJCCD-020-2). Coltrane's first recording as sole leader in 1957. Includes three Coltrane compositions including "Bakai" and "Straight Street," plus the standard "While My Lady Sleeps." (See Zita Carno's article, "The Style of John Coltrane," on page 7 of this anthology.)

Soultrane (Prestige OJCCD-021-2). This well-knit 1958 date with the Red Garland trio includes two classic ballads and several swingers.

Blue Note Recordings (1957)

The Ultimate Blue Train (Blue Note CDP 7243 8 53428 0 6). John Coltrane's breakthrough sextet recording from 1957 features classic Coltrane compositions such as "Locomotion," "Moment's Notice," and the master take of "Blue Train" discussed in Zita Carno's "The Style of John Coltrane" on page 7 of this anthology. This new "enhanced CD" reissue also includes alternate takes of "Blue Train" and "Lazy Bird," as well as CD-ROM-formatted interviews and photos. Highly recommended.

Atlantic Recordings (1959–1961)

Giant Steps (Atlantic 1311-2). A landmark 1959 quartet recording with the master takes of important Coltrane compositions such as "Giant Steps" and "Naima." Highly recommended.

My Favorite Things (Atlantic 1361-2). Coltrane's first-issued recordings on soprano sax. The hypnotic modal arrangement of the title song became a hit for Coltrane. Highly recommended.

The Heavyweight Champion: The Complete Atlantic Recordings (Atlantic/Rhino R2-72984). This seven-CD set brings together all surviving material that Coltrane recorded for Atlantic and includes alternate takes, many of which are grouped on the last CD. The size and cost of the set will be daunting to some listeners, but the music's excellence makes it a must for serious Coltrane fans.

Impulse Recordings (1961–1967)

Coltrane "Live" at the Village Vanguard (Impulse MCAD-39136). An early (1961) document of Coltrane's classic quartet including pianist McCoy Tyner, bassists Reggie Workman or Jimmy Garrison, and drummer Elvin Jones. Coltrane's "Chasin' the Trane" (a blues) and "Spiritual" show how he continued to find inspiration in African-American musical traditions.

Duke Ellington and John Coltrane (Impulse IMPD-166). Although they were born twenty-seven years apart, these two artists had much to say to each other. Each brought his own bassist and drummer to switch off on the various tracks. The version of "In a Sentimental Mood" is considered a classic.

A Love Supreme (Impulse GRD-155). Coltrane's 1964 four-part suite was an expression of his spirituality that he offered to God. This sometimes turbulent recording is an essential example of Coltrane's "classic quartet." Highly recommended.

A John Coltrane Retrospective—The Impulse Years (Impulse GRD-3-119). Coltrane's output for Impulse was so extensive and varied that this three-CD set covering 1961 to 1965 will be the place to begin for many listeners. Coltrane is heard with many groups, including the classic quartet, a studio orchestra and with Duke Ellington. The moods range from gentle to intense, and several selections were recorded live. Highly recommended.

The Major Works of John Coltrane (Impulse GRD-2-113). These challenging 1965 recordings on two CDs are highly energetic, lengthy, and often dissonant, featuring expanded instrumentations and compositions as well as solos influenced by the "free jazz" movement. Includes two versions of Coltrane's collective improvisation "Ascension."

Select Bibliography

Biographies

Porter, Lewis. *John Coltrane: His Life and Music*. Ann Arbor: University of Michigan Press, 1998. This most accurate of Coltrane biographies makes others obsolete. Includes extensive discussion of Coltrane's music with notated examples and a lengthy chronology. Essential.

Simpkins, C. O. *Coltrane: A Biography*. Perth Amboy, N.J.: Herndon House Publishers, 1975. The reproductions from Coltrane's notebooks are especially interesting.

Thomas, J. C. *Chasin' the Trane: The Music and Mystique of John Coltrane*. New York: Doubleday, 1975. Includes many quotations from Coltrane's friends and family.

Books with Chapters on Coltrane

Goldberg, Joe. "John Coltrane." In *Jazz Masters of the Fifties*. New York: Macmillan, 1965.

Gridley, Mark C. "John Coltrane." In *Jazz Styles*. 6th edition. Upper Saddle River, N.J.: Prentice Hall, 1997.

Hentoff, Nat. "John Coltrane." In *Jazz Is*. New York: Random House, 1976.

Porter, Lewis, and Michael Ullman. "John Coltrane." In *Jazz: From Its Origins to the Present*. Englewood Cliffs, N.J.: Prentice Hall, 1993.

Williams, Martin. "Man in the Middle." In *The Jazz Tradition*. New York: Oxford University Press, 1970.

Technical Studies

Demsey, David. "Chromatic Third Relations in the Music of John Coltrane." *Annual Review of Jazz Studies,* vol. 5 (1991).

Jost, Ekkekhard. "John Coltrane and Modal Playing." *Free Jazz*. Graz, Austria: Institut für Jazzforschung, 1974.

———. "John Coltrane 1965–1967." *Free Jazz*. Graz, Austria: Institut für Jazzforschung, 1974.

Kernfeld, Barry. "Two Coltranes." *Annual Review of Jazz Studies*, vol. 2 (1983).

Porter, Lewis. "John Coltrane's 'A Love Supreme.'" *Journal of the American Musicological Society* (fall 1985).

John Coltrane in His Own Words
"Brief Interview with John Coltrane." *Jazz & Pop*, March 1968.

Coltrane, John, with Don DeMicheal. "Coltrane on Coltrane." *Down Beat*, September 29, 1960.

DeMicheal, Don. "John Coltrane and Eric Dolphy Answer the Jazz Critics." *Down Beat*, April 12, 1962.

Feather, Leonard. "Blindfold Test: Honest John." *Down Beat*, February 19, 1959.

Colleagues and Family Remember John Coltrane
Heckman, Don. "Jimmy Garrison: After Coltrane." *Down Beat*, March 9, 1967.

Palmer, Robert. "From the Inside Out: Bob Palmer Interviews Bob Thiele." *Coda*, June 1971.

Rivelli, Pauline. "Alice Coltrane." *Jazz & Pop,* September 1968.

Wild, David. "McCoy Tyner: The Jubilant Experience of the Classic Quartet." *Down Beat*, July 12, 1979.

Permissions

Index

About the Editor

Carl Woideck teaches jazz history at the University of Oregon. He is the author of *Charlie Parker: His Music and Life* and the editor of Schirmer's *Charlie Parker Companion*.